THE REAL REAGAN

☆

THE REAL REAGAN

☆

What he believes
What he has accomplished
What we can expect from him

☆

FRANK VAN DER LINDEN

William Morrow and Company, Inc.
New York   1981

Library of Congress Cataloging in Publication Data

Van der Linden, Frank.
   The real Reagan.

   Includes Index.
   1. Reagan, Ronald.   2. Presidents—United States—
Biography.   I. Title.
E877.V36   973.927′092′4   [B]   81-903
ISBN 0-688-00386-9   AACR2

Printed in the United States of America

   2 3 4 5 6 7 8 9 10

Book Design by Bernard Schleifer

This book is dedicated to my wife, Lyn;
our son, Bob; and our daughters, Margaret and Anne.
I am grateful for their love and their unwavering faith in me.

☆

FOREWORD

ON A SUNDAY AFTERNOON in September, 1945, I stood at Harry Truman's elbow and watched him win $807 in a poker game with several other distinguished Democrats. At that time, Captain Ronald Reagan, reveling in his freedom after four years in the army, was cruising around in a speedboat on a lake in California. No one could have dreamed that the Hollywood actor of that faraway time would be occupying the Oval Office today. But that is one of the fascinations of history and of biography: Anything can happen!

One of my grandfathers was a Dutch immigrant. The other was a Confederate Army captain. Perhaps that heritage has made me stubborn and independent.

So, in 1975, when Ronald Reagan's bid for the presidency was being ridiculed by nearly all the experts in Washington, I took a different view. Incredible though it may seem, I believed the former motion picture star could reach the White House. I began a long and intensive study of Reagan for the purpose of writing this book.

I approached the Reagan Phenomenon from a dual perspective: as a White House correspondent and as a historian. I have known eight Presidents and have written three books about the presidency.

I saw Reagan mature from his early role as the White Knight of the Right to his present one as Chief Executive of all the American people. I knew the inside story when he turned down the conservatives' demand, six years ago, that he run as an independent candidate. I had my first in-depth interview with him at his Pacific Palisades home in 1976 and my latest one shortly before his inauguration.

I am grateful to the President, the First Lady, Vice President George Bush, numerous aides and advisers, senators, congressmen, cabinet members, and friends who have shared their knowledge of Reagan with me. Especially helpful were Edwin Meese III, Michael Deaver, Peter Hannaford, William Casey, Richard Allen, Adm. Robert Garrick, Richard Wirthlin, Jim Brady, Lyn Nofziger, Richard Williamson, Nancy Reynolds, Robert Carleson, Charles Black, Gerald Carmen, Paul Russo, Chuck Tyson, Ed Gray, Joe Holmes, Ken Towery, and other associates of the President; Lt. Gen. Daniel Graham; Sens. Paul Laxalt, Jesse Helms, Strom Thurmond, Orrin Hatch, S. I. Hayakawa, Gordon Humphrey, Howard Baker, and Bob Dole; former Sens. George Murphy, Bill Brock, and Richard Schweiker; Congressmen Tom Evans, Phil Crane, Bob Dornan, Mickey Edwards, Jack Kemp, Trent Lott, Bud Shuster, and Robert Walker; also conservative leaders John Laxalt, Paul Weyrich, Morton Blackwell, Howard Phillips, Tom Ellis, Jerry Falwell, and Bob Billings.

Frank van der Linden
WASHINGTON, D.C.

☆
CONTENTS

THE REAL REAGAN

☆

1

☆

PORTRAIT
OF A
PRESIDENT

SHORTLY BEFORE HIS inauguration as the fortieth President of the United States, Ronald Reagan's foreign policy advisers briefed him about the many burdens that would fall upon his shoulders at a time of great danger to the future of the Republic.

Reagan was already fully aware that as his first priority, he must reverse the nation's economic decline and control the inflation that was a major cause of the people's decision to take a chance on a new President, whom millions scarcely knew except from his image on their television screens.

Now his advisers were telling him that the latest intelligence estimate showed the steady build-up of the Soviet Union's armed forces would require the production of new weapons by the United States, as Reagan had advocated in his successful campaign to take the White House away from Jimmy Carter.

The new President would be fully justified in his plan for restoring this nation's "margin of safety" before entering into any talks with the men in the Kremlin about another series of Strategic Arms Limitation Talks to replace Carter's SALT II, which could not be rammed through the Senate.

Reagan listened to the experts' litany of problems he would inherit: the Soviet threat to Poland, trouble with Iran even after the release of the American hostages, possible new bloodshed in the Middle East and in Latin America. . . .

With a rueful smile, he quipped: "I think I'll demand a recount!"

13

Reagan and his aides also joked about the ceremony in which Carter had kissed Leonid Brezhnev in a sentimental scene after they had signed the SALT II pact in Vienna.

"There's just one thing we ask," one of the briefers told the incoming President: "We don't ever want to see a picture of you kissing Brezhnev."

Oh, there was no reason to worry about that, Reagan fired back. "You won't even see me kissing Brezhnev's wife!"

It was typical of Reagan, the Great Entertainer, that he could not resist an opportunity to mask his inner uneasiness with a flash of humor. His delight in wisecracks comes as naturally to him as does breathing. The only President who ever earned his living as a performer in motion pictures and television, he loves to make an audience applaud. Whether speaking to one listener in the Oval Office or to millions on TV, he strives to please.

Some critics claim he was playacting when he repeated The Speech, which made him a star on the banquet circuit, year after year, appearing everywhere in the same role as the somewhat elderly All-American Boy. "When he wets his lips with his tongue and bends his head at a slight angle," one reporter wrote after seeing that familiar gesture, "you can almost imagine a straw dangling from the corner of his mouth and hear him say, 'Shucks, Ma'am.'"

While campaigning, Reagan never tired of retelling the jokes that had proved to be durable, surefire laughter lines. Samples:

" 'Status quo'—that's Latin for 'the mess we're in.' "

"Herbert Hoover was the first President to return his entire salary to the government. Now we're all doing it."

Upon meeting a friend, Reagan will often open the conversation by relaying the latest joke he has picked up; and he enjoys telling tales about his early days in radio and in Hollywood. He is an artless, charming man.

With his fondness for storytelling, he resembles another man who grew up in poverty in small-town Illinois and climbed all the way to the White House. Abraham Lincoln's thigh-slapping barnyard yarns, however, were sometimes so smutty that they would have shocked Ronald Reagan, who is a puritan at heart.

Lincoln, the first President elected by the present-day Republican party, and Reagan, the latest one, share another trait: Both were underestimated and came to their high office against the opposition of the old power structure.

In 1861, the self-appointed arbiters of Washington fashion trembled with indignation when the crude, awkward, loose-limbed lawyer from Illinois, with his limited education and his undistinguished single term in Congress, moved into the White House. Likewise, today's Establishment greeted Reagan with mingled envy and fear tinged with ridicule about his record as a movie actor and his total lack of familiarity with Washington and foreign affairs. The skeptics waited eagerly to see the old trouper slip and fall flat on his face.

In his eight years as governor of California, Reagan acquired the image of a "nine-to-five" administrator who shied away from conflict, liked compromises, and yielded to the faction that applied the most pressure. "Whoever got in there and fought the hardest and presented the best case," one former associate once said, "was generally able to prevail."

It is true that like every other successful executive, the President delegates an enormous amount of detail. He does not waste long hours in line-by-line scrutiny of reports nor does he determine which assistants can use the tennis courts.

Much of the work of running the White House is done by Edwin Meese III, his counselor and trusted confidant for many years going back to their days together in Sacramento. Meese, holding cabinet rank, is The Man to See on all major policy decisions; the Keeper of the Flame. If he is against a proposal, it is unlikely to go very far.

James Baker III, the chief of staff, is a recent convert from Texas who backed Gerald Ford and George Bush in their efforts to block Reagan out of the presidency. Baker keeps the machinery of the executive branch humming and the paper flowing smoothly in and out. Michael Deaver, his deputy, is a longtime friend of the President's and enjoys his total trust.

But it is a mistake to assume that the Washington gossips are right—that Reagan is a lazy, easygoing fellow who merely presides over the government in a vague sort of way; an affable, accommodating figure pulled to and fro by strong-willed men.

The error of the theory became clear in the well-orchestrated campaign intended to frighten Reagan out of naming Gen. Alexander Haig as his Secretary of State. It was a classic example of a Washington power play involving influential Eastern newspapers, Democratic senators determined to make mischief for the new President, and Nervous Nellie Republicans in the Senate and in the Reagan camp, afraid of making a mistake that could again light the fires of Watergate and of Vietnam.

The New York Times fired the opening volley in a column a month after the election, even while the Washington *Post* publisher, Katharine Graham, was coyly courting Reagan by having a dinner in his honor. Senate Republican Leader Howard Baker took his cue from the *Times* and scurried into action. Baker dispatched to the Reagan forces a memorandum warning that if Haig's name came up to the Senate for confirmation as Secretary of State, the Democrats would surely rake over the coals of Watergate to find out the role that Haig had played as Richard Nixon's chief of staff in the President's efforts to stonewall the investigators and withhold tape recordings of Nixon's Oval Office conversations from special prosecutor Leon Jaworski.

Baker, vice chairman of the Senate Watergate hearings, dreaded the thought of seeing the horror figures of that era paraded about in another long round of televised confrontations, to the embarrassment of the Republican party. Certain Democrats also vowed to question Haig about his actions during his four years as deputy to National Security Adviser Henry Kissinger, in the secret bombing of Cambodia, the B–52 raids on Hanoi that hastened the end of the Vietnam War, and the earlier orders that resulted in taps on the telephones of some officials and newsmen suspected of leaking national security secrets. Furthermore, both friends and foes agreed, the General was ruthless, tough, and ambitious. He wanted to be President himself.

Haig's enemies also repeated the old whispers that he had somehow arranged for President Ford to grant the Nixon pardon. West Virginia's Sen. Robert C. Byrd, then the majority leader, said the General might not be confirmed if all the secrets of his past as a Nixon aide came out. Byrd implied that naming Haig to head the State Department would be the same as sending him before a Senate firing squad.

Byrd's shotgun blast backfired. Friends of Haig's on the Reagan transition team immediately warned the President-elect that he could not allow Bobby Byrd to dictate his cabinet. If the Senate bosses could get away with one bullying act, they would keep kicking Reagan around throughout his term. They would never stop. Reagan must show them that he really would be the boss.

By this time, Reagan's Irish was up. He had not run from a fight since his grammar school days, and he would not run from this one. After checking by telephone with Ford to make sure the Nixon pardon story was untrue, Reagan went ahead with the announcement: Haig would be his Secretary of State. "There's nothing uninvented that can be brought up against him," Reagan said. "I think he is the man for the job."

Reagan admired the General's total record, as a combat officer in Korea and in Vietnam, as an aide in the White House, as Army chief of staff, and most recently, as the commander of the North Atlantic Treaty Organization. Leaders of the Western European nations had come to respect Haig for his firm stand against Soviet adventurism and his call for a stronger NATO alliance.

Reagan tapped the retired General to be his deputy in carrying out a bold new "grand strategy" for the dangerous decade ahead, and in making sure that the State Department personnel would follow it faithfully. Reagan had spelled out months before his proposed change in foreign policy from "the vacillation, appeasement, and aimlessness" of the Democratic administration. Under Carter, he charged, "we apologize, compromise, withdraw and retreat; we fall silent when insulted and pay ransom when we are victimized."

Reagan intended to change all that. Haig, he felt confident, would enforce his tough new policy. It would be quite a switch from the practice of seeking "accommodations" with the Soviet Union on any terms and of going along with revolutions if their leaders claimed to be bringing in a people's democracy to replace a repressive regime.

The Washington *Post* revealed the real basic reasons underlying the objections to the General. "The installation of Haig," it said, "means the new administration will have a team of hard-liners throughout the key policy centers, and also that the potentially most influential voice for a stiffened foreign and defense policy may come from State, which in the past has been a spokesman for moderation."

The hard-liners smiled over the prospect that the dovecote in Foggy Bottom might be cleaned out at last.

Lt. Gen. Daniel Graham, U.S. Army, retired, one architect of the President's "peace through strength" program, applauded his moves to take a firm grip on the foreign policy-making machinery. General Graham, a former chief of the Defense Intelligence Agency, said:

"In the Reagan administration there will be a basic framework of grand strategy. From that concept will flow the military decisions. The President is not interested in the systems analysis-cost effectiveness of weapons. One of the most touching things to me, personally, about him is that he doesn't pretend to know our Pentagon jargon. I've briefed other officials who would nod wisely rather than admit they didn't know what I was talking about. Reagan doesn't do that.

"The President is able to sense, 'What am I going to need to know?' and he asks for the details. In the campaign, he stuck to his general line of attack—the failure of disarmament and detente, the bankruptcy of the notion that somehow we and the Russians can get together and cause a peaceful world to evolve. All this became clear to Joe Blow and now Reagan is President."

With Ed Meese as his mentor, the new President began an experiment in creating "cabinet government." He selected, as department heads, individuals who could join in discussing broad general issues as well as those in their own shops. Some were old friends from California, notably Caspar Weinberger, the Secretary of Defense, and William French Smith, the Attorney General, Reagan's personal lawyer.

The East provided an array of talent: William J. Casey of New York, the Reagan campaign chairman and World War II veteran of the Office of Strategic Services in Europe, became director of Central Intelligence. Donald T. Regan of New Jersey, chairman and chief executive officer of Merrill Lynch and Company, Inc., became Secretary of the Treasury; and Malcolm Baldrige of Connecticut, Secretary of Commerce.

Pennsylvania furnished three: General Haig at State; Sen. Richard Schweiker, Secretary of Health and Human Services; and Drew Lewis, Secretary of Transportation.

Also from the industrial East came Raymond Donovan, the New Jersey contractor tapped as Secretary of Labor; and Samuel Pierce of New York, Secretary of Housing and Urban Development, the only black in the cabinet.

Reagan selected one woman, Georgetown University professor Jeane Kirkpatrick, as ambassador to the United Nations; and former South Carolina governor James Edwards as Secretary of Energy. The youngest cabinet member is former Michigan congressman David Stockman, thirty-four, director of the Office of Management and Budget. The President chose James G. Watt of Colorado to head the Interior Department; John Block of Illinois, Agriculture; Terrel Bell of Utah, Education; and former Tennessee Senator Bill Brock as Trade Representative.

When you meet Ronald Reagan, your first impression is this: Here is a warm, genial man who is not at all arrogant or overbearing although he occupies the most powerful position in the land. He feels at home in the White House and he wants you to feel comfortable there as well.

Visitors who are privileged to enter the Oval Office see a handsome, broad-shouldered, vigorous man who looks like a ranch hand. He is tall, tanned, trim, with bright blue eyes and dazzling white teeth. His face is lined with tiny wrinkles; it seems to have weathered like fine old leather.

There are creases around his mouth, and beneath his jaw are other signs of age—the "turkey neck" caused by long hours of exposure to the sun. He has always had a ruddy complexion, and he likes to say he was one of the few actors in Hollywood who seldom had to wear make-up. He also swears that he has never had a face-lift. By turning his head, he can show you that he has no telltale scars behind his ears.

His incredibly thick thatch of dark-brown hair has a few streaks of gray. Ironically, he welcomes these as proof that—contrary to the jokes about his "prematurely orange" hair—he has never dyed it. When he was governor, some skeptics stooped so low as to pick up clippings of his hair from the barbershop floor and test them, only to find to their dismay that the verdict was: "No dye."

The President's midriff is as flat and hard as an athlete's. At 185 pounds, he is only five pounds heavier than in the days when he played right guard for the Red Devils football team at Eureka College half a century ago. It is difficult to believe that this virile, muscular man is seventy. Physically and mentally, he is in his prime.

Reagan's life as an outdoorsman—riding horseback, chopping wood, and performing other chores at his California ranch—is one reason for his good health. On his travels, he exercises each day with a wheel. He had a prostate operation in 1967 that ended a series of urinary tract infections, and six physicians in 1980 found no evidence of serious ailments in his annual check-ups.

Reagan is slightly deaf; you notice that he sometimes leans forward to hear questions better. He cannot hear a watch tick with either ear. He explains that his ears were hurt while he was filming a motion picture in which another actor fired a pistol so close to his head that Reagan staggered three feet from the concussion.

The President has a form of hay fever aggravated by airplane trips and by the artificial air of hotels. He takes no drugs other than daily vitamins and an occasional antihistamine pill. During his career as an actor and as a public speaker, he learned to pace himself and that is another reason for his excellent physique. He would seldom sleep on his campaign plane but would put his feet up and relax like a cat while scanning his 4 x 6 cards or the text of a speech or background material from his "Brain Bag," the briefcase filled with papers supplied by his staff. He prefers eight hours of sleep at night but seldom has that much.

Reagan has never consulted a psychiatrist. He is remarkably calm. He does not suffer from the sharp swings of elation and depression that afflicted some predecessors in his place of power and great responsibility.

In seeking the nation's highest office, through years of effort, Reagan did not try to gratify an oversized ego or to overcome a sense of insecurity or to get even with his enemies. Nor did he aspire to loll about in the Executive Mansion. For years before his election, he had been enjoying a full and happy life, and his shrewd investments in California real estate had made him a millionaire.

Reagan is a driven man only in the sense that he has an inner compulsion to "make America great again." "He feels that he was meant to do this," said one woman who knows him well, "and his feeling of destiny is part of his charm. He is the most secure man, emotionally and psychologically, that you'd ever want to meet. He has his own solid feeling of self-worth. He has a normal amount of ego, but there isn't a mean-spirited bone in Ronald Reagan's body."

Charles Black, a political strategist who was tossed overboard by Reagan in early 1980 but still admires him, commented: "He is relaxed and paces himself mentally. He gets mad but doesn't stay mad about anything. When Jimmy Carter lost a primary, it just tore his guts out. When Reagan lost a primary, he went out to win the next one.

"Being easygoing is a great asset to Reagan; he doesn't get ulcers over mistakes. I'd rather have him in the Oval Office from nine to five every day, making carefully calculated judgments, than have a President running around eighteen hours a day, always uptight about something."

Morton Blackwell, who accurately predicted in The Right Report of March 24, 1978, that "Reagan could win it all in 1980," observed: "President Reagan, unlike Johnson, Nixon and Carter, would keep his popularity over the long haul. He's a nice guy and he shows it."

But, skeptics may ask, isn't this all an act—a carefully polished image of Mr. Nice Guy, who loves everybody while he's on camera but is a cold and calculating politician otherwise? Isn't there an iron man behind that smiling mask?

Those who know him best say "No." They insist there is only one Reagan, that what you see is what you get.

Secretary Schweiker, tapped by Reagan as his potential running mate in 1976, found him "a very friendly, warm" person then, and after five years of close association, concluded: "The Reagan I met and got to know was the same Reagan I know today. There is no hidden Reagan."

It is ironic, Schweiker believes, that Reagan is sometimes distrusted as a former movie star, while the real "actors" in public life are politicians who "put on a big show and double-talk while Reagan is straightforward and tells it like it is."

Yes, the witnesses agree, the President is a square. So is his wife. Warm, gracious, and lovely but strong-willed and independent, Nancy Reagan plays an extremely important role in his life —not as a co-star but as a counselor exerting her influence in private. Reagan calls her "Mommy" and welcomes her advice. Contrary to some reports, the First Lady does not dictate policies for her "Ronnie." She does not care to be called the power behind the throne.

Their marriage has endured for more than a quarter of a century for one simple reason: They are deeply in love.

The President is not only a devoted husband; he is also an indulgent father. The four young Reagans agree that he is a "soft touch." Maureen, his eldest daughter, whose mother was Reagan's first wife, Jane Wyman, calls him "Dear Old Dad" or "D. O. D." and campaigned for him all across the country although she is strongly in favor of the Equal Rights Amendment and he is against it.

Michael, the adopted son, also a tireless campaigner, owns a company that sells equipment to farmers for the production of gasohol. He and his wife, Colleen, have a son, Cameron Michael, the lone Reagan grandchild. Patti, the daughter of President and Mrs. Reagan, was a rebel in the era of the Youth Revolt of the

1960's but has made her peace with her parents—or, at least, detente—amid mutual respect. Ronald Prescott Reagan, her brother, dances with the Joffrey II ballet ensemble in New York. Soon after his father's election to the presidency, Ron married Doria Palmieri, a dancing school classmate, with whom he had been keeping house for more than a year.

Nancy Reagan is happy to have her "Ronnie" all to herself by taking refuge in their ranch in the California hills, when they can escape from the press and almost everyone else except the Secret Service. The road to Rancho del Cielo, "Ranch in the Sky," is narrow and crooked and the asphalt strip winds through seven miles of twists and turns as it rises from the blue Pacific Ocean to a high ridge in the sun-browned hills north of Santa Barbara.

Driving along a gravel lane through a forest of live oaks, a visitor suddenly looks down across a meadow toward a group of farm buildings on a saddle ridge in the Santa Ynez mountains, overlooking the ocean on one side and the valley on the other. The main house is a century-old adobe structure that was not much more than a tin-roofed shack before it was remodeled and enlarged by the Reagans.

Reagan bought the 667-acre property in December, 1974, the last month of his service as governor. He likes to tell how he improved the place with his own labor and the help of Nancy and some friends. He renovated the kitchen, ripped off a screened porch, put on a family room, and hauled flat rocks up to make a patio.

One associate, who helped him paint and lay tile at the ranch on weekends, said: "He loved all the physical labor, dragging big boulders around, digging holes for the fence posts. He got a lot of fun out of that, the pleasure of being able to do things with his hands."

"Barney" Barnett, who had been assigned by the state highway patrol to guard Governor Reagan, stayed on after retirement. The two men together put in the fence. They sawed the bottom off more than 100 telephone poles and set them in the ground as posts, then placed crosspieces into the notched poles to complete the fence.

Since the only heat for the two-bedroom house comes from fireplaces, a lot of wood must be cut. The President likes to do that; the exercise keeps him fit. Sometimes he fixes the fences or repairs a washed-out road—anything to give him the pleasure of hard physical exertion.

Because of his exercise, he does not have to diet. He eats a light breakfast of cereal and fruit; his lunch is usually a sandwich or a salad. When he tired of the beef and chicken so often served to him on the political banquet circuit, he would dine at home on Chinese, Mexican, or Italian food, or sometimes corned beef and cabbage. Another longtime favorite is macaroni and cheese.

For desserts, he prefers fruit, ice cream or sherbet, and lots of cookies. He drinks very little, only an occasional glass of wine. He has tragic recollections of his father, who died of a heart attack at sixty after years of heavy drinking and cigarette smoking.

Reagan learned to ride as a reserve cavalry officer when he was a radio sports announcer in Iowa. He rode a black mare named Baby in his movie *Stallion Road*. Reagan says, "It was love at first sight." He bought the horse, acquired a riding stable, and went into the business of breeding horses for market. He rode the mare again when he played the role of a Confederate cavalry officer in *The Last Outpost*. Baby has died and he now rides her son, Little Man.

Nancy Reynolds, who was Reagan's assistant press secretary in Sacramento before becoming a vice president of the Bendix Corporation in Washington, shares the Reagans' love of horses and once accompanied them on a pack trip to Yosemite. Several horses she owned at a ranch in Idaho were killed in a fire, which ruined her stables. Reagan gave her an Italian jumping saddle and said, "I hope this will make up for some of the hurt."

At an Idaho auction, Mrs. Reynolds bought a piece of wrought iron that had come off the gate to an old ranch. The iron had an "R" wrought into it, a perfect gift for the Reagans. In a handwritten thank-you letter inviting his "tycoon" friend to come out and see her present properly in place at Rancho del Cielo, Reagan wrote: "Who knows? We might be in line for buying what the h--l ever the company makes."

In the middle of the letter, he drew a pen-and-ink sketch of a twelve-button rattlesnake that had interrupted a recent horseback ride by his wife. "Nancy's horse must have heard one before," he wrote. "He went straight up in the air. Fortunately, Nancy was still with him when he came down. We'll show you his 'rattle'— the other end wound up under a rock. I'm talking about the snake now—not the horse!"

Reagan's image as an easygoing rancher or an old cowhand of the late late movie is deceptive. It does not show the quiet determination of the real Reagan, who pursued the presidency for years until he won it.

Some opponents pictured him as Don Quixote on his ancient nag, tilting at windmills, dashing off on a crusade into the past. He is quixotic in the sense that he has a romantic faith in his country and in his own mission to help preserve its freedom. Certainly, he is old fashioned. He clings to the traditions of courtesy, civility, and gentle manners. To the total disgust of sophisticates, he embodies all twelve traits of the Boy Scout Law: He is trustworthy, loyal, helpful, friendly, courteous, kind, obedient, cheerful, thrifty, brave, clean, and reverent. It's enough to cause weeping and wailing and gnashing of teeth over intimate dinners in Georgetown.

Reagan is like a Knight of the Age of Chivalry scarred by many battles but holding high his sword for one more charge. He was a Lone Crusader for years as the White Knight of the Right, while he was criticized as being far out of the mainstream of American life.

Winston Churchill endured similar shafts from the sophisticates of Britain during the armistice between the two world wars. Frozen out of the government, Churchill tried desperately to make his countrymen re-arm against the rising menace of the Nazi military machine. But they called him a boring old Tory and told him to let them sleep.

At long last, in 1940, when France had fallen and Adolf Hitler's bombers were raining death and destruction upon London, the British people admitted that "Winnie" was right. They called the Old Man to become prime minister at sixty-six and save them. Churchill shouldered the burden of command, not with fear but with a great feeling of relief, happy that after years of frustration, he could lead his country in its darkest hour.

Fortunately, the United States was not involved in a shooting war when it summoned Reagan to the presidency at an age even greater than Churchill's. But the parallel is there. Reagan also felt "called" to lead the nation, as ministers are "called" to their congregations and they pray that it is God's will. Often, he has expressed the firm belief that "God has a plan for each one of us." In one letter, he wrote: "I believe very deeply in something I was raised to believe in by my mother. I now seem to have her faith that there is a divine plan, and that while we may not be able to see the reason for something at the time, things do happen for a reason and for the best."

The President has a remarkable serenity that comes directly from his belief that God has a plan for his life. Call it mysticism, fatalism, or predestination, Reagan believes that he is ordained to fill his present role. Mentally and emotionally, he stands on solid rock. That rock is his religious faith.

Despite his many years before the public, Reagan has remained essentially a mystery to many of his fellow Americans; and they are surprised to discover that he is deeply religious. He has not paraded his piety or "merchandised" it for political purposes. He has not campaigned in churches. But he has a quiet faith derived in childhood from his mother.

Rev. Adrian Rogers of Memphis, president of the Southern Baptist Convention, who was debating his own course in the 1980 election, conversed with Reagan early in the primary campaign and cross-examined him at length. Rogers said afterwards: "Governor Reagan said that his faith is very personal, that God is real to him. He had a personal experience when he had invited Christ into his life. I asked if he knew the Lord Jesus or if he only knew 'about' Him. Reagan replied: 'I *know* Him.' "

George Otis of High Adventure Ministries in Van Nuys, California, asked Reagan in 1976: "Have you been born again?" Reagan said, "Yes," that he had made God the leader of his life. "I can't remember a time in my life," he went on, "when I didn't call upon God and hopefully thank Him as often as I called upon Him."

"Do you really believe somebody is listening up there?" Otis asked.

"Oh, my!" Reagan exclaimed. "If I didn't believe that, I'd be scared to death!"

Reagan, who was assailed in 1980 for voicing doubts about the evolution theory, wrote earlier: "I have never had any trouble reconciling spiritual and scientific versions of Creation. God's miracles are to be found in nature itself: The wind and waves, the wood that becomes a tree—all of these are explained biologically, but behind them is the hand of God."

Reagan affirmed his belief in "the old-time religion and the old-time Constitution" at the Religious Roundtable's rally of fundamentalist Christians in Dallas and later brought a similar message to an audience in New York. "We can rekindle the spirit of America," he said, "because God intended this land to be free; because we are free to dream, to plan, and to make our dreams come true."

This is not entirely campaign oratory to rally the faithful. This is the essence of the real Reagan. He is not only the Great Entertainer. He is also a philosopher and a moralist with firm convictions that he refused to compromise throughout his long quest for the presidency. He knows who he is; he knows precisely what he believes; he knows where he wants to take this country.

Well aware that he may have only a few years left on this earth, the President moves through the autumn of his life with a calm confidence that he conveys to a nation shaken by change and by fear of the future. Americans who look for a Big Daddy in the White House will not find one there. They will see, instead, a simple, earnest, courageous man who is seeking guidance from God.

2

☆

I REMEMBER,
I REMEMBER

PRESIDENT REAGAN was reminiscing one day about his childhood and his mother's heroic struggles to feed her family with very little money. Suddenly, his eyes brightened and he asked me: "Have you ever eaten Oatmeal Meat?"

No, I had to confess that I had not.

"We were too poor to afford enough meat," he explained, then rattled off the recipe: "You get some hamburger, make oatmeal, mix the hamburger and oatmeal together, put it in a pan and fry it. Then you make a little gravy from the hamburger and put gravy on the Oatmeal Meat and, oh, boy! It makes the meat go a long way. I thought it was a luxury. I loved it."

Nelle Wilson Reagan served large quantities of soup and oatmeal as the Reagans strove to survive in genteel poverty in a series of towns in Illinois. Yet the President, who can see in his mind's eye a series of motion pictures of those long-lost days, expresses no bitterness about his hardscrabble past.

"The funny thing was, in those days, you didn't feel poor," he told me. "The government didn't come around and tell you that you were poor. There was always someone worse off. My mother was always finding people to help. I can see her now with a dish, and a towel over the dish, taking food to a family that didn't have anything to eat."

The President loved his father, John Edward Reagan, a tall, handsome, athletic Black Irishman. He adored his mother, a small, lovely woman with auburn hair and blue eyes. "She was the gentlest woman, the kindest woman that anyone ever knew," he said softly.

"My father was orphaned when he was three," he continued. "He was born in Bennett, Iowa, and, after the death of his parents, he came to Fulton, Illinois, where he was raised by an aunt. My mother was born in Fulton and they became acquainted there. Her father was a Scot named Wilson. I discovered there is a Wilson plaid and I now have a sport jacket made out of the Wilson plaid."

In the spring of 1906 Jack Reagan, a Roman Catholic, and Nelle Wilson, a Protestant, were married by a priest in Holy Name Church in Fulton. A few months later, Jack became a clerk in the H. C. Pitney General Store on Main Street in Tampico, Illinois, and the young couple moved into a five-room flat upstairs.

Their first child, John Neil Reagan, was born in September, 1908, and was baptized as a Catholic over his mother's protests. According to one account, the priest said: "Nelle, you raise the boy any way you want. You can get him into Heaven. I'm not so sure about Jack, here."

Ronald Wilson Reagan was born in the flat above the store on February 6, 1911. "They say that babies don't have memories," the President said, but he recalls one: He was only a tiny tot, lying in bed one night, when his father tiptoed in and kissed him good-night. "I remember him bending his face down to kiss me, and he needed a shave."

The President's mental motion pictures flashed back to one day in Tampico, when he was three. By that time, his family had moved to a house in the middle of town.

"I remember distinctly," he said, "that there was a little park between our house and the railroad station. The ice wagon pulled up over there by the depot. All the kids used to follow the ice wagon and get a chunk of ice in the summertime. That was a big treat."

One day a train pulled into the station, but the Reagan brothers were determined to reach the ice wagon on the other side of the tracks, so they crawled under the train. "My mother, missing us in the yard, was on the porch in time to see us do that," the President said. "By the time we got the chunk of ice and turned around, the train had pulled out and there, in full view, was my mother coming across the park. She did not pause. We both got a larruping right there!"

Ronald had another narrow escape in an automobile accident. "We were riding in one of those old original Ford touring cars, with the brass radiator and lamps," the President remembered. "It had to be a neighbor's car, or a relative's, because it was a long time before we owned one. The car tipped over. Everybody got out all right except me. I was still underneath. They fished me out from under the car."

This frightening experience left such a scar on Reagan's psyche that he has felt ever since, he said, "a certain amount of discomfort when I get too enclosed." When he was a little older, and a gang of boys would be "piling on" in a wild amateur football game, he would make sure that he did not land on the bottom of the heap. He had a fear of being smothered under there.

Not long after their escapade at the Tampico depot, the Reagan brothers learned about life amid the perils of the big city. Jack Reagan moved his family to Chicago, where he worked as a shoe clerk in Marshall Field's department store. Much of his pay went to cover the rent on their flat on the South Side near the university. On Saturdays, Neil would be sent to the butcher shop nearby with a dime to spend for a soupbone. He would also beg some free liver for the "family cat" (which did not exist) and his mother would serve that for Sunday dinner.

"The big thing with the older kids—I was too young—was to hitch rides on the horse-drawn beer wagons," the President recalled. "They had big chain loops back there that held the tailgate up and those stacked cases of beer. One day, when my brother was sitting in one of those looped chains, he fell off. The wheel of the wagon went over his leg and opened it up from knee to ankle. I can remember them bringing him home.

"I remember also the Saturday night our parents went shopping and left us at home, told us they wouldn't be long. My brother got the idea that we ought to go look for them. So we took off. . . . Some drunk came out of a saloon and started telling us we were too little to be out on the street at night. That was about the time that our parents found us."

Jack and Nelle Reagan were distraught, and for good reason, the President explained. "Before we left the flat, my brother climbed up on a chair and very carefully blew out the gaslights. He did not turn off the gas. So, when my parents came home to our dark flat filled with gas, they rushed in and opened the windows, then started to search for us, thinking we were in there and something terrible had happened." Jack Reagan gave both of his boys a good spanking to make sure they never did such a foolish thing again.

"My other vivid memory of Chicago was a fire," the President said. "Down the street came those matched gray horses, pulling the fire engines, and the bells clanging. Oh, I lived for years with the desire to be a fireman!

"I had bronchial pneumonia when I was very young and, at that time, pneumonia was a very desperate and dangerous thing," he recalled. "A neighbor, who was much better off than we were, had a son who had a great collection of lead soldiers. He loaned them to me during my convalescence. I can see the scene yet: lying there in bed, with the sun coming in through the window onto the bed, and oh! I had those lead soldiers. I was having battles all over the bedcovers."

Jack Reagan, a restless, ambitious but constantly frustrated man, realized that he was on a treadmill to nowhere in Chicago. So he moved his family to Galesburg, where he found a better job and more pleasant living conditions in a community with green trees, parks, and dark-red brick streets, a picture that remains in the President's mind as a picture of "brightly colored peace."

Instead of being cramped in a flat, the Reagans rented a house which to Ronald seemed enormous. In the attic, to his delight, he found a huge collection of birds' eggs and butterflies, stored in glass cases, and left behind by the owner. The little boy spent hours alone in the dusty attic, admiring the fragile relics which, to his fanciful imagination, conveyed "the first scent of wind on peaks, pine needles in the rain, and visions of sunrise on the desert."

The Reagans were a close-knit family and each member respected the others' independence. Ronald acquired the nickname "Dutch" because, his father said, he looked like "a fat Dutchman." Neil was called "Moon" for some obscure reason, and both boys called their parents "Jack" and "Nelle," with an informality quite rare in those days. Nelle, who was loving and kind to everyone in need, went about the community helping others. She even visited the prisoners in jail on a weekly schedule.

Neither Jack Reagan nor his wife had attended any school beyond the elementary grades but they were determined that their sons would have more education. Every night, when the boys were in bed, Nelle would read books to them, running her finger carefully along the words on the printed page. One evening, before five-year-old Ronald had started to school, he was sprawled out on the living room floor with a newspaper.

"My father asked me what I was doing," he recalled, "and I said, 'Reading the newspaper.' He thought I was making-believe so he said, 'Well, read me something.' I did, and the next thing I knew, my mother had called all the neighbors in to see me perform and I was a one-night sensation there with my reading."

The papers were filled with news about the Great War, which the United States entered in April, 1917. Nelle Reagan took her sons to the railroad station to see troop trains coming through with doughboys bound for France. "Oh, it was just like some of the old movies, with the crowd of soldiers leaning out the windows, the Red Cross women handing them doughnuts," the President said, rerunning this old movie through his mind.

"I remember giving a young soldier a penny for luck. I've often wondered who he was, and where he went, and if the penny did bring him luck.

"We also have a photograph of the Silas Willard School where I was in first grade, my brother in third grade, and they had a big carnival to raise money for the war effort. They had everybody all dressed up. My father went as a female snake charmer with a wig and a fancy skirt."

That was a rare performance by Jack Reagan. Usually, it was his wife who starred in the local dramatic festivals. She gave regular readings for ladies' societies with the zest of a frustrated actress. She recited tragic passages from melodramas, reeled off verses of poetry, and occasionally stooped to comedy. Without realizing it, she also pointed her younger son down the road that led to Hollywood.

"My brother wouldn't do it, but when I was young, she taught me a couple of her readings," the President recalled, "and would bring me along to some ladies' aid society that had asked her to entertain its members. She would introduce me and I'd do one. She gave me a couple of funny ones and I know now that the bug was planted in me then, because I sure did love to hear them laugh! She always volunteered me for church pageants for the holidays, too; I was usually dressed in a sheet as The Spirit of Christmas.

"As a boy, of course, I had no idea of having a career in acting. In a little town in Illinois in those days, you didn't say, 'I want to be an actor.'"

The Reagans were living in Monmouth, Illinois, in a house near the Monmouth College campus in 1918 when Ronald did a good deed that made him a hero to the local Audubon Society. Inspired by the display of birds' eggs that he had found in the Galesburg attic, he started his own collection, roaming through the woods in search of new treasures.

"I was very careful, because Nelle could make you vividly believe that a mother bird was like a human mother and she knew how many eggs she had, so I never raided a bird's nest but what I took only one egg to a nest," the President remembered. "We used to play on the college campus and there, one day, I found a nest had spilled out of a tree and young birds were scattered in the street. I gathered up the birds, put them in the nest, and shinnied up the tree and put the nest back where I thought the mother could find it. Evidently, someone who was a member of the Audubon Society was looking out a window. The next thing I knew, they were calling to pat me on the head."

Little Ronald also had some less heroic moments. "I remember in Monmouth the first time I went to the dentist," the President said. "The drills were a little slower and ground a little bigger than today. Oh, gee! It seemed like it went on forever. I had about three or four lead fillings that had to be put in. Oh, boy! How I hated it! In those days, the dentists didn't want to use anything like Novocaine because your pain was their only signal that they were getting close to the nerve.

"To this day—you know, it's amazing—I start to tense up and sweat even if I'm going in to have my teeth cleaned, just for a check-up. My kids don't understand that, because modern dentistry is nothing horrible at all."

Life became miserable for Ronald in the third grade at Monmouth when a bigger boy began beating him up each afternoon on the way home from school. The bully would chase him past a house on the corner and then Ronald would race for the safety of his home next door.

"Boy, this bully would drive me home, day after day, and I'd be in tears," the President said. "One day, when I turned the corner and the bully was right there, having at me, I saw my mother standing there on our front steps.

"I thought, 'Oh, safety!'

"But she said, 'You can't come in the house until you turn around and fight him.'

"I was in tears but she said, 'Go back, you're not coming in here until you fight!'

"'Oh, betrayed by my only friend!' I thought.

"So I turned around, waded in and threw a couple of punches, tears streaming down my face. To my surprise, the bully took off and ran, and that was the end of him. I learned a very good lesson."

Reagan was seven when the Armistice brought an end to the Great War on November 11, 1918, and Monmouth, like the rest of the nation, went wild with joy. "Never, never had I seen such a celebration as there was for the Armistice," he said. "I remember Mother taking us downtown to see the parade, the fireworks, the crowds, and a great fire burning Kaiser Bill in effigy. All day long, it was a very exciting time."

That winter, at the close of the war, brought the terrible epidemic of influenza. As he walked to school, Ronald Reagan would pass by several houses, each with a wreath and black ribbon on the door. Each day, he would notice a wreath that had not been there the day before. "It was a frightening thing," he said. "It seemed that if you got the flu, you just died."

Then came the most dreadful day of all: Nelle Reagan fell ill. "Oh, this just can't happen," her young son thought, stricken with terror at the prospect of losing the sweet and gentle champion he adored. For a long time, her life hung in the balance. Jack Reagan lighted candles for her in the Catholic church.

The family doctor, after trying all the usual remedies without success, proposed this one: "Stuff her with old green cheese."

Nelle Reagan, on her diet of moldy cheese, made a recovery that seemed miraculous. "It was many years," her son said, "before we learned that the basis of that mold in the cheese was penicillin."

After Nelle was well again, Jack Reagan moved his family back to Tampico, where he became the manager of the general store on Main Street and once again they lived in the flat upstairs. The jeweler and his wife next door, who had no children, became especially fond of the quiet, studious younger son who loved books and birds and solitude while his older brother roamed around with a gang in search of rougher fun.

"Aunt Emma" gave Ronald ten cents a week as an allowance in addition to chocolate and cookies each afternoon, when he would come to spend hours in happy reverie in a rocking chair in her living room with its stuffed birds in globes of glass, its flowers and books and horsehair furniture. On other days he would hide in a corner in "Uncle Jim's" jewelry shop downstairs enjoying his own private dream world.

Eventually, the young dreamer went back out into the real world of other boys, roaming through the woods and swimming in the town canal. One day, Dutch Reagan, a pint-sized eight-year-old, became involved with a "shrimp" about his own weight in the park near the Tampico railroad station. "My father came wading through a bunch of older fellows who were egging us on," the President remembered. "His greatest anger was with them for not stopping the fight. He told them off in no uncertain terms and then he headed me for home. Every fifteen feet, he would kick me with the side of his foot, he would come up under me and boost me a step faster toward home.

"By this time, I was crying again, not from any pain he was inflicting upon me but from my reaction to the whole thing. The worst, though, was when with the last little lift of the foot, he said: 'And that isn't for fighting, that's for getting licked.'

"Then I really got mad—because I thought I was winning!"

When Dutch was nine, in 1920, the family moved to Dixon, a town of 10,000 people about 100 miles west of Chicago, and this became "home" to him until he was twenty-one. After years of struggle, his father started moving up in the business world. H. C. Pitney, the owner of the Tampico store, went into partnership with Jack Reagan and placed him in charge of a high-quality shoe store in Dixon, the Fashion Boot Shop.

"My father had become a pretty darned good authority on the structure of the foot," the President said. "I remember him taking a correspondence course on the subject and studying it night after night. He acquired quite a record of not just selling people shoes but, in fitting shoes and recommending arch supports where needed, he brought great relief to people who had thought they had rheumatism or lameness.

"Dixon is a beautiful town," he said, allowing his mind to roam backwards to the scenes of his youth along the Rock River, which flows through the center of the town. "That river, which has been called 'the Hudson of the West,' became a great part of my life. In the winter, I loved ice skating on it and in the summer I enjoyed canoeing and swimming there. I hiked along its shores, climbed its limestone bluffs, and went tramping around, exploring the wooded country nearby.

"I became a great nature lover. An aunt, who was breaking up housekeeping, sent us some books. One was called *Northern Trails*. It was about Alaska and the Arctic, and the salmon coming up the streams, and the great white Arctic wolves. I must have read that book six times, just fascinated by it."

Reagan the bookworm often borrowed other books from the Dixon Library; his favorite characters included Tom Swift, who "invented" everything from the "aeroplane" to the automobile; and John Carter, the hero of Martian adventures by the author of the Tarzan books, Edgar Rice Burroughs. He liked to watch his cowboy heroes, Tom Mix, William S. Hart, and all the rest in the flickering silent films at the Family Theater, "as they foiled robbers and villains and escorted the beautiful girls to safety, waving back from their horses as they cantered into the sunset."

With some hesitation, the President acknowledged that as a little boy, he was terribly afraid of the dark. "When they would send me to the store after dark, boy, that was an agonizing couple of blocks," he said. "I would usually wind up running like hell the last block home. I was ashamed of myself. I thought, 'My brother isn't afraid of the dark. Is it something I will outgrow or what?'"

He found the key to the mystery of his fear one afternoon when the family was out for a ride in the country. (By this time, his father could afford a second-hand car.) Riding in the back seat with his mother, Dutch noticed her reading glasses lying there. On an impulse, he put them on. "Suddenly," he said, "I discovered a world that I had never known existed. For the first time, a tree wasn't just a green blob. I could actually see the leaves; and buildings had a sharp, clean edge, not blurred."

The truth was that Reagan was afraid of the dark because he couldn't see. His eyesight was so poor that although he sat in the front row in school, he had trouble reading the lessons the teacher wrote on the blackboard. He bluffed his way through his classes.

After discovering the glorious new world of sight through his mother's spectacles, he was delighted to acquire some black-rimmed glasses of his own. "It was worth it," he said, "even though some of the other kids called me 'Four Eyes.'"

He quickly improved as a sandlot baseball player because at last he could see the ball.

"I was the last kid chosen for baseball because when I'd get up to the plate, I couldn't see that ball until it was right here and coming at me," he said. "I had what in the big leagues they called 'The Married Man's Stance.' I stood there on my right foot with my left foot kinda back and ready to move out when I saw that ball. Of course, you don't hit very well when you're standing that way."

Across the bright memories of Reagan's boyhood falls the shadow of his father's personal tragedy. Jack Reagan might have had a brilliant career in business but in all his life he never brought home more than fifty-five dollars a week. He suffered from a fatal weakness.

"I was eleven years old," Ronald Reagan recalled in his autobiography, *Where's the Rest of Me?*, "the first time I came home to find my father flat on his back on the front porch, and no one there to lend a hand but me. He was drunk, dead to the world. I stood over him for a minute or two. I wanted to let myself in the house and go to bed and pretend he wasn't there. . . .

"I felt myself fill with grief for my father. . . . Seeing his arms spread out as if he were crucified—as, indeed, he was—his hair soaked with melting snow, snoring as he breathed; I could feel no resentment against him. . . . I bent over him, smelling the sharp odor of whiskey . . . I managed to drag him inside and get him to bed. In a few days, he was the bluff, hearty man I knew and loved, and will always remember."

"My father didn't go to church as often as he should," the President told me. "In later life he did, but when he was young he didn't go too often. So my mother would take us to Sunday school." Thus, the Reagan brothers were brought up in Protestant churches in little Illinois towns where Catholics were in a minority and subjected to prejudice in the dark era when the Ku Klux Klan spread its venom of hate across the Midwest as well as the South.

"A lot of people today forget that religious prejudice was as great as racial prejudice in those days," Reagan said. "On the school grounds, the kids would talk about the local Catholic church and say, 'The basement is full of guns for the day when the pope comes to take over America and all the Catholics will be out shooting at us.'

"Some people in the campaign didn't understand what I meant when I said I remembered an era when we didn't know we had a race problem," the President continued. "We were accustomed to hearing everywhere, 'Well, they're fine—in their place.' They could be talking about Catholics or Jews or blacks.

"Both my father and my mother were the most unprejudiced, most unbigoted people I ever knew in my life, and the quickest we could get tromped on was to say any deprecatory remark about anything based upon prejudice or race.

"To this day, I have never seen the great motion picture classic *The Birth of a Nation*. No, sir! My father said, 'It's a picture about the Ku Klux Klan and no one in my family is going to see it.' I've sometimes been curious to see this famous old movie that did so much to change picture-making. But, no, I have a feeling that he was right."

Proudly, the President retold the story of the time that his father, trying desperately to earn a living on the road as a traveling shoe-salesman, checked into a small-town hotel one snowy night.

"That was after he lost his store at Dixon in the Depression years and he was driving around in a little Ford coupe trying to make a buck," Reagan said. "The clerk saw his name on the register and said, 'You'll like it here, Reagan; we don't let Jews in here.' My old man picked up his bag and said, 'Then you won't let *me* in.'

"The clerk thought he was joking but Jack said, 'No, if you won't let Jews in, the next thing, you won't let Catholics in, and I'm a Catholic.'"

Since the hotel was the only one in the little town, Jack Reagan spent the night in his car, parked out in a blizzard. "He came home with pneumonia," his son recalled, "and later had the first of his heart attacks that eventually caused his death."

During their early years in Dixon, the Reagans lived on the south side of the Rock River, on Hennepin Avenue. The boys of the neighborhood practiced football from the last days of summer until the first snowfall, every moment they could spare from school.

Despite his poor eyesight, Dutch Reagan could perform much better than in baseball for two reasons, he said: "Number One, the ball is big enough to see, and Number Two, it's body contact. You don't have to see very clearly to ram yourself into someone.

"I started out in just backyard football with my brother and the kids next door, but when I was in the seventh or eighth grade, we moved across the river to the north side and the house we rented was on an embankment about twenty feet high overlooking the high school athletic field. Great was my joy and delight! Home I would come, as fast as I could, in the fall days and down there to that field where my heroes were in the purple-and-white jerseys. I knew I was going to have to play there."

Reagan was a scrawny kid—five feet three, weighing 108 pounds and wearing his huge black-rimmed glasses—when he entered high school at thirteen in the fall of 1924. But he was determined to go out for football and told his father so. "If you want to do something that foolish," Jack Reagan replied, "go ahead, but you'll get your neck broken."

In the first year, Dutch Reagan was such a runt that the team had no pants small enough to fit him. He could not even make the scrub squad. But he never missed a practice. He learned the fundamentals of the game so that someday, when he grew up, he could star on the varsity, just like big brother Moon, who was a regular end. In his junior year, the President recalled, "I suddenly sprang up. I was five feet ten and a half, weighed about 135 pounds or so, and that was the year I made varsity. I was a late bloomer as to growth. As a matter of fact, I was still growing a year after I finished my college football."

Reagan also took part in the school plays, was a popular figure in the drama club, the Hi-Y, the track team, and was president of the student body. Under his picture in the yearbook of his senior year is this sentence: "Life is just one grand sweet song, so start the music."

For seven summers, starting in 1926, Dutch worked seven days a week as the lifeguard at Lowell Park on the Rock River.

Each morning, he would drive out to the park in a truck loaded with ice for the soft drinks and spend the rest of the day lifeguarding. He estimates that he saved seventy-seven people, few of whom thanked him for it.

Once, a family at Lowell Park gave a bottle of homemade wine apiece to Dutch and a friend, John Crabtree, for teaching their children to swim. This is Crabtree's story of the ensuing events: After polishing off the wine, the young men took a stroll through town. In those days, the stoplights were on top of short cement posts in the middle of the street intersections. Reagan climbed up on one of the stoplights and sat there. The police chief drove by in his Model T Ford and asked what he was doing.

"Twinkle, twinkle, little star, just who do you think you are?" Reagan replied.

The chief took him in and fined him a dollar.

The handsome lifeguard also fell in love. His sweetheart was Margaret Cleaver, nicknamed "Mugs," and her father was the minister of the church that Reagan and his mother faithfully attended.

Margaret would enroll at Eureka College, the school near Peoria maintained by her church, the Disciples of Christ. Reagan determined that he must enroll there, too. So, with the money saved from his lifeguarding and other jobs, he entered Eureka in the fall of 1928.

3

☆

"A LITTLE
STAR-STRUCK"

RONALD REAGAN was rolling toward his victory in the presidential election campaign when on Friday night, October 17, 1980, he made a nostalgic detour to little Eureka College and starred at a pep rally for the Red Devils football team, displaying the same boyish enthusiasm and "rah, rah" spirit he had shown at similar events as a student there half a century before.

It was like a journey into the past in a time machine. His old coach, Ralph McKinzie, still vigorous at eighty-six, called the future President "Dutch," and presented him with a red-and-white jersey bearing an American flag and the number "80." Dutch, the coach said, could wear it while jogging around the Rose Garden.

Amid cheers, Reagan took off his suit coat and put on the jersey, and beamed with delight, his eyes glistening with sentimental tears. He was home again at Eureka, which he considers one of the loveliest colleges in America, and he shared his pleasure with the students in a speech extolling the benefits of small, church-related schools.

As governor of California, he said, he had served on the board of regents of a great university system, but "if I had to do it all over again, I'd come right back here and start where I was before." Those large "diploma mills" could provide a good education and they "look attractive and glamorous on a Saturday with the stadium filled," he continued, but at Eureka "you will have memories, you will have friendships that are impossible on those great campuses and that just are peculiar to this place."

At the climax of the pep rally, Reagan lit the victory bonfire after Coach "Mac" McKinzie cautioned him, "Don't singe your eyebrows!" The Red Devils lost to Concordia College the next day, 14 to 7.

Reagan "fell head over heels in love" with Eureka on the day he enrolled there in the autumn of 1928. The ivy-covered red-brick buildings, framed by huge elms on rolling green lawns, would provide a second home for him for the next four years.

Dutch had dreamed of being the first member of his family to achieve a college education. He had saved $400 from his life-guard duties, and that paid for his room. But he needed help to cover the tuition of $180 a year. Through the influence of Margaret Cleaver's family, he was pledged by Tau Kappa Epsilon and lived in the "Teke" house. The college officials gave him a scholarship for half the tuition, and a job washing dishes in the fraternity house.

Eureka, with only 250 students, about equally divided between boys and girls, was already having financial problems because the Depression had come early to the Midwest. Gifts from churches, alumni, and endowment funds proved inadequate. Sometimes the professors had to go for months without pay, and the local merchants would carry them on credit for the bare necessities of life.

The new president, Bert Wilson, proposed a drastic cutback in the faculty to reduce expenses and to keep the school from being forced to close. This meant, however, that many juniors and seniors could not have the courses they needed to graduate in their chosen fields. Reagan and 142 other students signed a petition demanding that the president resign. On the night before the Thanksgiving vacation, the trustees met with Wilson until midnight. They refused the students' petition.

Then the college bell began tolling. Students poured out of their dormitories and fraternity houses—many wearing night-clothes under their overcoats—and most of the faculty members joined them in a protest rally at the chapel. Reagan was chosen, as a freshman on the strike committee, to speak.

He clearly outlined the students' plan—that they would go

home for Thanksgiving, return on the day the vacation ended, but no one would attend a class until their demands were met. It was his first experience as a speaker before such a crowd, and he discovered a secret known to veterans of the theater, that an audience has a "feel" to it. He felt complete rapport with his listeners that night. When he offered the motion to strike, they came to their feet with a roar of approval, and Reagan, at seventeen, savored his first taste of the delights of applause. He recalls: "It was heady wine."

The students carried out their strike. The professors attended the scheduled classes, marked the absentees "present," and left. Each afternoon, the strike committee sponsored a dance, which went on until basketball practice. Eventually, the president resigned, and classes resumed. The students had won.

Dutch Reagan had less success in athletics, at first. He had assumed that with his record at Dixon High School, he would be welcomed to the Eureka football team. But he spent the first season on the bench, complaining that Coach McKinzie disliked him, that he was the victim of prejudice. In retrospect, he wrote, "I needed a damn good kick in the keister."

Reagan was so disheartened that he nearly decided against returning to college the next fall. He had only $200 saved from his summer's work as the Lowell Park lifeguard. But he enrolled again, after he found a job washing dishes in the girls' dormitory and the college deferred half of his tuition until after graduation. He also arranged for his brother, Neil, who had been working in a cement plant, to become a Eureka student, too, with a football scholarship that required him to work in the Teke house kitchen.

Dutch determined that the only way to work off his anger against the coach was to make the team. He impressed McKinzie by doggedly working out on the second team in a long series of bruising battles, until finally the coach put him in the varsity line. Half a century later, the President recalled: "In my last three years in college, I averaged all but two minutes of every game.

"Night football came in my last year," he added. "In the first night game, against Milliken, the lights weren't as good as now. There were no rules then. The Milliken players came out with white headgear and blue jerseys and white facing. Well, when that ball was snapped, we had two or three guys tackling them but couldn't find the one with the ball."

The President is justifiably proud of having been a "sixty-minute man" playing both offense and defense. When the opposing team was threatening, he would say, "Let's hang out the old red lantern," meaning, "Let's stop them now."

Dutch became a Big Man on the Campus, as first string guard on the football team next to the right tackle, Pebe Leitch, who was also the captain and his roommate at the Teke house. The starting center was William Burghardt, another close friend and one of three blacks on the squad. One night, on a road trip, the Eureka players arrived at a hotel not far from Reagan's home, to stay overnight. The desk clerk refused to show them up to their rooms. He would not allow the blacks to stay there.

As Burghardt tells the story: "Reagan said, 'I think I have a solution. Give me the cab fare and I'll take the three blacks home with me to my parents' house.' So the three of us went to the Reagans' home at one in the morning and that sort of entrenched the friendship."

Reagan's memories of college life are a montage of scenes: walking home to the Teke house on crisp autumn evenings after football practice with Pebe Leitch and Bud Cole, his idols; dancing in the living room of a fraternity house with soft lights and sweet music while the chaperones dozed; taking his girl to the drugstore for a ten-cent cherry phosphate; strolling with her down Lovers' Lane to the cemetery, where each couple had its own favorite grave as a trysting place.

Reagan, an economics major, made no great record as a scholar. He studied enough to keep at least the "C" average required to remain eligible for his extracurricular activities. He was so busy being a football star, basketball cheerleader, swimmer, actor, and debater that he had little time for books. He was a quick study, then as now, and could absorb a textbook as easily as he could later memorize lines for his roles in motion pictures.

Dutch, after making his debut as his mother's assistant in her readings before the Dixon ladies' aid societies, had let his career in the drama lapse until high school. Then he appeared in a few plays under the guidance of his English teacher, B. J. Fraser: in Philip Barry's *You and I*, and in Walter Hackett's *Captain Applejack*. At Eureka, he had the good fortune to be taught by another talented instructor, Miss Ellen Marie Johnson, and he became a leading man in her drama class.

His first great achievement as an actor still shone brightly in the President's mind as he reminisced about it fifty years later. "Eureka," he said, "was accepted as one of the fourteen schools for the Eva Le Gallienne one-act play contest at Northwestern University. It was quite a tribute for a little college; no school of our size had ever been invited before. Hundreds of colleges and universities from all over the United States entered, including such groups as the Yale Playhouse and the Princeton Triangle Club."

The Eureka players achieved the finals with their presentation of *Aria da Capo*, Edna St. Vincent Millay's antiwar drama. Reagan and Bud Cole played a pair of Greek shepherds, in costumes sewn by coeds in the sororities. "My high spot," Reagan recalled, "was a death scene wherein I was strangled by Bud."

Eureka's "little band of Greeks" achieved second place honors, and Reagan won a prize for his individual performance. He stumbled down the aisle at the presentation ceremony to receive his award "in stunned ecstasy."

"The director of the Northwestern University School of Speech sent for me," the President remembered. "I went to his office and he asked me if I had ever thought seriously about acting as a profession, and I said, 'No.'

"'Well,' he said, 'you should.' He talked to me about it and I went, a little star-struck, back to Eureka College. For the first time, really in any adult way, I knew that I wouldn't be happy just getting a job behind a counter."

But his dreams of a career in the drama seemed impossible to fulfill, for in the world outside Eureka's ivy-covered sanctuary walls, the Depression was deepening. It killed the Fashion Boot Shop in Dixon and forced Jack Reagan to take a job as the manager and sole clerk of a hole-in-the-wall chain store, selling cheap shoes. Nelle went to work in a dress shop for fourteen dollars a week.

On Christmas Eve, 1931, when the four Reagans were at home for the holidays, a special delivery letter arrived for Jack. In his mind's eye, the President can still see the tiny living room and his father opening the envelope and reading the single blue page it contained.

"Well," Jack murmured, "it's a hell of a Christmas present." He had received the traditional blue slip. He was fired.

The following June, Dutch Reagan and Margaret Cleaver and their fellow seniors stood in a circle on the Eureka campus, holding a long chain of ivy taken from the old brick buildings and woven together. In keeping with tradition, the chain was cut, symbolizing the separation of the forty-five graduates.

Margaret left to become a high school teacher and she and her college sweetheart drifted apart. As he expressed it, "our lovely and wholesome relationship did not survive growing up," and so they bade "farewell to the romance of youth."

Reagan yearned to break into show business, but how could a greenhorn from a small town in Illinois do that? "Broadway was a thousand miles away one way and Hollywood was two thousand miles away the other, and what could I do?" he recalled, as President. "I got to thinking: Radio was relatively new and sports announcing had become something tremendous in a very short time. There were only a few well-known names, or household words, in sports announcing: Graham McNamee, Ted Husing, Quin Ryan. Finally, I conceived the idea, 'Gee, radio sports announcing might lead me where I wanted to go. That wouldn't sound the same as saying you wanted to be an actor.' "

Reagan hitchhiked to Chicago and tramped from one radio station to another asking for any kind of a job—even sweeping floors—just to get started in the business. He learned that he must start, not in the big city, but "in the sticks." He then tackled station WOC in Davenport, Iowa.

Its program director, Peter MacArthur, a vaudeville veteran from Scotland who spoke with a strong Highland burr, gave the neophyte a tryout. When the red light came on in the studio,

Reagan reeled off a fast, play-by-play account of the fourth quarter of the Eureka Red Devils' game against Western Illinois State University, which they had won in the last twenty seconds, 7 to 6. He made his narration so vivid that old Pete told him: "Be here Saturday. We'll give you bus fare and five dollars. You're doing the Iowa-Minnesota game."

"In the week before that game, I would go over to the Dixon High School football practice, sit in the stands, put down on a piece of paper the numbers and names of the players," the President reminisced. "I knew all the kids on my hometown team, then I'd sit up there by myself seeing how quickly I could catch the numbers and names of the players. On a big sheet of paper, I wrote the names and numbers for each position right side up and upside down. When they changed, all I had to do was to turn the sheet upside down."

Reagan didn't dare tell Pete MacArthur that the radio fans in Dixon, Illinois, seldom tuned in to the Davenport station. "We listened to the Chicago stations—WGN, WBBM, WMAQ—but we could get WOC in Dixon and, oh, boy! My folks had everybody in Dixon listening to the Iowa game that day," he said, recalling the great day of his debut in radio. The newcomer found out that MacArthur, the canny Scot, had hired him as back-up insurance. "He really covered himself," the President said. "They had sold the broadcasts of the Iowa games, then they found they didn't have anyone good at that from their regular announcing staff. Pete brought along one of the fellows that had done the first few games of the season, and I was to open the game and do the first quarter."

Reagan, who had never even been inside a press box before, was vibrating with excitement when he looked down from the grandstand of the Iowa City stadium and heard the other announcer say, "And now to begin the play-by-play, here is Ronald Reagan."

With surprising ease, Reagan glided through the first quarter and turned the microphone over to his rival, whose knowledge of football was limited. "It was so obvious that he knew so little about football that my confidence just blossomed, listening to him," the President recalled. "He held the mike for the between-halves stuff and pretty soon he was running down.

"So I wrote a little note saying, 'I have something I could say, if you need me.' He turned the microphone over to me and I described the formations the two teams were using—how they differed, what the terms were—and I did the third quarter. Then I saw a note coming down from the old Scotsman. It said: 'Let the kid finish the game.' Oh, boy! I could have *played* the game by then!"

Afterwards MacArthur told him, "Ye'll do the rest of the games." He did, for a doubled fee, ten dollars each plus bus fare. Then "the kid" went home to Dixon and waited for weeks for a telephone call from old Pete who had spoken vaguely about a regular assignment, saying: "Keep in touch."

Franklin D. Roosevelt was elected President in November, 1932, and Jack Reagan, a volunteer worker in his campaign, was rewarded with a position in the government's relief program, handing out surplus food and WPA jobs to his neighbors. Then, one day in February, 1933, MacArthur called. One of the staff announcers at the Davenport station was leaving, and Dutch would replace him. "He told me to get down there," President Reagan recalled. "I did, and I started at a hundred dollars a month.

"Many years later, when I was governor, a foundation sent some interns to the state Capitol. One day when we were having a luncheon, an intern asked me how I got started after school, so I told the story. A very antagonistic young black lady spoke up and said: 'Yes, but do you think opportunities like that exist to-day? Do you think that young people today can get a chance like that?'

"Before I could answer, another black lady said in a soft little voice from the other side of the table: 'Yes, if you know what to say when the red light goes on.'"

Dutch always had something to say. Soon he became a regu-lar staff announcer for WHO, Des Moines, the 50,000-watt, clear channel station for NBC in the Midwest. During the next five years, he developed his velvet voice and his superlative skills as a sportscaster, describing football and baseball games, boxing matches, swimming and track meets. His imaginative, exciting words made his listeners see the events in their minds.

His creative powers were at their best when he gave vivid play-by-play descriptions of a Chicago Cubs or White Sox baseball game, for he had to make up the action from nothing more than a series of typed notes that a Western Union telegraph operator passed to him through a slot as the news came over the wire from the stadium.

"It's a hit!" Reagan would shout; the engineer would crack a small bat against an imitation baseball and turn up a phonograph record of crowd noises that sounded like the cheers of thousands in the stands at Wrigley Field.

As the telegraph operator would type out another dispatch off the wire from Chicago and slide it through the slot in the studio window, Dutch would go through a spiel that recounted the action as if he were actually in the press box seeing the game. On a few occasions, when the wire went dead, he could even cope with that dire emergency. He would rattle off ad-lib chatter— such as a pitcher going through his wind-up or an endless series of foul tips at the plate—until the wire came to life again. Without realizing it, he was perfecting his technique as an off-the-cuff speaker, an art that would make him a poised and polished performer in political campaigns many years in the future.

His mother had taught him to "tithe," to give a tenth of his income to charity. So, out of the $100 a month he earned in his early days in Davenport, Dutch sent $10 to his brother, who was working his way through Eureka College. After graduating, Moon came to Des Moines, helped out in the WHO studio, then moved up the ladder of radio as an announcer, program director, network producer, and finally vice president of an advertising agency in Los Angeles.

The President looks back at his young manhood in Iowa with nostalgia: "Those were wonderful days." He had youth, friends, an exciting profession, and a steadily rising income that enabled him to send home a monthly check that removed his parents' chronic financial worries. Because of a heart ailment, Jack Reagan was unable to work anymore. At last, he could rest after his years of toil—a life that his son once described as one of "almost permanent anger and frustration."

Ronald Reagan's dreams of becoming an actor lay dormant through his five years in radio. But they revived in 1937 when the Oklahoma Outlaws, a hillbilly band featured on the "barn dance" programs of the Des Moines station, were hired by Gene Autry to appear in one of his western movies. Reagan persuaded WHO to let him spend his vacation time accompanying the Chicago Cubs to California for their spring training sessions on Catalina Island.

In Hollywood, Reagan called upon Joy Hodges, a WHO graduate who was singing with Jimmy Grier's orchestra at the Biltmore Bowl. He sent a note backstage and she joined him for dinner.

Reagan told her about the Oklahoma Outlaws and his own hopes that he, too, might make it in the movies, that his sports announcing could be a stepping stone to an acting career.

She arranged for him to meet the next day with an agent, Bill Meiklejohn. "But, for heaven's sake," she said, "don't see him with those glasses on!"

Meiklejohn looked over the broad-shouldered, handsome young man the following morning, listened to his somewhat embroidered account of his experience in the Eureka Dramatic Club, and telephoned Max Arnow, the casting director at the Warner Brothers studio. "Max," he said, "I have another Robert Taylor in my office."

"God made only one Robert Taylor!" Arnow retorted.

Warner Brothers gave Reagan a screen test—a scene from Philip Barry's play *Holiday*—and told him to wait around several days until Jack Warner could see the film.

"No," said Reagan, "I will be on the train tomorrow—me and the Cubs are going home."

On the way home, he worried: "Have I blown the whole thing?" Actually he had made, through ignorance, the smartest possible move, for, as he discovered, "Hollywood just loves people who don't need Hollywood."

Home in Des Moines, he received a telegram from Bill Mei-klejohn:

WARNER'S OFFER CONTRACT SEVEN YEARS, ONE YEAR'S OPTIONS, STARTING AT $200 A WEEK. WHAT SHALL I DO?

Reagan sent this reply:

SIGN BEFORE THEY CHANGE THEIR MINDS.

4

☆

AN INNOCENT
IN TINSELTOWN

LATE IN MAY, 1937, Ronald Reagan bade farewell to his friends at radio station WHO, bought his first convertible, and drove west from Des Moines—a handsome, clean-cut Midwestern innocent of twenty-six, heading for Tinseltown, U.S.A. The sunscorched desert rushed by his car in a blur, and he soon found himself cruising between long rows of orange trees along the highway from San Bernardino to Los Angeles.

He came to Hollywood, a sports announcer with no record as a professional actor, "filled with all the star-struck awe of one who had from childhood been entertained in the house of illusion, the neighborhood theater." He felt proud and excited but a little frightened, too, as he entered a strange new world where he might become a star or a dismal failure.

He was a green amateur from the Corn Belt and the professionals at Warner Brothers knew it. The studio's chief hairdresser took one pitying look at the newcomer's crew cut and sighed, "Bowl Number Seven," then gave him a more sophisticated hairstyle.

Reagan had to learn the tricks of the trade in a hurry: How to walk onto a set without looking down at the chalk marks drawn on the floor to show him where to stand; how to avoid abrupt head movements in close-ups; how to kiss the heroine very lightly on the lips and not to push her face out of shape. He picked up many tips freely given to him by the stars he had idolized on the screen. These veterans of show business amazed

him with their warmth and generosity and their willingness to
accept a beginner and help him master their craft.

Brynie Foy, the Warners B-picture executive producer and
eldest of the Seven Little Foys of vaudeville, cast Reagan in a
series of low-budget action pictures. The first was *Love Is on the
Air*. It was a remake of *Hi, Nellie!*, the Broadway play in which
the ace reporter on a big city newspaper is relegated to the Advice to the Lovelorn column as punishment for his cockiness.
Warner Brothers had filmed it before with Paul Muni as the star.
Reagan recalls that in his own part as a fast-talking radio news-
caster he rushed to the telephone and yelled to his boss, "I've got
a story that will crack this town wide open!"

His parents saw *Love Is on the Air* in Des Moines and his
mother wept. "That's my boy," she cried. "That's my Dutch.
That's the way he is at home. He's no Robert Taylor. He's just
himself."

Grinding out eight pictures in his first eleven months in Hollywood, Reagan became "the Errol Flynn of the B's." He fought
villains in airplanes, in the cavalry, in a submarine, in a dirigible
down at sea. Once, when ordered to fake a punch, he caught a
stunt man squarely on the jaw and knocked him out. "Naturally,
I felt terrible," he recalled, "but it was kind of nice knowing I
could do it."

Warner Brothers began building up the broad-shouldered
young athlete with fan magazine publicity. Once, at the studio's
request, he escorted a beautiful, buxom blond actress to a movie
premiere. Both, he recalls, were "very scared," she in a gown borrowed from the wardrobe department, he in a dinner jacket from
the same place. Reagan was afraid to drive his old convertible
and did not know about renting a limousine, so he and Lana
Turner went to the premiere in a taxicab.

When his screen career was assured of success, Reagan
brought his parents to California and gave them the first house
they had ever owned. He arranged for his father to take charge
of handling his fan mail so that Jack Reagan, despite his heart
ailment, could be happy again with a useful job. Every morning,
Jack would take a slow, careful walk prescribed by his doctor.

But he was unimpressed by California. "There's nothing, by God," he said, "but real estate offices and hot dog stands."

Gradually, Ronald Reagan became an accepted figure in the Warner Brothers repertory company, appearing often on the screen with Dick Powell, James Cagney, Humphrey Bogart, Pat O'Brien, and the character actors Frank McHugh and Allen Jenkins. Reagan, Wayne Morris, and Eddie Albert portrayed three mischievous cadets at the Virginia Military Institute in *Brother Rat*. But it was Albert who walked off with the acting honors in that comedy, which also featured a pretty young actress named Jane Wyman.

Reagan asked Warner Brothers to film the life story of Knute Rockne, the Notre Dame football coach, and talked about writing the script himself. One day Brynie Foy told him the studio was already selecting the cast of the Rockne feature. Reagan pleaded for the role of George Gipp, a legendary hero of the Fighting Irish, but was rebuffed as unsuitable for the part. Reagan rummaged through his trunk at home and found some photographs of himself in a Eureka College football uniform. He slapped the pictures down on the producer's desk and won the part. Pat O'Brien played Rockne.

Gipp died in the movie and made a deathbed request of Rockne—that when Notre Dame was behind in a game someday, the coach would ask the team "to win one for the Gipper." Reagan turned in a touching performance that identified him forever after as "the Gipper."

Shortly before the Rockne film had its premiere at Notre Dame, Nelle Reagan told her son that his father's last great dream of his life was to accompany him there for the ceremonies. Jack Reagan was an Irishman who worshiped the Notre Dame football team, although he had never seen it play; he idolized Pat O'Brien. But his family had lived so long with his "black curse," his weakness for alcohol, that his son felt a chilling fear about bringing him along.

Nevertheless, the studio agreed that Jack could go, and he had a wonderful time. He and O'Brien stayed out all night after a university banquet but the next day Jack proved a delightful guest at luncheon, carrying on a nonstop conversation with the Mother Superior. On the way out of the dining hall, the Mother Superior told "Gipper" Reagan: "Your father is the most charming man I have ever met."

Home again, Jack Reagan informed his family that he had enjoyed the most wonderful time of his life, and he would not mind now if his ailing heart finally quit. Not long afterward, it did.

The big brawny Irishman, whose own life was a tragic series of frustrations, lived long enough to see his actor-son achieve stardom.

Reagan was not happy in all of his roles. He was upstaged by two old pros, Wallace Beery and Lionel Barrymore, in *The Badman;* he made several B-grade pictures with the Dead End Kids; he had only a secondary part with Bette Davis, George Brent, and Humphrey Bogart in *Dark Victory;* and he appeared as young Lieutenant George Custer, with Errol Flynn starring as the future Confederate cavalry officer, J. E. B. Stuart, in *Santa Fe Trail,* a pre-Civil War drama about John Brown. He played second fiddle to Flynn again in *Desperate Journey,* in which they were two R.A.F. crewmen shot down behind enemy lines but eventually rescued from the Nazis.

In 1941, Reagan reached the zenith of his career with his superlative performance in *Kings Row,* which he considers his finest picture. Kings Row is a small town, like the Dixon, Illinois, of Reagan's own idyllic memories, but beneath its placid surface lurk hints of evil in some of its residents: sadism, incest, insanity. Reagan portrays Drake McHugh, an attractive man-about-town who is injured in an accident. A sadistic physician, to punish him for romancing the doctor's daughter, amputates both of McHugh's legs—unnecessarily.

Awakening in bed, the young man looks down at his body and screams: "Where's the rest of me?"

In his autobiography, which derives its title from that anguished cry, Reagan remembers how he agonized over the scene in advance, trying to imagine how awful he would feel if he found his legs cut off. After a sleepless night, he wandered over to the sound stage where the prop men had cut a hole in the mattress of the bed and put a supporting box beneath. On impulse, he climbed into the rig and spent an hour there, gazing at the smooth, flat place on the covers.

Gradually, he began to feel terrified, as if something horrible had happened to his body. Sam Wood, the director, moved the camera, lights, and crew into place and ordered: "Let's make it."

There were cries of "Lights!" and "Quiet, please!" Then "Action!" Reagan opened his eyes, slowly let his gaze travel downward, then groped for the place where his legs should have been.

"Randy!" he screamed.

Ann Sheridan, playing Randy, burst through the door, and Reagan, in a strangled voice, asked: "Where's the rest of me?"

Kings Row won acclaim from the critics and the public. It brought Reagan a new seven-year contract with Warner Brothers for a total salary of $1 million.

Reagan and Jane Wyman had met while filming *Brother Rat*. She had divorced Myron Futterman, a businessman, the previous year. Ronald and Jane were married January 26, 1940, at the Wee Kirk O'Heather, honeymooned in Palm Springs, and moved into Wyman's apartment in Beverly Hills. They basked in the glow of favorable publicity about their "ideal Hollywood marriage" in gossip columns and movie fan magazines. A Warner Brothers publicity release in 1941 said the Reagans and their baby Maureen Elizabeth were becoming "one of the important First Families of the Film Colony."

In April, 1942, Army Reserve Second Lieutenant Ronald Reagan kissed his wife and baby good-bye and reported for active duty at Fort Mason near San Francisco. A few weeks later, he was ordered back to Los Angeles, to spend the remainder of the war making training films for the Air Corps. Thirteen hundred men with skills as screen technicians made up the unit, commanded by a stunt pilot, Major Paul Mantz. Their headquarters at the former Hal Roach Studio in Culver City soon won the nickname, Fort Roach, or Fort Wacky, for the men's notorious aversion to discipline.

One afternoon, when an officer marched the celluloid soldiers four abreast to the flagpole, shouting orders like a drillmaster, Lieutenant Reagan could not resist shouting: "Splendid body of men! With half this many I could conquer MGM!" The ranks dissolved.

The "Culver City Commandos" performed valuable work, which aided in the war effort. Some of their films aided in the destruction of the Nazi missile launching sites at Peenemunde. Replicas of the site were built of concrete and steel at a Florida base, and bombers experimented with methods of destroying them.

"Day after day," Reagan recalls, "we sat in a projection room in Culver City and saw fantastic slow motion films of huge bombs bouncing off these concrete buildings as if they were pebbles, until one day we saw on screen armor-piercing bombs dropped from low altitudes going through the huge concrete walls as if through cheese. Those films were flown directly to the Eighth Air Force and the launch sites were knocked out in time to postpone the V2 launchings, long enough for D Day to take place on schedule."

Reagan served as the narrator for the most secret project, *Target Tokyo*. This was a motion picture that helped American bomber crews to prepare for raids on Japan. Special effects men, working from newspaper photographs, books, and travel brochures, built a complete miniature of Tokyo covering most of a sound stage floor. They intercut their films of the miniature with real ones taken from flights over Tokyo so that the pilots could identify landmarks on their flights from Saipan to the targets.

Bombing crews in the Pacific would view a motion picture apparently taken from a plane flying at 30,000 feet, and Reagan's voice would be heard over the roar of the motors: "Gentlemen, you are approaching the coast of Honshu on a course of three hundred degrees. You are now twenty miles offshore. To your left, if you are on course, you should be able to see a narrow inlet. . . ." And he would close at the target point by saying, "Bombs away!"

*   *   *

"By the time I got out of the Army Air Corps all I wanted to do," Reagan wrote in his autobiography, "was to rest up awhile, make love to my wife, and come up refreshed to a better job in an ideal world. (As it came out, I was disappointed in all these postwar ambitions.)"

For months after V–J Day, he simply drifted along enjoying the pleasures of civilian life. He took a vacation at Lake Arrowhead and rented a speedboat around the clock. At thirty-four, he became obsessed with a schoolboy's hobby and spent weeks making two model boats. With $3,500 a week coming in under his Warner Brothers contract, he was a wealthy, healthy playboy, and he admits, "I didn't have a practical thought in my head."

When he finally went back to work in March, 1946, Reagan found Hollywood in turmoil over a series of strikes caused by the rival ambitions of two unions. The International Alliance of Theatrical Stage Employees (IATSE), an American Federation of Labor (AFL) craft union, was fighting the Conference of Studio Unions (CSU) to control the studios' workers. Earlier, two alliance bosses, George Browne and Willie Bioff, had been sent to prison for extorting $550,000 from five major studios.

Roy Brewer, the alliance's new chief, waged bitter warfare against Herbert Sorrell, who led the Conference of Studio Unions. A committee of the California legislature later branded Sorrell "a secret member of the Communist party" but he denied the charge.

The Screen Actors Guild (SAG) intervened in the dispute to protect its own members, who were thrown out of work when the strikes disrupted the studios and halted production of films. Reagan played an active role in the peace-making efforts as a member of the SAG board. As a newcomer to Hollywood, he had complained about having to join the guild until the distinguished actress, Helen Broderick, cornered him in the Warner Brothers commissary one day and gave him an hour-long lecture about the need for a union to improve the pay of the contract players and free lancers. She converted him into "a rabid union man."

In 1938, the green young actor from the Midwest was appointed to the board of directors as a spokesman for the contract

players, and he accepted "with awe and pleasure." He still remembers how thrilled he was when he first walked into the
boardroom and found it filled with stars. Robert Montgomery,
Cary Grant, Dick Powell, George Murphy, Eddie Cantor, James
Cagney, Charles Boyer, Fredric March, Gary Cooper, and
Spencer Tracy were among the leaders who had organized the
guild in 1933 and made it work.

In mid-1946, when Reagan was picking up the threads of his
interrupted screen career, the unions began battling over control
of the set designers. The Screen Actors Guild called the rival parties to a meeting at the Beverly Hills Hotel and this session led
to a temporary truce called "the Treaty of Beverly Hills." In
August, however, the American Federation of Labor handed
down a ruling that Sorrell interpreted as giving his Conference
of Studio Unions sole jurisdiction over the set decorators. He
called his men out in September in a strike that led to violence
involving clubs, chains, bottles, bricks, and two-by-fours. Reagan
recalls that the homes of some IATSE members were bombed by
night; other workers were ambushed and slugged.

Sorrell said he did not "advocate" violence but could not control his members. The guild leaders became certain that Sorrell
was condoning violence in his attempt to capture AFL unions
and make himself the labor boss of the motion picture industry.
Reagan was assigned to make a report to a general guild meeting,
recommending that the actors side with the International Alliance, cross Sorrell's picket lines, and keep the studios producing
films.

Reagan recalls that while he was filming location shots at the
beach for his next picture, *Night unto Night*, shortly before the
scheduled SAG session, he was called to the telephone at a
nearby filling station. "I was told," he later testified, "that if I
made the report, a squad was ready to take care of me and fix my
face so I would never be in pictures again."

For months after that threat to throw acid in his face, he carried a loaded .32 Smith and Wesson in a shoulder holster provided by the police, who also guarded his house at night. Once,
during the strike, three federal agents came to him and reported

that one of his enemies had said at a meeting: "What are we going to do about that sonofabitching bastard Reagan?"

Reagan escaped harm, and in early 1947 the guild led the way in a joint declaration by twenty-five Hollywood unions, denouncing the ever recurring strikes by the small "rump organization," the CSU, and declaring that anyone backing the current strike would be aiding in "the destruction of AFL unions in the studios." The strike fizzled out and Sorrell's CSU, Reagan says, "dissolved like sugar in hot water."

On the basis of evidence obtained by the guild, the FBI, and investigating committees of Congress and of the California legislature, Reagan became convinced that "the Communists . . . were the cause of the labor strife . . . Their aim was to gain economic control of the motion picture industry to finance their activities and subvert the screen for their propaganda."

"The direct link to the international Communist organization," he said, "was Gerhard Eisler, who at one time took personal charge of the Hollywood strike maneuvers." Exposed as a foreign agent, Eisler fled to East Germany where he carried on a radio campaign of vituperation against the United States for several years.

"Some of the people against us," Reagan concluded, "were Communists, some were knowing fellow travelers, and many were innocent dupes."

He was an "innocent dupe" himself in the immediate post-war era when, in his zeal to assure a peaceful future, he was blindly joining every organization that would guarantee to save the world. He knew nothing about Communism; the Russians then still seemed to be our gallant wartime allies, and Reagan admits he was "unusually naive."

Eagerly, Reagan joined the American Veterans Committee (AVC); the United World Federalists, which promoted world government; and the star-studded Hollywood Independent Citizens Committee of the Arts, Sciences and Professions (HICCASP). He loved making speeches, his ego inflated by the acclaim, not realizing that he was being "spoon-fed," that both his script and his audiences had been handpicked by the masterminds of the Left. Once, in the spring of 1946, he evoked riotous applause with his standard address excoriating Fascism. Then he added a sentence also denouncing Communism. The silence was shocking.

Another rude awakening came when the AVC called Reagan to report in full Air Corps uniform to picket a studio. He found the picketing decision had been made by only seventy-three of the 1,300 members. Finding out that the AVC had become "a hot-bed of Communists in Hollywood," he resigned.

Naively, Reagan had felt honored when chosen for the board of the Hollywood Independent Citizens Committee, but in his first encounter with some fellow members, he got another shock. James Roosevelt, the late President's son, expressed concern that HICCASP had been accused of being a Communist front group. To reassure the public, Roosevelt proposed that the board sign a declaration repudiating Communism.

A torrent of abuse poured forth, and Reagan leaped to endorse Roosevelt's remarks. "Well, sir," he remembers, "I found myself waist-high in epithets such as 'Fascist' and 'capitalist scum' and 'enemy of the proletariat' and 'witch-hunter' and 'Red-baiter.' . . . You can imagine what this did to my naiveté." As the distinguished board members broke up their session with a Kilkenny brawl, Dore Schary, then head of MGM, whispered to Reagan, "Come up to Olivia de Havilland's apartment."

There, he met with about a dozen other Hollywood celebrities who shared his newly awakened aversion to Communists. Reagan remembers grinning at Olivia de Havilland until she asked, "What's so funny?"

"Nothing," he said, "except that I thought you were one."

"I thought *you* were one," she replied, "until tonight."

Roosevelt and Reagan immediately resigned from the HICCASP board, and ere long, it expired.

As the new president of the Screen Actors Guild, Reagan joined two previous presidents, George Murphy and Robert Montgomery, as friendly witnesses before the House Un-American Activities Committee (HUAC), detailing SAG's efforts to battle Communism. Reagan said a small clique had been suspected of using Communist tactics but had failed to dominate the guild. He opposed the idea of outlawing any party on the basis of its ideology, but if it was proved to be the agent of a foreign power, "that is another matter."

Ten screenwriters and directors who refused to answer any questions about their political beliefs or party memberships, asserting their rights under the First Amendment, were cited for contempt of Congress and later convicted. The "Hollywood Ten" became martyrs when the Motion Picture Association of America blacklisted them. Powerful figures of the Left, who remained in high places in the studios, struck back by subtly sabotaging the career of conservative and moderate actors.

Reagan thinks his career suffered because of his efforts to combat Communism. He was targeted by the Left for special treatment. Sterling Hayden, an actor who gave the House Un-American Activities Committee an account of the Communists' attempts to take over Hollywood, was asked who stopped them. He replied: "We ran into a one-man battalion named Ronnie Reagan."

For Reagan, 1947 was a year that combined achievements with personal tragedies. The Screen Actors Guild, under his leadership, negotiated for five months with the producers for a new contract and finally won excellent terms, which raised actors' salaries from 52 to 166 percent and improved their working conditions. But the strain of double duty, making motion pictures and working at night for the guild, broke Reagan's health. He fell ill with a severe case of virus pneumonia, which nearly proved fatal. Delirious with alternate chills and fever at Cedars of Lebanon Hospital, he did not know that in another hospital his wife had lost their baby by miscarriage.

Both Reagan and Jane Wyman survived, but their marriage did not. When he came home from the HUAC hearings in Washington, she told him they were through.

He tried desperately to avoid a divorce, telling Hedda Hopper, the columnist, in December: "We had a tiff. That's right. But we've had tiffs before, as what couple married eight years hasn't. But I expect, when Jane gets back from New York, we'll get back together all right."

Jane sued for divorce in Los Angeles County Superior Court and won the decree on grounds of extreme mental cruelty. At the divorce hearing in June, 1948, she indicated that her husband had become obsessed with the Screen Actors Guild and political activities. He insisted that she take part in long, boring meetings with his friends but her ideas "were never considered important." "Most of their discussions," she said, "were far above me. Finally, there was nothing in common between us, nothing to sustain our marriage."

Jane won custody of daughter Maureen, eight, and Michael, the adopted son, who was three.

Reagan, who was not in the courtroom, refused to discuss the collapse of his marriage. But he expressed his pain and bewilderment in his memoirs, long afterward: "I suppose there had been warning signs, if only I hadn't been so busy. But small-town boys grow up thinking only other people get divorced. Such a thing was so far from even being imagined by me that I had no resources to call upon."

Although the public may imagine that divorce is not a tragedy among Hollywood people, he added, "that isn't true. If you hit us, we bruise, if you cut us (forgive me, Shakespeare) we bleed . . . There is no easy way to break up a home, and I don't think there is any way to ease the bewildered pain of children at such times."

At thirty-seven, Ronald Reagan found himself a bachelor again, with a Cadillac convertible, a luxury apartment, and a screen star's large income, free to play the field of desirable women in Hollywood. Yet he felt lonely and unhappy, hurt by the failure of his marriage and subconsciously afraid that his career was also sliding slowly downward. He had reached undisputed stardom in *Kings Row*, but his four years in the Army Air Corps had interrupted his career, and he had to compete with younger actors more attractive to a new generation of movie fans.

Reagan yearned to make "cavalry and Indian" action epics like those that kept John Wayne, Gregory Peck, and Errol Flynn at the top as superstars along with Clark Gable, who also made a couple of westerns. Instead, Warner Brothers cast Reagan in its version of several plays—*The Voice of the Turtle, John Loves Mary*, and *The Hasty Heart*. Over his angry protests, he played the lead in *That Hagen Girl*, featuring Shirley Temple in her first adult role, and it was a box-office flop. He appeared with Virginia Mayo in two comedies, *The Girl from Jones Beach* and *She's Working Her Way Through College*.

He quarreled bitterly with Warner Brothers over the roles he disliked. His agent, Lew Wasserman, negotiated a new agreement under which the studio would pay Reagan $75,000 for one film annually over a three-year period, with full rights to freelance elsewhere. Then Wasserman lined up a five-year five-picture deal for him with Universal. But Reagan won no Oscars for the ensuing films. With Ginger Rogers and Doris Day, he starred in *Storm Warning* as a lawyer battling the Ku Klux Klan. He played the father of a teen-ager, Piper Laurie, in *Louisa;* and a Confederate cavalryman in *The Last Outpost*, which partially fulfilled his desire to star in a western. To this day, Reagan is ridiculed for his part in the comedy, *Bedtime for Bonzo*, in which the central character was a chimpanzee.

Reagan was drifting along in his career and in his private life, free-lancing in both, but dissatisfied with his solitary state. "All of us, I suppose, have a lonely inner world of our own, but I didn't want to admit to mine," he commented later. "My loneliness was not from being unloved, but rather from not loving. . . . I wanted to care for someone."

One day in 1951, he received a telephone call from director Mervyn LeRoy, who requested his help as president of the Screen Actors Guild. A young actress at MGM, Nancy Davis, was worried because her name kept appearing in print on petitions of Communist front groups and she was receiving mail about meetings covered by the *Daily Worker*. Reagan, by checking the files at the guild office, found that there was no detrimental information about her there; she need have no fear of being blacklisted.

He reported the facts to LeRoy and promised that the guild would defend Miss Davis' name if necessary. She told the director that she would feel much better if the president of the guild would explain it all to her in person. So Reagan telephoned her and agreed to meet her, if she didn't mind an early dinner date; he had a very early studio call on a film the next morning. She replied that she had an early call, too; that would be fine.

He came to her apartment the next evening, balancing himself on a pair of canes. He had broken his right thigh in a charity baseball game. "The door opened," he recalls, "on a small, slender young lady with dark hair and a wide-spaced pair of hazel eyes." They dined at La Rue's on the Sunset Strip and enjoyed two opening-night performances by Sophie Tucker at Ciro's. They did not go home until after three o'clock in the morning, but that did not interfere with their film-making work. Neither Nancy nor Reagan really had an "early call" at the studio the next day, anyway.

In Nancy's opinion, it was either love at first sight or something close to it. A series of dinner dates quickly followed. Reagan learned that Nancy had been christened Anne Frances Robbins when she was born July 6, 1923. Her mother, Edith Luckett of Petersburg, Virginia, had starred on the stage in New York with George M. Cohan and Spencer Tracy, and her godmother was Alla Nazimova. Nancy's father was Kenneth Robbins but her parents were divorced. In 1929, her mother married Dr. Loyal Davis, a distinguished Chicago neurosurgeon. Nancy, a Smith College graduate, acted in eight motion pictures before she met Reagan.

She appeared with Fredric March in an episode of *It's a Big Country;* with Ray Milland in *Night unto Morning;* with Glenn Ford in *The Doctor and the Girl,* and with James Mason and Barbara Stanwyck in *East Side, West Side.*

In the months that followed their first meeting, Nancy and Reagan made the rounds of the Hollywood nightclubs and then had many dates at the home of Bill Holden and his wife, Ardis, the actress Brenda Marshall. One night, while attending a Motion

Picture Industry Council meeting with Holden, Reagan scribbled a note to him: "To hell with this, how would you like to be best man when I marry Nancy?"

"It's about time," Holden said, aloud, and the two actors walked out.

The wedding ceremony took place on March 4, 1952, in the Little Brown Church in the Valley, with Holden as the best man and his wife as the matron of honor. The Reagans spent their wedding night in the old Riverside Inn, then drove to Phoenix for their honeymoon at the Arizona Biltmore, where her parents were vacationing.

"Dutch" Reagan, the former sportscaster, thoroughly enjoyed making the 1952 movie, *The Winning Team*, the life story of baseball pitcher Grover Cleveland Alexander. He still likes to do imitations of the "hungry ballplayer's stance" and other techniques he learned from Bob Lemon and Jerry Priddy, two major league players who coached him in pitching skills as technical advisers for the film.

After that picture, which won good reviews as well as box office success, Reagan slid steadily downward. He made "a couple of turkeys," *Tropic Zone* and *Law and Order*, and, to his dismay, shoestring producers who would not have dared to approach him in his days of stardom were telephoning him with offers to appear in B-grade quickies. The whole motion picture industry was in a panic over the loss of its mass audiences to television and the decline of the major studios that had reigned supreme in Hollywood's Golden Age.

Reagan, too, felt panic as his screen career seemed to be collapsing while he was still burdened with high income taxes overdue from his days of great prosperity. He was paying for his ranch and his home in Pacific Palisades out of current income and carrying three mortgages.

To save his status as a star, Reagan resorted to drastic measures. He rejected three scripts offered by Universal at $75,000 apiece. He refused to appear in a Broadway play or a television series. For fourteen months, he went without steady work, turning down half a million dollars worth of films, simply to avoid ruining his reputation by appearing in trash. At the end of that time, he was $18,000 in debt.

He accepted a few respectable offers: *Prisoner of War* for MGM, a film about the mistreatment of American soldiers captured in the Korean conflict; and *Cattle Queen of Montana,* which he had great fun filming with Barbara Stanwyck amid the beautiful scenery of Glacier National Park.

At the bottom of his long slide, Reagan received an invitation to appear in a Las Vegas nightclub act. "The idea scared hell out of me," he later admitted, but he accepted because he needed the money. For two weeks, he acted as the master of ceremonies for a variety act that included a male quartet called The Continentals. He scored a hit. Each night was a sell-out and he received offers from the Waldorf in New York and nightclubs from Miami to Chicago. But he and Nancy did not feel at home amid the late-night drinking crowds in Las Vegas.

When the two weeks ended, the Reagans rushed back to Pacific Palisades and their baby daughter, Patti, the "tiny queen" of their home.

At last, in 1954, came the big break that eventually would lead Reagan to his political career.

Taft Schreiber, who headed Revue Productions for the Music Corporation of America, offered the General Electric Company a new half-hour television series, featuring guest stars. Reagan would appear in a few of the weekly dramas but introduce all of them as Robert Montgomery had done in his previous TV programs. G.E. also wanted the host to visit its plants on personal appearance tours to improve the employees' morale.

Reagan was chosen because he had already made an impressive record as president of the Screen Actors Guild and had made many speeches across the country for the motion picture industry. Schreiber signed him to a contract at $125,000 a year, later increased to $150,000.

Thus Reagan moved into the national television scene, which in time would become his field of political action. As he expressed it, he "came out of the monastery of the movies into the world."

5

☆

REAGAN
DISCOVERS
AMERICA

WITHOUT REALIZING IT, Ronald Reagan took precisely the right step in the long road that would lead to a future in national politics when in the fall of 1954 he became the host of *General Electric Theater*. The dramas on network television, featuring the top stars of Hollywood, proved to be an instant success. They made Reagan's face and voice familiar to a large national audience. They dominated the ratings in prime time at nine o'clock Sunday night for seven years out of eight.

Even more important for Reagan's future, G.E. sent him out on the road making personal appearance tours. He personally greeted a quarter of a million employees in 135 plants across the country. After his years in the motion picture studios, a place of make-believe, the actor emerged into the real world outside where he found out how ordinary Americans earned their incomes in industry. Reagan, who had seldom performed before a live audience, suddenly discovered how much fun it was to meet people and see them reaching out eagerly to touch a genuine movie star.

It all began at the giant turbine plant at Schenectady, when Reagan walked down from a balcony outside G.E.'s executive offices and waded into a sea of workers on the factory floor. It was like a movie premiere: Machines ground to a halt; the aisles filled with men and women holding out autograph books. For four hours, the delighted actor walked through the mob, grasping hands and signing his name. After his depressing year and a half of financial problems, and times when he wondered if he had any future, it was balm for his wounded ego to bask in such glory.

The scenes of hero-worship were repeated as Reagan would visit several groups of employees in a factory, sometimes as many as fourteen sessions in a single day. He felt like a vaudeville trouper in the oldtime "five-a-day" routine. At each stop, he would stand up—sometimes on a cafeteria table, sometimes on a truck—make a little speech and answer questions, usually about movie-making techniques, how stunt fights were filmed, what the glamorous stars did in Hollywood at night. The one comment he heard most often about *General Electric Theater* was "Thank you," because the shows never embarrassed the workers in front of their children.

Reagan, who had once lived the pampered life of a $3,500-a-week film star, learned to like and respect the average Americans working at hard jobs for much less money. "These employees," he wrote in his autobiography, "were a cross-section of America and, damn it, too many of our political leaders, our labor leaders and certainly a lot of geniuses in my own business and on Madison Avenue have underestimated them. They want the truth. They are friendly and helpful, intelligent and alert. They are concerned, not with security but their personal liberties; and they are moral."

Because he disliked flying, Reagan usually traveled by train on the tours, which averaged about three weeks apiece and were "murderously difficult." He could lose ten pounds in three weeks while eating anything he wanted, and he seldom enjoyed a full night's sleep. But, he insisted, "I enjoyed every whizzing minute of it. It was one of the most rewarding experiences of my life. There was an understandable glow at being welcomed so warmly; it was wonderful to encounter the honest affection most people had for the familiar faces of Hollywood.

"No barnstorming politician ever met the people on quite such a common footing. Sometimes I had an awesome, shivering feeling that America was making a personal appearance for me, and it made me the biggest fan in the world."

Reagan's travels not only taught him how to meet and greet the people. He also learned how to make speeches on "the mashed potato circuit." When the noon whistle would interrupt his hikes up and down the factory aisles, he would be rushed in a car to a civic club luncheon, rattle off his remarks to some assembled businessmen, and hasten back to the plant. At first, he spoke about the one subject he knew: the motion picture industry and its complaints about high taxes, government regulation, and the Communists' efforts to take it over. Later, as his horizons widened and his knowledge increased, Reagan expanded his topics to cover a broader field.

His philosophy steadily changed from naive liberalism to conservative concern about "the swiftly rising tide of collectivism," which he perceived as threatening the free American economy. He found that his audiences, too, began to reflect public concern about the growing power of a permanent bureaucracy in Washington.

His experience as a speaker taught him how to achieve quick rapport with his listeners with a few one-line jokes, how to gauge an audience's reactions, how to evoke emotions. He was unintentionally taking his own "show" on the road for a tryout all through his eight years with G.E., never dreaming that he was preparing for a political career.

Reagan also found new security and happiness in his personal life. In 1956, he and Nancy built their dream house on San Onofre Drive in Pacific Palisades in the hills off Sunset Boulevard, high above Los Angeles and the Pacific Ocean. The house—which G.E. filled with every conceivable electric gadget as a gift—is spacious but not as large as some of the neighboring mansions that are surrounded by carefully manicured lawns in an exclusive enclave sheltered by the Santa Monica Mountains. The rooms in the Reagans' home are filled with flowers and books and photographs of their old friends in the movie industry. A den looks out on a small swimming pool and a patio where the Reagans and their guests like to relax in the brilliant sunshine.

In 1957, Nancy and Ron made the only motion picture in which they starred together: *Hellcats of the Navy*. This was the true story of an undersea mission in World War II filmed aboard a submarine docked in San Diego. For several days as many as sixteen people in the cast were crammed into the conning tower, along with lights, microphones, and cameras. Reagan, the skipper in the film, worried about his reaction to this imprisonment because of his lifelong tendency toward claustrophobia, dating back to childhood days when he was afraid of being smothered beneath a pile of bigger boys in their football games.

Reagan solved his claustrophobia problem aboard the submarine by hoisting the periscope between camera shots and watching all the other ships moving about in the harbor.

Nancy, too, had an emotional problem. She was playing Ron's fiancée, and in a moonlight farewell scene, when she had to send him off to risk his life at sea, the situation became so real to her that she broke down and cried. Then she giggled between her sobs, in embarrassment, as the scene was shot over and over. "I must say," she remarked in her memoirs, entitled *Nancy*, "the love scenes in this film were the easiest I ever had to do."

She then retired completely from film-making and devoted herself to her favorite roles of wife and mother. The Reagans' son, Ronald Prescott, was born on May 20, 1958.

The next year, Reagan was called back for another term as president of the Screen Actors Guild. He led the union in a long and successful strike for an agreement whereby the producers gave the performers a fair share of the money received from the sale of 1948–59 films to television, plus a percentage of revenues from future motion pictures shown on the home screen. With the first $2 million of this fund, the studios set up a pension and welfare plan for the guild members.

As the audiences for his speeches expanded from local luncheon clubs to state Chamber of Commerce banquets and national business conventions, Reagan began attracting not only bouquets but brickbats. As he was preparing to address a Los Angeles convention in 1959, a G.E. executive told him that a government official objected to his using the Tennessee Valley Authority (TVA) as an example of federal programs' expanding beyond their original aim. Reagan understood that unless he dropped his reference to the TVA he could be fired and G.E.'s millions of dollars worth of government business could be taken elsewhere.

Reagan telephoned G.E.'s president, Ralph Cordiner, and

said, "I understand you have a problem and it concerns me."

Cordiner replied that he would handle it personally; that G.E. would not tell any individual what he could not say.

Reagan did not want to risk having several thousand G.E. workers laid off because of contracts canceled in the wake of his speech.

"Mr. Cordiner," he said, "what would you say if I said I could make my speech just as effectively without mentioning TVA?"

After a long pause, Cordiner answered: "Well, it would make my job easier."

"Dropping TVA from the speech was no problem," Reagan later commented. "You can reach out blindfolded and grab a hundred examples of overgrown government. The whole attempt only served to illustrate how late it is if we are to save freedom."

Reagan, the old-line Franklin D. Roosevelt Democrat, thought it strange that his attacks against Big Government in the Eisenhower administration were accepted as nonpartisan, but after he campaigned for Richard Nixon against John F. Kennedy in the 1960 presidential election, the same speeches were denounced by the liberals. Sadly, he realized that the modern, self-styled liberals were not like the classic liberal who believed the individual should be the master of his destiny; that had become the conservative position. Now, those claiming the liberal label believed in a stronger central government, run by Big Brother.

Reagan found, to his sorrow, that after all his years of leadership in the Screen Actors Guild, and his arduous struggles for better contracts for the workers in the film industry, his former friends at the top of the AFL-CIO were branding him a "right-wing extremist."

A teachers federation at St. Paul, Minnesota, tried to block him from speaking to a student assembly there in 1961, branding him a "controversial personality." But he defied the ban and made his speech against Big Government, and the students gave him a five-minute standing ovation. "They damn well didn't want someone telling them," Reagan commented, "whom they could or couldn't listen to."

The next night just across the river in Minneapolis, where

Reagan addressed a banquet, a St. Paul teacher made a public apology for the teachers' resolution against him. Only a few teachers out of a membership of 1,200 had attended the meeting at which the resolution was adopted.

In its eighth year, *General Electric Theater* finally lost its first place on Sunday night television to a western show, *Bonanza*. Reagan, who personally liked to watch *Bonanza*, explained: "Our half hour, black and white, was up against an hour color program with four permanent stars, plus a weekly guest star, all wrapped in a budget several millions of dollars greater than ours."

General Electric proposed that Reagan limit his speeches to strictly commercial pitches for its products, and quit talking about political affairs. He refused to do such huckstering. Twenty-four hours later, the company canceled *General Electric Theater*.

Reagan never could find out the real reason his show was so abruptly killed. But he later wrote: "I traveled coast to coast speaking on behalf of conservative principles. Indeed, I chose to continue speaking even when to continue meant the loss of my television show." Congressman Phil Crane of Illinois, who first met Reagan while he, Crane, was an obscure college professor doing research for a book, *The Democrat's Dilemma*, in 1963, said: "I was told that part of the settlement of the G.E. antitrust suit when Attorney General Robert F. Kennedy went after G.E. was to get Reagan off the air, because he was reaching the blue-collar workers."

Reagan walked away with his head high, after eight years of "tremendous success," in his own estimation. He later spent two years as the host of *Death Valley Days*, a television show sponsored by the U.S. Borax Corporation. His brother, Neil, now senior vice president of the McCann-Erickson advertising agency, arranged that contract.

Having developed into a polished speaker and a superb campaigner during his years on the G.E. factory tours and the banquet circuit, Reagan now moved forward to the threshold of an entirely new life as a politician.

In his Pilgrim's Progress, he had already gone far from his

days as a "hemophiliac liberal" embracing a vague, naive idealism and voting for Franklin D. Roosevelt. He simply followed the faith of his father, Jack, who always voted the straight Democratic ticket. To millions of Americans frightened by the Depression, F.D.R. became the Big Daddy who would bear all burdens, solve all ills, pull the country out of economic chaos, and lead the free world to victory over the Nazis and the Japanese in World War II.

To these Americans, Roosevelt served as a surrogate father, and his passing in 1945 grieved them like the death of a beloved relative. It was a shocking personal loss that left them bereft and bewildered.

Reagan also lost a lot of his juvenile naiveté when he felt betrayed by the ultraliberals in the Hollywood "front" groups and he became convinced that the Communists had sought to muscle in on the trade unions in the film industry. He voted for President Truman in 1948; for Helen Gahagan Douglas, the liberal Democrat and onetime actress (and wife of screen star Melvyn Douglas), who lost a bruising U.S. Senate race to Richard Nixon in 1950.

Reagan, still a Democrat, supported Dwight D. Eisenhower in both of his victories over Adlai Stevenson. In 1960, Reagan made 200 speeches for Nixon, who lost the presidential battle that year to John F. Kennedy. Two years later, Reagan changed his registration to Republican.

In the autumn of 1964, Reagan campaigned for Barry Goldwater and presented a moving appeal at a thousand-dollar-a-plate dinner in Los Angeles. It was a successful event at a time when the Arizona senator was trailing far behind President Johnson on the road to a disaster at the polls.

Reagan's speech made such a hit that his California friends televised it, added a "trailer" that asked for contributions to the Goldwater campaign, and offered it to the Republican candidate's headquarters in Washington. The intellectual leaders of the Goldwater camp looked askance at the script at first as too negative, too "emotional," and not quite erudite enough for a national audience. But yielding to an order from the Goldwater TV committee, they put the speech on nationwide television on the night of October 27.

Reagan, the onetime voice of G.E., electrified the nation with his address. Lifting a sentence from Franklin D. Roosevelt, he declared with great fervor: "You and I have a rendezvous with destiny. We will preserve for our children this, the last best hope for man on earth, or we will sentence them to take the first step into a thousand years of darkness."

The speech brought an outpouring of money into Republican campaign offices, perhaps as much as $1 million. It also created a new conservative hero overnight, a man with star quality, who could become a leader to achieve future victory out of the ashes of Goldwater's defeat.

Reagan looked like a knight in shining armor to three rich Southern Californians who were seeking just such a hero to rescue the Republican party from ruin: Holmes Tuttle, a Los Angeles Ford dealer; Henry Salvatori, founder of the Western Geophysical Company; and A. C. (Cy) Rubel, chairman of the board of the Union Oil Company. They felt sure that the genial actor, with his gift for plucking the heartstrings of the average American via television, could be built up into a credible candidate for governor of California.

Not long after Goldwater's defeat, the three millionaires met at Tuttle's home for a long discussion and Tuttle remembers saying: "Gentlemen, I think we've got a candidate right here. How about Ron?"

They agreed. Then Tuttle and his wife visited the Reagans at Pacific Palisades for a series of sessions in which the automobile mogul repeatedly begged the reluctant film star to run, saying, in effect: "If you run, we'll see that you get the money."

Reagan could not help being flattered. Nancy wanted him to accept. But both had doubts, based upon the cold realities of politics: Goldwater had lost California by 1.3 million votes; the state Republican party was a broken, dispirited collection of factions, each blaming the others for the 1964 disaster. There was only one ray of hope amid the gloom: Reagan's old friend and fellow actor, George Murphy, swimming upstream against the Democratic tide, had won a United States Senate seat despite the opposition's sneers that he was only "a song-and-dance man."

Murphy had run up a 200,000-vote margin over Pierre Salinger, former White House press secretary, who had been appointed to the Senate by Gov. Edmund G. (Pat) Brown after the death of Sen. Clair Engle. "Good old Murph" had shown how an affable actor with quick quips and a lighthearted manner could skillfully use television to overcome an overbearing opponent who came across to the viewers as "The Bad Guy in the Black Hat." Perhaps Reagan could do the same against Governor Brown, who was bidding for a third term.

While Reagan agonized over his decision, his wealthy advocates made overtures to Stuart Spencer and Bill Roberts, a top-rated team of political managers, who had handled Nelson Rockefeller's losing battle against Goldwater in the bitter California primary. Spencer and Roberts were far from eager to sign on with a potential candidate whom they distrusted as a "right winger." But they lunched with Reagan and several friends at a Los Angeles private club and had two more lengthy conferences with the actor at his home.

The two consultants frankly declared that they would not become involved in a Goldwater-type campaign appealing only to the Right, and that they must be treated with respect, not as errand boys for some Hollywood prima donna. If shocked by their frankness, Reagan did not show any resentment. He answered a fusillade of questions until finally, at the close of the third meeting in April, 1965, he turned the tables on his inquisitors by saying, according to one version of the story: "Now, goddammit, I want to get some answers from you guys. Are you going to work for me or not?"

They said "Yes," and Reagan telephoned Tuttle to begin a quiet, undercover campaign to determine over the next few months that there was overwhelming support from California Republicans to win—not just a primary, but the battle against Governor Brown.

Reagan moved around the state through the spring and summer, sounding out potential supporters and learning details of California's geography and problems, which were all brand-new to him. In Los Angeles, Tuttle, Rubel, and Salvatori opened an office in the Union Oil Building for "Friends of Ronald Reagan" and collected donations by a successful direct mail appeal. The response to the letters and to Reagan's travels proved so positive that he officially plunged into the race for the governorship on the night of January 4, 1966, with a speech that presented him as a thoughtful, moderate leader with a vision of a greater California.

Spencer and Roberts engaged a pair of psychologists, Dr. Kenneth Holden and Dr. Stanley Plog of the Behavior Science Corporation, to instruct the candidate in a "cram course" about his adopted state. When the two academic experts first met Reagan, they were amazed to find he had piles of newspaper clippings, books, and magazines which he had been reading to form the basis of his firm political philosophy. Holden concluded: "Reagan knows who he is and what he stands for."

Plog and Holden collected information about major state issues, ranging from taxes to education, and condensed the facts in several black books, which the candidate carried around with him throughout the campaign. He would copy details onto his ever present four-by-six cards, writing his speeches by hand, often while traveling by bus or plane. If he could not answer a question at a press conference, the experts would be summoned to supply the missing facts. Sometimes, however, the "citizen-politician" frankly confessed that he just didn't know. Such an admission, accompanied by a boyish smile, disarmed his critics and turned a minus into a plus.

Only once in the campaign did Reagan lose his composure. In March, 1966, he and his principal primary opponent, George Christopher, former mayor of San Francisco, appeared before a black audience in Santa Monica. Christopher needled Reagan for defending Barry Goldwater's vote against the 1964 civil rights bill. Reagan said that if he did not know personally that Goldwater was "the very opposite of a racist, I could not have supported him." Christopher retorted: "Contrary to my opponent, I would have voted for the bill if I had been in Congress."

Jack Reagan's son completely lost control of his hot Irish temper and let it flare up like a rocket.

"I resent the implication that there is any bigotry in my nature!" he shouted. "Don't anyone ever imply that I lack integrity. I will not stand silent and let anyone imply that—in this or any group!" With tears in his eyes, he stalked out of the hall growling, according to one witness, "I'll get that son of a bitch."

Holden, who was horrified by the outburst, telephoned Reagan at home and persuaded him to come back and explain to the delegates that he was not angry at them. Reagan's return soothed many hurt feelings and he frankly confessed, "I got mad." Christopher tried to cite the incident as a symptom of "emotional disturbance," but Reagan turned the charge aside by recalling that Hollywood gossip columnists had called him "a Boy Scout and a square." "Fellows," he told reporters, "you can't have it both ways. You can't be a wild-eyed kook and a square."

The Democrats believed that Reagan would be easily defeated as a right-wing "kook" and an actor with no experience in government. They thought Governor Brown should be more afraid of Christopher, who could appeal to labor, liberals, and minorities— basic elements in their own coalition. So the Brown organization took part in a smear job on Christopher, to make sure that he lost the primary to Reagan.

Twenty-eight years before, Christopher had been convicted and fined for violating milk price regulations in his dairy business. Drew Pearson, the columnist, revived the old case and copies of a police photograph of the defendant began circulating across the state. Brown admitted that one of his assistants had fed the information to Pearson.

Reagan won the Republican primary with 1.4 million votes to 675,683 for Christopher. Brown ran poorly in the Democratic contest. He defeated Los Angeles Mayor Sam Yorty but only by 1.3 million votes to 981,088. Yorty played on the fears of Los Angeles white voters, alarmed by the riots that had cost thirty-four lives in the Watts slums the previous year. The same law-and-order issue would continue haunting the Governor through the fall campaign.

Brown, who had soundly trounced two nationally prominent Republicans—William Knowland and Richard Nixon—did not take Reagan seriously. He could not bring himself to believe that a mere actor, closely allied with the Right, could actually become governor of the nation's largest state.

The Democrats decided to emphasize two issues, which they perceived as sure-fire winners: "extremism" and inexperience. They issued a twenty-nine–page document, "Ronald Reagan, Extremist Collaborator," saying "he has collaborated directly with a score of top leaders of the super-secret John Birch Society."

Also, State Controller Alan Cranston claimed to have a document proving anti-Semitic forces at work inside the John Birch Society, and this was so important that he must hand it personally to Reagan. Cranston pursued the Republican candidate around the state and handed the dossier to him at Sacramento Airport, with full television coverage of the dramatic scene. "All right, you've made your grandstand play," Reagan told the controller, who later became a United States senator. "Now why don't you run against your opponent?"

Much earlier, Reagan had issued a statement criticizing Robert Welch, the founder of the John Birch Society, and saying that "any members of the society who support me will be buying my philosophy, I won't be buying theirs."

Too late, the Democrats realized that the voters cared very little about imaginary "extremists" but worried a lot about real criminals killing, looting, and burning in Watts and students staging riots on the Berkeley campus of the University of California. Reagan, promising to preserve order, said: "Preservation of free speech does not justify letting beatniks and advocates of sexual orgies, drug usage, and filthy speech disrupt the academic community and interfere with our universities' purpose."

Hale Champion, who was Brown's finance director and political adviser, later commented that Reagan proved to be "kitchen smart" in sensing the issues that really mattered to the voters;

that he exploited their resentments and emotions not by being a loud and threatening figure but by making wisecracks or poking fun at his foes. Reagan realized, Champion concluded, that "you can get away with being a thundering conservative if you don't thunder."

With his mastery of the smile, the jest, the art of gentle ridicule, the former film star easily surpassed the Governor in television performances that influenced mass voter preferences. When asked what was the best thing he knew about Brown, Reagan grinned and replied, "Well, I know he's fond of his family, because he's put so many of them on the state payroll."

Brown became furious every time he thought of an uninformed, wisecracking actor, with not a single day of experience in government, even in a city council or a legislature, aspiring to become governor of California. In a television documentary entitled *Man vs. Actor*, the Governor was shown in a schoolroom informing the students, "I'm running against an actor and you know who shot Lincoln, don't you?"

Brown clung to his belief that Reagan would ruin himself by some totally devastating mistake somewhere during the long campaign, but the error never happened.

On November 8, 1966, the voters of California gave the governorship to Reagan by a majority of nearly a million votes. The totals: Reagan, 3,742,913; Brown, 2,749,174. Reagan carried fifty-five of the fifty-eight counties, the Governor running ahead only in his home county of San Francisco as well as in Alameda and Plumas counties.

So Pat Brown retired involuntarily amid a crushing defeat for himself and the Democratic party, and the stage was set for Reagan's performance in his first starring role in big-time politics.

6

☆

THE
SACRAMENTO
STAR

RONALD REAGAN came to the governorship of California as an outsider who had never administered anything bigger than the Screen Actors Guild in Hollywood. His years as the star of the political scene in Sacramento would provide an out-of-town try-out for Washington, a dress rehearsal for the presidency of the United States.

Reagan had the leading role in a scene of high drama in the State Capitol a few minutes after midnight January 3, 1967, when he was sworn into office in a ceremony that mingled show biz and government. George Murphy, the former song-and-dance man who had played the part of Reagan's father in the film *This Is the Army*, appeared this time as the Hero's Best Friend. United States Senator Murphy led the inaugural procession into the Rotunda and onto a platform bathed in blazing lights for the television cameras.

The State Senate's chaplain, Rev. Wilbur Choy, administered the oath first to Lt. Gov. Robert Finch and next to Reagan. Then the new Governor turned to Senator Murphy and quipped: "Well, George, here we are on the Late Show again."

Suddenly solemn once more, the Governor made a brief, emotional speech quoting Benjamin Franklin as saying that any man who dared to bring the teachings of Jesus Christ into public office would revolutionize the world. Reagan promised to follow the precepts of the Prince of Peace but would not be so presumptuous as to imply that he would do so completely. "I can tell you this," he said, his voice husky with emotion. "I'll try very hard. I think it is needed in today's world."

At a prayer breakfast during Inaugural Week, Reagan said: "Faith in God is absolutely essential if a person is to do his best. Sometimes we're afraid to let people know that we rely on God. Taking this stand just seems to be a logical and proper way to begin."

In his formal inaugural address on the Capitol steps, the new Governor renewed his campaign pledges to provide more jobs in private industry, to promote law and order, and to reduce the cost of government. To a state fearful of racial disorders and campus violence, he said: "Lawlessness by the mob, as with the individual, will not be tolerated. We will act firmly and quickly to put down riot or insurrection."

"We are going to squeeze and cut and trim" to slash expenses, he promised, and he left the door open to higher taxes "if it becomes clear that economies alone cannot balance the budget."

Reagan discovered to his dismay that California's finances were in even worse condition than he had charged in his campaign. His free-spending predecessor had left the state $194 million in debt. To avoid an election-year tax increase, Governor Brown had resorted to a sleight-of-hand device that speeded up the collection of all taxes paid on the installment plan. He had covered his last year's expenditures by spending fifteen months' income—like a man who stalls his creditors by paying last month's bills with next month's paycheck. Now there were no more funds to tap to cover the current bills. Pat Brown had presided over a lavish banquet for his friends and left Reagan stuck with the check.

In a televised "Report to the People," Reagan asserted that the state had been "looted and drained"; that it had been spending $1 million a day more than its income. He took drastic measures: He ordered a temporary hiring freeze on state employees; reduced out-of-state travel and the purchase of state automobiles; and sold the state's airplane, the *Grizzly II*. He asked every agency to reduce its spending by 10 percent.

The Governor even dared to assail the Holy of Holies and

hold down expenditures for higher education. The University of California wanted a record $278 million for the coming year; he offered $236 million and proposed that $20 million should come, for the first time, from students' tuition payments.

Dutch Reagan, who had worked his way through Eureka College by washing dishes and saving his summertime wages as a lifeguard, thought it reasonable that young people in the richest state should pay a small part of the cost of the college education provided by the taxpayers. But the pampered Californians were outraged. At Fresno State College, the Governor was hanged in effigy. His home in Pacific Palisades was picketed. Students on several campuses staged protest rallies.

More trouble ensued when the University of California regents, meeting for the first time in the Reagan regime, voted fourteen to eight to fire President Clark Kerr. Infuriated friends of Kerr's claimed that Reagan showed his anti-intellectual bias by purging the controversial scholar. But for more than a year, Kerr had been in trouble with the regents because he could not maintain order on the Berkeley campus, where the Free Speech movement and demonstrations against the Vietnam War were creating much turmoil.

In February, a group of demonstrators mobilized by the American Federation of Teachers marched on the State Capitol in protest against the budget cuts and the tuition plan. To their surprise, the Governor confronted them on the steps. They responded with a chorus of "Boos."

"Ladies and gentlemen, if there are any," he began, and the booing grew louder. "The people do have some right to have a voice in the principles and basic philosophy that will go along with the education they provide," he said. "As governor, I am going to represent the people. . . ." More booing drowned out his voice and he left, remarking in disgust: "If they represent the majority of the student body of California, then God help the university and the college system."

Reagan stirred up another hornet's nest in March by proposing to abolish 3,700 jobs in the Department of Mental Hygiene. He explained that in four years the number of patients in the state mental hospitals had declined from 37,000 to 26,000 yet the staff had shown no similar cutback. California was transferring most patients to smaller local centers and away from large state institutions which, Reagan said, "in too many instances had simply become warehouses providing only custodial care."

Under Governor Brown's administration, the state paid 50 percent to 75 percent of the county clinics' expenses. Reagan increased the subsidy to 90 percent. Nevertheless, resentment against his reductions in state mental hospital funds persisted.

In driving ahead with his determination to "squeeze and cut and trim," the new Governor surprised many politicians by actually trying to carry out his campaign promises. "I didn't know you weren't supposed to do that," he told reporters on April 4, when he completed his first hundred days in office.

"I had been led to believe there was a honeymoon period," he said, "but evidently I lost the license on the way to the church."

Governor and Mrs. Reagan incurred more criticism when they left the official governor's mansion, a Victorian Gothic "fire trap" on Sixteenth Street, choked with heavy traffic between Reno and San Francisco. Reagan complained that the trucks interfered with his sleep. "Kathy, those damn trucks!" he once exclaimed to his secretary, Kathy Davis. "I think they shift gears every time I begin falling asleep!"

The Reagans were also concerned that the old gingerbread-style house, in a business district of filling stations and motels, provided no safe play areas or playmates for eight-year-old Ronald, nicknamed "Skipper," and his sister, Patti, thirteen. So with their own money they leased a two-story white brick Tudor house with a swimming pool in an exclusive enclave of quiet streets, green lawns, and lush gardens in East Sacramento.

"If there are some civic-minded citizens who want to give the state of California a mansion," Reagan quipped at a press conference, "I'm not one to look a gift house in the mouth."

In April, 1967, Reagan faced his most agonizing decision when he had to determine the fate of Aaron Mitchell, a black man sentenced to die in the gas chamber for killing a policeman during an armed robbery. Mitchell had first been sentenced in 1963 and Governor Brown had refused clemency. The State Supreme Court ordered a new trial, and the death sentence was reconfirmed. From Death Row in San Quentin prison came an appeal to the new Governor.

Reagan studied the plea for clemency. He also believed it was his duty to uphold the law and the courts and punish a man convicted of killing a policeman, the father of two children. On April 11, he said to Edwin Meese III, his adviser on capital punishment cases: "It will be my decision not to intervene."

Telephone calls and letters poured into the Governor's office, warning him not to let Mitchell die: "We'll kill you if you kill him!" "There'll be blood in your coffee!" "Murderer! May your soul roast in hell!"

Reagan went to bed early that night, but did not sleep. In the middle of the night, he looked at the demonstrators marching back and forth, carrying lighted candles in front of his house in a vigil of protest. Searching his conscience and praying for guidance, he concluded that he had done his duty by his decision.

Some Sacramento church bells were tolling when Mitchell died in the gas chamber the following morning. "Kathy, nobody rang bells when that policeman was killed," the Governor said to his secretary as he sat alone in his office, where the drapes were drawn because of the death threats. Mrs. Davis said she believed his difficult decision was correct. "Thank you, Kathy," he replied, and his eyes filled with tears.

The first execution in Reagan's administration was the last.

Threats against the Governor continued during the era of racial unrest and campus violence. Bulletproof glass was installed in the windows of his private office under orders from his security staff for fear of snipers.

Reagan recoiled from the blasts of criticism that assailed him from every side. Having sailed serenely into the governorship on a wave of acclaim with a majority of nearly a million votes, he had believed in his own popularity. He was shocked to discover how many people hated him. Not since the days of the fight over control of the motion picture studio unions, when he had carried a .32 pistol for protection, had he felt the sting of so many enemies' hatred.

In his time of trial, Reagan fell back upon the faith instilled in him by his mother many years before. He had not mentioned religion very often during his halcyon days when he was riding high in Hollywood. But as he became more mature and had to wrestle with the responsibilities of high office, he acquired a new appreciation of the time and effort his mother had spent in teaching him the need for daily prayer.

His mother, who had died in 1962, left him with many memories of her courage and faith under trying circumstances. "She had an abiding faith in the necessity to believe and trust that everything happens for some good reason . . . and that if a person faces up to the situation without rebellion and bitterness and is willing to wait for a time, he will learn the reason and discover its place in the divine scheme of things," he said after a few months in the governor's office.

"I have spent more time in prayer these past months than in any previous period I can recall," he said. "The everyday demands of this job could leave me with many doubts and fears if it were not for the wisdom and strength that come from these times of prayer."

The Reagan family attended services at the Bel Air Presbyterian Church and often sought spiritual guidance from its pastor, the Reverend Donn Moomaw, former All American linebacker at UCLA. Moomaw told an interviewer, "We've spent many hours together on our knees."

William Rose, religion writer for the Oakland *Tribune*, asked the Governor if it was true that he had committed his life into Christ's hands before his election. "Yes! Yes!" Reagan replied. "I've always believed there is a certain divine scheme of things. I'm not quite able to explain how my election happened or why I'm here, apart from believing it is part of God's plan for me.

"There's nothing automatic about God's will," he added. "I think it is very plain that we are given a certain control of our destiny because we have a chance to choose. We are given a set of rules or guidelines in the Bible by which to live and it is up to us to decide whether we will abide by them or not."

Reagan promised himself that he would try to make every decision on the basis of right and wrong, as if he never intended to run for office again. "I didn't mean that I wouldn't run," he explained to one friend, but he thought that whenever an official strayed from strict principle in quest of votes in the next election, he started down "the path of compromise from which there is no turning back."

With the zeal of an idealist, he told his cabinet and staff: "We belong here only so long as we refer to government as 'they' and never think of it as 'we.' "

Reagan ran the state as if he were the chairman of the board of a corporation. He persuaded business and professional men to give up high incomes and come into his administration at a financial sacrifice. He appointed judges of high caliber based upon the recommendations of the bar associations—not political hacks. He relied upon his department heads and assistants to do most of the detail work, so his office ran efficiently. Sometimes he was accused of delegating too much and shying away from resolving conflicts among his subordinates.

One early admirer, who later became disenchanted, described cabinet meetings in these jaundiced words: "Ed Meese, the executive secretary, would prepare the agenda. Reagan would be at the head of the table, Meese at the foot. Meese would introduce a speaker. Reagan would sit there and not say a goddam word. When the time for decision came on that item, Reagan would synthesize all the arguments. But he dodged the tough decisions. He'd say, 'Let's think about it.' "

But Robert B. Carleson, Reagan's chief lieutenant in his successful fight to reform California's costly welfare system, indignantly defended him against the oft-repeated canard that Reagan was "a nine-to-five governor who liked to take naps."

"First of all, he's organized," Carleson said. "I've been a city manager and head of two departments at the state level and I know you can make any job a twenty-hour-a-day job if you do everything yourself. The important thing is that he organized his administration in such a way that things got done properly; he participated in the decisions and did not in any way abdicate or buck them."

There is a tremendous difference between "delegate" and "abdicate," Carleson said. Reagan, he explained, would delegate details to trusted assistants, check on them to "make sure that the shop was run correctly," and save his own time for more important things.

Critics have poked fun at the "mini-memos," which the staff would prepare for the Governor, summing up the main points on both sides of an issue on a single sheet of paper with a space provided for him to indicate a choice. Usually, the papers would come back marked, "OK, RR."

The "mini-memos" are cited as evidence that Reagan did not want to be bothered with reading a lot of material but preferred to let others do it. But Carleson, praising the system, said: "Yes, each issue was condensed, but there was plenty of back-up material. If it was a routine decision, it didn't take a lot of time. If it required greater depth, he could go into that with longer discussions."

Carleson, a professional city manager, turned down two job offers from the Reagan regime before he finally went to Sacramento as Number Two man in the Department of Public Works, later renamed the Department of Transportation. He admits having had much "reticence" about Reagan but was pleasantly surprised at the high caliber of his administration and the Governor's own ability to grasp facts quickly.

Once, Carleson was called in to brief Reagan about some heavy flooding that had damaged roads in Northern California. "I was struck by how quickly he assimilated the information and then asked the second and third and back-up questions; then he went into a press conference and gave exactly the right answer when asked about the damage in some small county," Carleson said. "I remember the chagrin of the reporters, who used to try to catch him up by asking ridiculous questions."

Nancy Reynolds vividly remembers when Reagan's Irish temper exploded in the bitter dispute over a plan to build a high dam on the Eel River and transport large amounts of water from Northern to Southern California. The U.S. Army Corps of Engineers and the state water bureaucracy strongly backed the project but conservationists warned that it would flood Round Valley along with hundreds of archaeological sites of the Yuki Indians.

Mrs. Reynolds, then Reagan's assistant press secretary, said: "The corps of engineers came in and said they were going to flood Round Valley and it meant displacing forty-five Indian families. The Governor absolutely blew sky high. He threw his glasses across the table and said, 'We've been doing the worst things to the Indians over the years—it's a shame!' The result was, there was no flooding of that valley.

"Generally, ninety-eight percent of the time, Reagan is easygoing," she added. "But you can't manipulate him. You can push him so far, but don't think you can fool him."

Although he was kind and considerate, Kathy Davis wrote: "There was always a distance between the Governor and his staff. He did not wish to be anyone's buddy. After the working day, the blinds were drawn and a veil of privacy separated the Governor from his public life. Usually, he spent the evening at home with Mrs. Reagan and Skipper." (Patti was then away at school.)

Having come into the governorship as a "citizen-politician" with an amateur's ideas about how to run a people's government, Reagan somewhat resembled the starry-eyed young senator portrayed by his friend, James Stewart, in *Mr. Smith Goes to Washington*. Reagan disliked the wheeling and dealing and after-hours carousing that went on among the legislators and lobbyists in Sacramento. At first, they greeted him as if he were Little Lord Fauntleroy, arrayed in ruffles and silk knee pants, tripping off to his music lesson. They waylaid this new boy on the block and mussed him up.

But Dutch Reagan, who had gloried in the bloody cuts and bruises that he sustained in football scrimmages as a boy, soon learned how to fight back. He let the legislators know that they could not get away with assailing him verbally on the floor and then greeting him the next day as if they were friends. He took each battle personally.

Frequently, Reagan mobilized public support for his policies by going over the heads of the legislators and appealing directly to the people. He used his great talents as a television performer as his former idol, Franklin D. Roosevelt, had done with radio in his "fireside chats."

Reagan convinced Californians that he had inherited a fiscal mess, the $194-million deficit, and he deserved credit for trying to trim the state's expenditures although some of the cuts proved unwise and were later restored. The steadily rising cost of providing services to more than 20 million people in the nation's largest state compelled the Governor to approve a $5-billion budget during his first year in office.

Through a temporary alliance with the Democrats' "Big Daddy," House Speaker Jesse Unruh, Reagan won the legislature's approval of a billion-dollar tax increase. It boosted levies across the board—on personal and corporate income, sales, cigarettes, and liquor—balanced the budget, and began a reduction in the property taxes that especially burdened elderly homeowners.

Reagan did not look like Little Lord Fauntleroy in his repeated efforts to curb the violence that marred several state colleges and universities. He pleaded with the administrators to show moral courage enough to cope with white students protesting the Vietnam War and blacks accusing officials of racism. He charged that the academics' own "so-called liberal philosophy, making them sympathetic to the announced aims of the riots, blinds them to their responsibility to offer protection to the others on the campus."

At one session, the Governor listened for two hours as the university officials told him how terribly complex the campus problem was, how complicated it was to discipline those who were beating fellow students, breaking windows, planting bombs. Finally, he asked one question: " 'How complex would it be if the mob outside was under the auspices of the Ku Klux Klan?"

He concluded that if the Klan were involved instead of some leftist group, "they would know how to handle this in about three and a half minutes."

When the campus authorities fail to do their duty and stop the "physical assaults, arson, bombing, destruction of property, the law must be called in," the Governor told one critic of his firm policy.

"This administration will do whatever is possible to maintain order on our campuses so that the vast majority of students, who attend to learn and to study, can have that right," he said in a televised report to the people after his first year in office. "Currently, the taxpayer foots a bill that averages out to two thousand nine hundred dollars per student at the university level."

Reagan reacted with sorrow and disgust when a band of students insulted the regents at a meeting in October, 1968, at the University of California, Santa Cruz. He was shocked by "the sad experience of seeing students on that beautiful campus rioting, threatening physical harm to the regents assembled there, and cursing the regents with profanity and unrepeatable obscenities."

But, he added in a letter to Bing Russell of Thousand Oaks, "out of all this came one bright moment: On the bus tour of the campus, students had been assigned to the buses as guides. I found myself seated beside one of the nicest, most ladylike young women one could hope to meet—your daughter.

"After hearing her good common-sense reaction to all that was going on, I finally had to ask how she had been able to maintain such a sense of values in the atmosphere so prevalent there. She stated very simply, 'That's the way my mother and father raised me.'

"You must be very proud and you have every right to be."

San Francisco State University, repeatedly disrupted by violence, closed down completely in November, 1968, and President Robert Smith resigned. His predecessor, John Summerskill, had left in May to take a job in Ethiopia. Reagan called the closing of the university a "surrender to a small, unrepresentative faction of faculty and student militants." He proposed that the next president be a strong man chosen from the faculty and asked: "What about this man, Professor Hayakawa?"

The Governor had never met S. I. Hayakawa, who had won a

national scholastic reputation as a semanticist and had recently spoken out against radical elements attempting to destroy great universities.

This is Hayakawa's own version of the events that would later lead to his election as a United States senator:

"The trustees, having lost two presidents in one year, were really at the bottom of the barrel. I was so angry about the campus violence that I said in a speech in November, 1968, that racial injustice in America and the war in Vietnam were no reason for disrupting our classes; we could make a better world only by educating our students. The remark was so unusual, coming from a faculty member at that time, that it was reprinted in the San Francisco and Los Angeles papers.

"The trustees asked, 'Who is this guy Hayakawa? Would he take the presidency of San Francisco State?'

"Chancellor Glenn Dumke said, 'Oh, no, he wouldn't take it, he's a scholar, wrapped up in his semantics studies—besides, he's working only half time.' Well, they decided, 'Call him up; all he can do is say no.'

"So they called by telephone from Los Angeles and asked if I would accept the temporary presidency. I said, 'Yes, I will—under one condition. . . . That I may use as many police as are necessary to keep order on the campus.'

"They agreed, and I am told that Governor Reagan said, 'If Hayakawa can get that college straightened out, we'll forgive him for Pearl Harbor.' "

Hayakawa, who took over the presidency on December 2, cracked down on the militants, who mistakenly assumed that they could make him cave in as they had bullied his predecessors. He banned campus demonstrations that would disturb the students who were studying for their midwinter examinations. The dissidents disobeyed his order, and about 400 were arrested in one mass sweep.

Hayakawa, with his colorful, knit tam-o'-shanter cocked jauntily on his head, became a folk hero when he was seen on national television, pulling out the wires of a sound truck the radicals were using in defiance of his authority. The scholarly man of words proved himself a man of action in his fight for the rights of the orderly students to pursue their education in peace and safety.

Reagan backed him all the way. "Those who want to get an education, those who want to teach, should be protected at the point of a bayonet if necessary," the Governor declared in January, 1969. "I don't care what force it takes. That force must be applied."

When students trying to attend classes were beaten up by strikers from the Third World Liberation Front in February, Reagan ordered in the highway patrol. "Students have been assaulted," he said. "Arsons and fire bombings have occurred and the university property has been destroyed." At Reagan's invitation, the beleaguered Hayakawa often went to Sacramento and conferred with him about the strategy for maintaining order on the campus.

"With the help of the Governor, Chancellor Glenn Dumke, San Francisco Mayor Joseph Alioto, and the Police Department, we restored order on the campus of San Francisco State," Hayakawa said. "I remain grateful to all of these strong leaders."

As a university president under fire, Hayakawa learned that "the most important thing is a prompt decision: Make up your mind and do something."

Reagan showed that capacity for making decisions, the senator said. Disputing the claim that "Reagan goes with the last person who talks with him," he declared: "Not Reagan! He is a man who takes his position and doesn't change his mind."

The liberal arts professors considered Reagan "a villain" and claimed he was "stingy" in funds for education, Hayakawa said. "Actually, the period in which he was governor was a time of rapid growth of all the colleges in the state system. We had great increases in enrollment and appropriations. The students still don't pay tuition. They pay certain fees, but nothing compared to the three-to-five thousand dollars charged by private universities."

As for the academics' charge that Reagan was "anti-intellectual," Hayakawa snapped: "That was always rubbish. But it was the position of the compulsive liberals of that period. If you didn't agree with them on every issue, then you weren't an intellectual."

Reagan's political sex appeal and his eloquence as a speaker at Republican fund-raising affairs throughout the country made him a natural prospect for a place on his party's national ticket in 1968, despite his brief experience as governor. He became California's favorite son candidate for the presidential nomination, chiefly as a device to prevent a bitter, divisive primary battle like the Rockefeller-Goldwater fight which had contributed to the debacle of 1964. In effect, Reagan posted a "no trespassing" sign on California. He carefully balanced the state's delegation to the Miami Beach convention to include leaders from all factions, for the sake of unity.

While the Governor refused to be an active candidate, several of his aides worked like beavers behind the scenes to make him one. Lyn Nofziger, his press secretary, was the ringleader, and Tom Reed resigned as appointments secretary to promote the subtle noncampaign among Republicans across the nation with financial support from millionaires Holmes Tuttle and Henry Salvatori.

F. Clifton White, the premier delegate-hunter who had engineered Goldwater's nomination, was hired to contact key Republicans in various states, ostensibly for the purpose of briefing the California delegation on the prospects of the contenders for the White House. Richard Nixon emerged as the front-runner through a series of primary victories over token opposition. Michigan's Gov. George Romney pulled out after discovering that he was merely being used as a stalking horse by New York's Gov. Nelson Rockefeller, who did not dare to battle Nixon in the primaries, for fear of defeat.

Nixon's foes persistently spread the word that "he can't win," citing his double defeats—by John F. Kennedy in the close presidential race of 1960 and by Gov. Pat Brown in 1962. Nofziger and Company never tired of pointing out that the same Pat Brown, who had conquered Nixon, was crushed four years later by the handsome giant-killer, Reagan, by nearly a million votes. Republicans who had doubts about "loser" Nixon should, they argued, swing to Reagan.

Rockefeller tried to block Nixon from a first-ballot nomination by persuading a flock of favorite sons to hold on to their states' delegates and thus produce a convention deadlock that could throw the nomination to him. The liberal New York Governor also sought an alliance of convenience with the conservative California Governor by spreading stories that they might combine forces to create a "dream ticket"—with Rockefeller, of course, on the top.

Reagan angrily denied press reports that he had made any kind of deal, "tacit or actual," with any presidential contender regarding the vice presidency or any other political post. He declared in a Sacramento statement May 10, "I will not accept the vice presidential nomination regardless of who the nominee for President may be. I have made no deals . . . Those who say or write differently have either been duped or are dispensing deliberate falsehoods."

On May 20, both Reagan and Rockefeller were interviewed at length by the Southern Republican chairmen at New Orleans. While Reagan was dressing in his hotel room that morning, Rockefeller barged in and, after some pointless conversation, came out to meet the press, declaring that there was "no gulf in ideology" between him and Reagan. Rockefeller reiterated his claim on national television, further infuriating Reagan.

On the night of June 4, after his triumph over Eugene McCarthy in the California Democratic presidential primary, Robert F. Kennedy was fatally shot in Los Angeles. The Reagans sent a letter of sympathy to Ethel Kennedy and the Governor wrote to their daughter, Patti, at her school in Arizona: "I've been here in the office all day, and feeling almost sick most of the time. Even though I disagree with him on political matters and even though I disapprove of him and his approach to these problems, I still feel very deeply the tragedy of this young man taken from his family in this way. . . .

"There are many times when I have wondered why I'm doing what I'm doing. Now is one of those moments when I'm grateful that I can be in a position to perhaps change things to see that we do start a return to sanity and law and order and turn away from this whole creed of violence that seems to be so prevalent in our land."

The following month, Reagan made a flying swing across the country, meeting privately with Republican convention delegates, with special emphasis on the South, where he had great popularity. He found, however, that nearly all the Dixie delegates had been locked up by Nixon, largely through the influence of South Carolina's Sen. Strom Thurmond and by Barry Goldwater.

Cliff White, Reagan's companion on his travels, gave him his first lessons in delegate-hunting on the national scene and found him an eager student, quickly absorbing the lore of Republican politics in various states. Reagan officially became a presidential contender at the opening of the Miami Beach convention and began a whirlwind courtship of the Southern delegates.

White believed that the Florida delegation, locked in for Nixon under the unit rule, which gave all its convention votes to the candidate with a mere majority, could be swung over to Reagan if only one or two wavering conservatives could be switched. Mississippi also hung in the balance, and White had several delegates in Thurmond's own South Carolina bloc eager to declare for Reagan.

Reagan made personal appeals to the doubtful Dixie delegates in his campaign trailer parked outside the convention hall. Several women wept as they avowed that their hearts were truly with Ronnie, but their votes were pledged to Richard, and they could not be released. White sarcastically commented that the floor of the trailer was flooded with the dear ladies' tears.

But Nixon's agents frightened the ultraconservative Southerners by warning that if their man lost on the first ballot, the nomination would eventually go, not to Reagan but to the liberal they feared most of all—Rockefeller. Nixon achieved his victory by a narrow margin without California's delegates. Reagan then marched up to the podium and moved that the decision be made unanimous.

At his next press conference in Sacramento, the Governor was asked, "Is the presidential bug finally out of your system?"

"There never was a presidential bug in my system," he retorted, his anger rising. He had been amazed to find how many people at the convention believed he should be the nominee, he said.

No harm had been done. While Reagan may have looked a little too eager to reach the White House after a brief sojourn in Sacramento, he actually strengthened his claim to be considered seriously as a future candidate for the presidency. His friends had begun to form the nationwide network of zealous admirers who would keep his flame of hope alive through the years until 1980.

Reagan's popularity remained so high that in 1970 he easily won a second term, defeating Jesse Unruh by a majority of about half a million votes.

As his first priority when his second term began in January, 1971, Governor Reagan set out to reform the welfare system, which in California as in the rest of the nation was completely out of control. Robert B. Carleson became director of the Department of Social Welfare with orders to design a program that would stop the skyrocketing growth of the welfare rolls and produce savings that would increase the benefits paid to the truly needy people as well as the aged, blind, and disabled.

Carleson reluctantly left the highway department, which spent about $1.5 billion a year on the biggest road program of any state. He was amazed to find that the welfare program, not counting Medicaid, had soared to $2.5 billion annually in the previous decade; the welfare rolls had risen from about 600,000 to more than 2.2 million persons, a tenth of California's population; and experts predicted the growth would continue indefinitely, requiring huge tax increases. The welfare system in Carleson's view was "literally a mess."

Reagan had a lot of advice from within his administration not to take on the Welfare Monster, that it was a no-win cause. "We are going to have some dark days because the Welfare Rights groups will fight us at every step of the way," Carleson warned him.

Reagan replied, "We have to do it." He was convinced that he must reform the welfare system to be an effective governor; he didn't care how the fight might affect his future.

Carleson called on Ronald Zumbrun, a lawyer, and John

Svahn, an analyst, both from the Department of Public Works, to help him in a top-to-bottom reorganization of the Department of Social Welfare. They tightened eligibility standards, simplified procedures, and stressed requirements that employable recipients of welfare payments must actively seek work. A team of auditors from the Department of Finance found the state was losing more than $50 million a year through eligibility errors alone. Tighter audits aided in the crackdown on welfare fraud.

Reagan studied the welfare system in depth and on March 3, 1971, delivered to the legislature a comprehensive message on the subject—a 175-page book proposing more than seventy changes. The immediate response was hostile: His plan was "too complicated." It could never be enacted. The leaders were dead set against it.

The Democrats, controlling the legislature, had no desire to give another victory to the newly re-elected Republican Governor. Reagan went over their heads directly to the people by television to build up support for his bill. He appointed a bipartisan citizens' committee, headed by Al McCandless, chairman of the Riverside County board of supervisors, and more than a hundred local committees of the same kind were created across California. Reagan, Carleson, and a few associates flew around the state, briefing newspaper editorial boards and making a sales pitch for the proposed reforms. Letters and cards backing the welfare changes poured into the legislators' offices in Sacramento.

As a result of the pressure, House Speaker Bob Moretti went to the Governor and called for a truce. According to the speaker's own version of the incident, he walked into Reagan's office and said, "Look, I don't like you, and I know you don't like me. But if this state is going to function, we had better try to work together and I suggest we start."

Carleson's recollection is somewhat different: Moretti threw up his hands and said, "Governor, stop your cards and letters." In either case, the two rival political leaders began to negotiate.

Reagan gained an initial advantage by arranging for the bargaining to take place in his own office. Then he said, "Let's use our welfare bills as the basis of discussion." The legislators agreed. They sat on one side of a long table with their staffs, facing the Governor, Carleson, Zumbrun, and other aides.

As Reagan went down the list of proposed changes in the law, Moretti would usually say, "That sounds good to me," or "Let's go on to the next item." His staff members, opposing any changes in the welfare bureaucracy, would beg him to reconsider his approval; in Carleson's words, "they were having conniption fits."

As Carleson recalls the sessions, Moretti and John Burton (who later went to Congress) would use "very strong language" in an effort to shock and intimidate Reagan into giving up major parts of his plan. But they found out that he was not Little Lord Fauntleroy. Reagan held his ground and he pounded the table a few times to make his point.

In the week of intensive negotiations, both sides favored increasing the benefits to welfare recipients for the first time in thirteen years. At that time a needy family of four in California was receiving $221 a month plus food stamps through Aid to Families with Dependent Children. Reagan said, according to Carleson, "We want the increase but we can't finance it unless we have corrections in the system to cut out the waste." In the end, a compromise bill emerged, including most of the Governor's proposed reforms and a 26 percent boost in benefits, later raised to 43 percent.

The technicians on both sides engaged in ten more days of heated discussions over the details of the legislation. It cleared both houses and Reagan signed it into law on August 13, 1971.

California's welfare rolls, which had been climbing at the rate of 40,000 persons per month, began declining in April as a result of Carleson's administrative reforms, which the new law made permanent. By the end of November, they were down by 180,000, despite a series of lawsuits intended to nullify the rules changes.

Critics of the welfare reform plan continued their efforts to scuttle it in the courts and in the legislature. Sen. Anthony Beilenson, the nominal author of the bill and later a congressman, staged a series of hearings to investigate charges that the law was not being carried out correctly. Carleson, who called the sessions "a kangaroo court," endured long days of hostile cross-examination.

Reagan wanted to attend as a spectator so that if the attacks became too abusive he could take his cabinet officer by the arm and say, "Come on, Bob, let's get out of here." But the Governor's staff persuaded him not to make such a defiant gesture. Instead, Reagan told Carleson, "When they get abusive again, you just get up and leave. Tell 'em I told you to leave."

Carleson never staged such a walkout. Still, he appreciated the way the Governor "hung in there when most politicians would have caved in or compromised or fired some scapegoats." Carleson became the United States Commissioner of Welfare in March, 1973.

"We not only avoided the five hundred thousand growth in California's welfare rolls, which the experts predicted for the decade of the 1970's," he said. "There were still three hundred thousand fewer people on family welfare and general assistance in 1980, nine years after we started the reforms in March, 1971."

Looking back on his eight years as governor, which he called "the most fulfilling" of his entire life, Reagan commented: "The two things I'm most proud of in those years were, first, the restoration of solvency to the state, getting it out of debt and then returning to the taxpayers some five point seven billion dollars in tax rebates; and, second, the welfare reforms which reduced the rolls by some three hundred thousand people who were not really eligible for help. We saved the taxpayers two billion dollars in three years and raised the grants to the deserving needy by forty-three percent."

For the first time in three decades, California bonds were raised to the highest possible rating in the market, Moody's Triple A. A San Francisco newspaper said of Reagan: "We exaggerate very little when we say that he has saved the state from bankruptcy."

Reagan suffered a setback in 1974 when the California voters rejected Proposition One, which he strongly advocated. It would have placed an eventual 7 percent ceiling on the amount of taxes the state and local government could impose. The beneficiaries of the spending programs, fearing sharp cutbacks, waged a furious fight against the proposal and beat it by a margin of 54 percent to 46 percent.

However, Sen. S. I. Hayakawa, who calls himself Reagan's "Samurai Warrior," said: "Reagan deserves the credit for starting the tax reduction movement. It led directly to the approval of Proposition Thirteen, for the limit on property taxes in 1978. In perceiving and responding to the profound public discontent with the costs of government, Ronald Reagan was, as wise men are, well ahead of his time."

Reagan, who had come into the governorship as an amateur, derided by his foes as merely a "Hollywood actor," developed over the years in Sacramento into a tough executive who learned how to deal with the legislature and to rally the people to his cause. The Los Angeles *Times* said he left office "an accomplished practitioner in the art of government, a proven administrator and a polished and potent force in conservative national politics."

In January, 1975, Reagan transferred the reins of office to his successor, Edmund Brown, Jr., the son of the man he had beaten in 1966.

Serving as governor, Reagan told one constituent in a letter, "has been the most soul-satisfying thing I've ever done, because I believed in a principle and am realizing the joy of battling and sacrificing to implement that principle."

As a private citizen once again, but more zealous than ever in his dedication to principle, Reagan looked eastward from California in quest of new worlds to conquer.

7

☆

THE
HOLLYWOOD
HAMLET

> To be, or not to be, that is the question. . . .
> —*Hamlet*

WHEN HE LEFT SACRAMENTO early in 1975, after his eight years as governor, Reagan reveled at first in his new freedom from official cares and the endless vistas of time ahead to be enjoyed with Nancy in the privacy of their ranch in the California hills. But he also had to wrestle with the question of making a second bid for the presidency.

The fires of his ambition had been ignited at Miami Beach in the summer of 1968 when, as a neophyte totally unsure of himself in the national political arena, he had made his brief race as California's favorite son candidate at the Republican convention. He felt relief, rather than keen disappointment, when his eager associates, working secretly with aides of Nelson Rockefeller, had failed to bring about a deadlock and block Richard Nixon from his first-ballot victory. Reagan was unready for the presidency then, and he knew it. But his promoters resolved that they would move into the White House next; so, early in Nixon's second term, they began quietly lining up pledges of support for 1976.

As one small example of the soft-sell campaign, North Carolina's influential Sen. Jesse Helms received a telephone call from the Governor while attending a convention in San Francisco in August, 1973. Could the senator spare the time to have lunch the next day with the Reagans at their Pacific Palisades home?

Helms did, and he recalls that "Ron and Nancy impressed me as sincere, decent people who were deeply concerned about their country." Helms raised the subject of a second Reagan bid for the presidency and, to his surprise, found his host seemed less than enthusiastic.

"Well, if you ever decide to run for President," the senator said, "and, if you feel that I can be helpful, count me in. I'll be honored to do whatever I can."

Robert Walker, the Governor's political adviser in the Sacramento years, slipped into Washington in early 1974 and recruited a young lawyer named John P. Sears III to begin making sub rosa plans for a presidential campaign. They were old friends who had opened the first Nixon-for-President office in 1967 in a Pennsylvania Avenue storefront near the White House.

In 1968, at twenty-seven, Sears took leave from the Nixon law firm in New York for his first round of delegate-hunting; and, after the Republican victory, was rewarded with a job as deputy counsel on the White House staff. He aligned himself with the liberal faction in its tug-of-war with the conservatives for control of the new administration. Sears had a weakness: He liked to talk and to have lunches with reporters. He did entirely too much of both, in the opinion of John Mitchell and Bob Haldeman and others in the Palace Guard who distrusted the media as The Enemy. They soon suspected, too, that Sears was maintaining too many convivial ties with liberals in the Rockefeller camp. So Sears lost his White House job.

Practicing law in Washington in 1974, Sears eagerly accepted Walker's offer to play a major role in a Reagan presidential campaign, assuming the Governor could be persuaded to make one. Sears was no conservative. His political philosophy—if any—derived from his association with Nixon. Sears dreamed of remaking Reagan into a moderate, in a Pygmalion-style operation, by steering him into more liberal stands on issues and selling him to the voters as Mr. Nice Guy.

Sears did not believe a conservative could win the presidency without being disguised in a moderate's costume. He interpreted Barry Goldwater's 1964 defeat as a repudiation of the Right and as proof that the way to win was to straddle divisive issues as Nixon did in 1968.

But the timetable of Sears and Company was thrown completely awry when the Watergate scandal forced Nixon out of the White House and genial Gerald R. Ford moved in. Although Ford, while Vice President, had repeatedly vowed that he would run for no office in 1976, he quickly changed his mind. He also placed a new obstacle in Reagan's path by naming Rockefeller as the new Vice President.

At first, Ford basked in the glow of almost unanimous praise from the media, the Democrats, and the moderate-to-liberal Republicans for placing the longtime Governor of New York in direct line of succession. Amid the applause, the new President failed to hear the rumble of discontent from the conservatives, many of whom had wanted Reagan for the vice presidency.

Ford gave no serious thought to choosing Reagan but cultivated the Eastern Establishment wing of the G.O.P.

Reagan's feelings were hurt as he watched this accidental President moving to freeze him out of the Oval Office forever. Reagan had hoped for a wide-open race in 1976, and he could not help recalling that no one had ever seriously mentioned good old Jerry Ford, the House minority leader, as a contender until Nixon placed Ford in the vice presidency after Spiro T. Agnew left that office under fire in the fall of 1973.

"After the 1972 election, everyone's eyes focused on '76 and there were a number in the Republican party whose names were frequently mentioned—Sen. Charles Percy, John Connally, Nelson Rockefeller, and myself, and one or two others—but not Gerald Ford," Reagan confided to a friend. Ford, he thought, should have stuck to his pledge to Congress when he was confirmed as Vice President, that he would not run for any office in 1976.

"The unusual circumstances should have led that appointed incumbent to take the lead early on in saying, '1976 should continue to be an open year,'" Reagan complained. But the once-modest Michigan congressman learned to love the imperial splendor of the presidency. He asserted that the Republican ticket next time would be "Ford and Rockefeller."

Ford did not realize how deep and emotional was the reaction of those who feared that Rockefeller would use his new political power base to become Deputy President, in fact, while his protégé, Henry Kissinger, would dictate foreign policy for the inexperienced new President, leaving Ford as a mere figurehead.

Ford's critics considered him not quite bright enough for the presidency. They ridiculed him as a Mortimer Snerd on Kissinger's knee, mouthing the honeyed words of "detente" whispered to him by his brilliant and iron-willed Secretary of State, who was busily promoting trade deals and arms cutbacks with the Soviet Union.

Some conservatives even feared that Ford might resign before the 1976 election, thereby making Rockefeller the President. They yearned for Reagan either to challenge Ford in the Republican primaries or to run as the nominee of an independent "third force," which would wreck the old Republican party.

Though some of Ford's advisers might dismiss Reagan as an aging right-wing after-dinner speaker or as an evangelist exhorting the Republicans to abandon their sinful liberalism and return to the Faith of their Fathers, Ford took him seriously as the only threat to his own dream of an uncontested nomination.

Ford, therefore, moved to take his potential rival into camp by making him a member of the administration. Twice the President dangled a cabinet post before Reagan's eyes, and twice the bait was refused.

"The first time, he offered me literally a choice of several cabinet positions," Reagan recalled. "In late 1974, he said, 'I'm going to be making some cabinet changes. There could be a choice of several.' I thanked him, told him I was greatly honored, but I thought I could do more for what I believed in—and what I thought he believed in—as an independent, with my radio program, newspaper columns, and speeches."

The second cabinet offer came early in 1975 when Reagan was in Washington, attending a meeting of Rockefeller's commission investigating the intelligence agencies. Donald Rumsfeld, then White House chief of staff, offered Reagan the post of Secretary of Commerce. Again, the answer was "No."

Reagan was torn between two desires: He wanted the presidency, but he did not wish to play the role of the Bad Guy in the Black Hat, challenging an incumbent of his own party. So he could not make up his mind "to be, or not to be," a candidate. Even some of his friends began calling him the Hollywood Hamlet.

A movement to launch a third party was all greased to go, when several hundred conservative activists gathered at the Mayflower Hotel in Washington February 15–17, 1975, for a political action conference. Its sponsors, the American Conservative Union (ACU) and Young Americans for Freedom (YAF), were fed up with Ford. Stanton Evans, the ACU president, and Ron Docksai, the leader of YAF, openly demanded an independent party and called for Reagan to be its presidential candidate.

But Reagan, welcomed as the hero of the hour, refused to challenge Ford. "I'm not going to join the chorus who say 'the honeymoon is over,'" he said. "I think he's entitled to a little longer honeymoon because he was an Instant President." Reagan argued that it was premature to make an open break with the Chief Executive; Ford should be given a few months more to return to conservative principles.

Reagan irked his fanatical followers by refusing to go along with their dump-Rockefeller movement, either, saying: "Nelson Rockefeller and I have a very congenial relationship."

Nor would Reagan accept the idea of running for President with George Wallace for Vice President, a "dream ticket" promoted by the soothsayers of the New Right.

In their fevered vision, a slate combining the former Hollywood star with the crippled ex-Governor of Alabama could bring together many Republicans—plus Democratic blue-collar voters in the Northern cities and rural Southerners—to reunite the coalition that had enabled Nixon to crush George McGovern.

Shying away from any link with Wallace, the former defender of segregation, Reagan said: "Well, he's a Democrat and I'm a

Republican. Besides, I think we have certain philosophical differences."

Reagan won the cheers and applause of a packed ballroom with a banquet speech in which he criticized Ford for his big budget deficit and questioned the SALT II arms agreement, which the President and Soviet boss Leonid Brezhnev had agreed upon at Vladivostok. But he threw a bucket of cold water on the independent ticket fire by saying:

"Is it a third party we need, or is it a new and revitalized second party, raising a banner of no pale pastels, but bold colors which make it unmistakably clear where we stand on all of the issues troubling the people?"

Unlike so many other meetings of conservatives, this one in Washington did not end with a lot of rhetoric. The thirteen-member Committee on Conservative Alternatives (COCA) was set up "to review and assess the current political situation and to develop future political opportunities." Chosen as chairman was the same Senator Helms who had endorsed Reagan for the presidency in 1973 and who also had many friends in the Wallace camp.

COCA launched a study of the election laws of all fifty states to find out how to field an independent ticket in each. "We mean business," Helms said. "We intend to work—not flake out. Conservatives have been talking to each other too long. Now we intend to act." The message to Ford from the conservatives was loud and clear: Shape up or we will see about launching a third party ticket.

Sen. Hugh Scott of Pennsylvania, the minority leader, struck back by circulating a resolution of support for the President and demanding that all Republican senators sign it. Several refused. On June 3, a group led by New York's Sen. James Buckley issued a manifesto calling for the Republicans to choose their nominees for both President and Vice President in an "open convention."

On the night of June 16, Reagan attended a very private dinner in a Madison Hotel suite in Washington. The guests ranged across the political spectrum from party-line Republicans to George Wallace Democrats and self-styled "counter-revolutionaries" of the Right. Among them were Richard Viguerie, the direct mail czar who had raised millions for George Wallace's presidential dreams; Robert Walker, Reagan's former aide now organizing a sub rosa Reagan-for-President effort; and Joseph Coors, the tall, soft-voiced brewer from Golden, Colorado, who had invested millions of dollars in conservative action causes.

Present also were three former officials of the Nixon administration: Patrick Buchanan, columnist and former speech writer for Nixon; Kevin Phillips, columnist and onetime employee of John Mitchell's Justice Department; and Howard Phillips, the Conservative Caucus director who had tried to scuttle the federal antipoverty program when he was chief of the Office of Economic Opportunity.

There too were Neal Freeman, a New York newspaper syndicate executive recruited for Viguerie's expanding empire; and Paul Weyrich, former aide to ex-Sen. Gordon Allott, Colorado Republican, now director of the Committee for the Survival of a Free Congress.

George Wallace was represented by his principal political manager, Charles Snider, and Bill France, a rich behind-the-scenes operator who promoted the Alabama Governor's varied interests in his home state.

Participants in the secret session recall this sequence of events:

Howard Phillips, a dark, burly young man from Massachusetts, said the Republican party was visibly disintegrating. Quoting Abraham Lincoln, he said the G.O.P. was "a house divided" that could not stand, an unreliable instrument to pursue the great opportunity for a history-making realignment of political parties in the United States.

Reagan retorted that the Republican party was still alive and not ready for the boneyard yet. His nomination, he said, would change it into a "different kind" of party with a much broader appeal to voters in all walks of life.

Kevin Phillips delivered a philippic on his favorite theme: "The Republican Party Must Die." It must be destroyed so that a new coalition, purified and cleansed of the liberal element, could achieve national power, the columnist said. He derided the

Republicans as a modern version of the Whig party, which collapsed and died in the late 1850's; he likened Ford to Millard Fillmore, the last Whig President.

When the Whigs fell apart, a fresh coalition of Whigs and Democrats, who were fired by zeal to stop the extension of slavery into the territories, created the modern Republican party and in 1860 made Lincoln President. Lincoln won an electoral-vote majority although he polled only 39 percent of the popular vote in a four-man race. In much the same way, columnist Phillips argued, a new coalition could elect Reagan or Wallace with less than half of the popular vote, if the Republicans fielded their Ford-Rockefeller team and the Democrats chose a presidential candidate as obviously liberal as McGovern.

"Suppose you get the Republican nomination," Phillips pressed on. "Would you actively seek the Wallace constituency and bring it into the party?" Reagan said he would, but he refused to offer the vice presidency to Wallace who, he observed, was busily pursuing the Democratic presidential nomination.

Then the columnist said he had seen enough of the Republican "politics of Chevy Chase and Wilshire Boulevard," that Reagan would have to choose between the conservatism of Big Business and the conservatism of the average man.

Reagan bristled at that. For the first time under the harsh interrogation, his temper flared. He did not need this fellow, Kevin Phillips, lecturing to him about how to get votes from Democrats; Reagan, being a former Democrat himself, was the very embodiment of the New Majority. He had the support of hundreds of thousands of Democrats when twice elected governor of California. As for the crack about the politics of "Wilshire Boulevard" in Los Angeles, he said, "the big businessmen are all for Gerald Ford; they're not for Reagan."

"If the Republicans nominate you," Phillips demanded, "would you cater to Ford's close advisers—Melvin Laird, Rogers C. B. Morton, and Donald Rumsfeld—to promote party unity, or would you choose the Wallace constituency? Would you make a deal with the moderate Republicans?"

"Absolutely not!" Reagan declared. While he might give lip

service to unity, he would never accommodate the Republican liberals. They would have to go their own way as they did when they left Goldwater in 1964.

Paul Weyrich warned Reagan that he was "putting yourself in a box" by delaying a decision on a new bid for the White House, that many conservatives in Congress were announcing their support for Ford on the grounds that apparently no one intended to challenge him.

Senator Goldwater had been "very naughty," Reagan said, by calling a group of Republican senators together and telling them he knew for sure that Reagan would not run. Reagan had telephoned several of the senators and set them straight. He mentioned Helms, James McClure of Idaho, and Carl Curtis of Nebraska as among the senators who would be on his side when the right time came.

"Did Curtis tell you that a few days ago he signed a loyalty pledge to the Ford-Rockefeller administration?" Weyrich asked.

Reagan seemed stunned. No one had told him that before.

"This is just an example of the kind of conservative people who are going into the Ford camp because of your inactivity," Weyrich said. "They are men of principle; they will keep their word."

Reagan held fast to his own "game plan" and refused to be rushed into an announcement of his candidacy, and that frustrated his warmest supporters.

"We haven't seen any fire in your belly," Robert Walker complained. "You don't seem to have any desire to rule."

Reagan agreed with his friend's analysis. "I don't see how anyone could have the gall to say, 'I *want* to be President of the United States,'" he said modestly. However, he added, if he honestly decided that it would be in the best interest of the nation, he would run. True, he did not have the "fire" now, but if he determined to make the race, he would pull out all the stops.

Joseph Coors expressed a burning desire to get out front in a strong, positive way to work for Reagan at once, without further delay. "We have only ten or fifteen years left," the Colorado brewer said, "before we turn into a Socialist country."

"I disagree," said Reagan. "This is the last opportunity to turn this country around."

Wallace's spokesmen held out the hope of a possible independent ticket, should Reagan and Wallace be blocked from their own parties' nominations. "I am committed to Governor Wallace," Charles Snider said. "But I think you should not foreclose the option of running as an independent candidate." Reagan replied that he had not foreclosed it.

Richard Viguerie insisted upon the independent route. Through sad experience, the money raiser said, he had found the Republican party "unmarketable."

Conservatives won elections more easily, he said, by playing down the party label. How could Reagan then say the Republican party could become the vehicle to unite the New Majority?

In response, Reagan made his most significant statement of the evening. As the Republican presidential nominee, he disclosed, he would appeal to the independents and conservative Democrats and propose a merger; then, if desirable, he would urge that the Republican party change its name.

"That," he said, "is my dream."

Reagan made a strong impression upon his listeners by his proposal to transform the Republican party. But they were displeased by his unwillingness to challenge its Establishment. His attractiveness and his ability to articulate the issues were offset by his lack of comprehension of practical politics. Despite his youthful appearance and vigor, they felt, he was a figure who was almost past his time.

The dinner in Washington marked the last serious effort by the men of the New Right to persuade Reagan to head an independent ticket and form an alliance with Wallace. They realized that Reagan would cling to the Republican party and try to lead it to victory. So their Reagan-Wallace "dream ticket" faded into the mists of Never-Never Land.

Sen. Paul Laxalt of Nevada, one of the few Republican senators brave enough to stick out his neck for Reagan, recalls that he first discussed a Reagan-for-President Committee at a dinner with "the Governor, Mike Deaver, and John Sears at the Madison

Hotel" in the summer of 1975. "They wanted my appraisal of where I thought the President was going," Laxalt said. "I told them I didn't think he was doing well, that he had serious political problems, and that Ron probably should be taking a look at running." Out of that conversation came Laxalt's "exploratory committee" on July 15, while the reluctant Reagan continued his columns, radio shows, and speeches on the banquet circuit.

One of the few outsiders who could penetrate the defenses around Reagan and visit his Pacific Palisades home was Frank Walton. Having served in the Governor's cabinet at Sacramento before going to Washington to become president of the Heritage Foundation, Walton felt close enough to his old boss to speak to him frankly.

"Look," Walton said, "if you want to retire to your ranch and say, 'I've had enough of it,' OK, but you know you won't enjoy your retirement years as you see the country decline and you know you didn't do anything about it."

To counteract the pressure from the Right, the President and his friends fired a barrage of appeals to Reagan to stay out of the race. They appealed to his party loyalty and his patriotism. They argued that it was not right for him to fight an incumbent President, a decent, honest, hard-working fellow trying his best to pull the shattered country together after the long nightmare of Watergate. To their pleas, Reagan would reply that this "incumbent" was the choice of Richard Nixon, not of the party. "If there's no sentiment out there for me," he would say, "we'll find out."

While Reagan toured the "mashed potato circuit," the President made a frenetic series of campaign swings across the country in early autumn, concentrating on California. He wanted to show that he could draw wildly cheering crowds and win endorsements from rich and powerful politicians right there in the state that had twice elected Reagan as its governor by big majorities.

According to the White House game plan, Reagan would realize that challenging Ford would waste a lot of time and money and split the already weak Republican party. Then Ron, always the Good Guy in the White Hat, would ride off into the sunset.

Twice, in Sacramento and in San Francisco, the President narrowly escaped being the victim of a gun-toting woman from the Fruits-and-Nuts Fringe. Yet he persevered at the risk of his life, through a series of motorcades, televised interviews, hand-shaking with the common people, and attending high-priced cocktail parties with the Republican elite; but it was all for naught.

Finally, after much meditation and prayer, Reagan made up his mind. "Nobody in the world could have prayed harder than I did that there would be no need for my candidacy," he confided later. "I prayed also that the administration would be successful in solving the domestic and the international problems. Finally, it became apparent to me that Washington wasn't doing what was needed.

"Ford started out with the right idea—with his 'WIN' buttons. We were going to 'Whip Inflation Now.' That is the fight I've always believed we should make. This recession, the unemployment, the economic dislocations, are the result of that inflation. But suddenly we find that in this administration we're going into debt at the rate of one hundred billion dollars a year."

In November, Nelson Rockefeller removed himself from the vice presidential race in a move interpreted as a sacrifice to appease the Right and finally persuade Reagan not to challenge the President. Whatever the motive, the maneuver did not work. On November 21, Reagan finally announced his candidacy at a press conference at the National Press Club a couple of blocks from the White House. He accused Ford of being linked to the Washington Establishment, which he blamed for most of the nation's woes.

"Our nation's capital has become the seat of a buddy system that functions for its own benefit—increasingly insensitive to the needs of the American worker who supports it with his taxes," Reagan charged. "Today it is difficult to find leaders who are independent of the forces that have brought us our problems: the Congress, the bureaucracy, the lobbyists, Big Business, and Big Labor."

Reagan's crack at Big Business came as a surprise to *The*

New York Times, which said that for twenty years he had championed the free enterprise system. Obviously, the Good Gray *Times* had not yet realized that Reagan was making a pitch to the blue-collar voters and he knew that most of the Big Business money in the campaign was going to Jerry Ford.

James Reston, in a column in the *Times*, sneered that Reagan's bid for the presidency "really should be tossed to the movie critics" because "it's the best script the old trouper ever had."

"The astonishing thing is that this amusing but frivolous Reagan fantasy is taken so seriously by the media and particularly by the President," Scotty scoffed. "It makes a lot of news, but it doesn't make much sense."

This was the standard line of attack from critics who wrote off the challenger as merely a has-been movie actor running for President, the candidate of a tiny right-wing splinter group, doomed to a crushing defeat. Sen. Charles Percy of Illinois, for instance, predicted that with Reagan as their nominee, the Republicans would even see "the beginning of the end" of their party.

Senator Laxalt retorted that the primary battle would not split the party but would provide "much-needed excitement, which will stimulate interest in the race." It was a paradox, he observed, that the self-styled moderates backing Ford favored the status quo, while the conservatives following Reagan were the ones advocating change by the overthrow of the "buddy system" in Washington. If Reagan sounded like a populist, it was worth remembering that he was once a Democrat who voted for Presidents Franklin D. Roosevelt and Harry Truman while Gerald Ford was voting for Thomas E. Dewey.

So Reagan at last abandoned the role of the Hollywood Hamlet, seized his sword, and rode forth to battle as a knight errant challenging Good King Jerry in the royal palace, in a modern-day War of the Roses.

8

☆

REAGAN'S
REBELLION

RONALD REAGAN began his 1976 presidential campaign with a "game plan" that called for him to score a quick knockout over the faltering President Ford in the early primaries in New Hampshire and Florida. Then, according to the scenario, party professionals elsewhere would accept him as the inevitable winner.

Early polls did indicate a lead for Reagan but this only made the party regulars more determined to block him at any price. They quailed at the mere idea that a broken-down movie actor—and a Franklin D. Roosevelt Democrat at that—should take over the party of Lincoln. At least, by keeping Ford in the White House, the old-line Republicans would continue in power, and when safely past the election, they could move him toward the Left on domestic issues. Furthermore, Henry Kissinger would continue to be the real President in foreign policy, so his patron, Nelson Rockefeller, would be a strong behind-the-scenes power even though unable to remain as Vice President and heir apparent.

In oversimplified terms, the Republicans waged a civil war between the moderates backing Ford and the militants championing Reagan. There was also a second civil war. This was an undercover struggle between two forces in the Reagan camp, and it finally resulted in the strange spectacle of two different Reagan campaigns.

First, the "movement conservatives," enthusiastic, high-principled people all over the country, devoted their time, energy, and money as volunteers in the Great Crusade to place him in the White House. Many of these self-starting zealots had been wild about their hero for years and they believed that at last he would come into his kingdom.

But the official Reagan campaign was run in the California style, first displayed by the men who were closest to Richard Nixon: an elite corps surrounding the candidate, isolating him, making decisions and issuing statements in his name. Knowing that Reagan enjoyed the seclusion of his Pacific Palisades home or his Rancho del Cielo in the hills, his managers kept a wall around him and rebuffed anyone who challenged them.

While John Sears directed the campaign from the Washington headquarters, as a combination of strategist, research man, and delegate hunter, the true center of power remained in Los Angeles, in the Wilshire Boulevard offices of Michael K. Deaver and Peter Hannaford, two very capable men who had long been trusted associates of their candidate.

Deaver, the chief of staff, and Hannaford, a speech writer, had formed a public relations agency at the close of Reagan's eight years as governor and successfully managed his career as a columnist, radio commentator, and banquet speaker. They handled him as a presidential candidate in the same way they scheduled his speaking tours. They did a first-rate professional job and he left the details to them. Reagan liked it that way.

"Mike Deaver and Pete Hannaford ran the whole show," one colleague said. "The Reagan campaign was really just an extension of the Deaver and Hannaford office in Los Angeles. Reagan is like a concert singer who has an agency booking him into various cities. He performs well for very high fees, and they manage him. But he delegates too much authority."

"Reagan's campaign is like a Hollywood movie," another associate said. "He's detached from it. He goes campaigning for a while like an opera star on a concert tour, he does his act, then he goes back to California and rests. He takes no phone calls. To his managers, Reagan is a product to be sold. He is an actor, not the center of the action. He really is not in charge of his own campaign. His act is completely natural; it has no pretense. He takes himself for real. He's been playing his role for so long, it seems real to him."

Robert Walker, who had recruited Sears in the undercover phase of the enterprise, later found himself frozen out of the inner circle and left, embittered and disillusioned. "The Governor is totally unaware of the campaign around him," Reagan's former assistant said. "He never understood the mechanics of the operation that elected him to the governorship twice and he has no perception of what a national presidential campaign should be like. He'd be a great knight on a white horse; he'd lead the people to victory. But he wouldn't know how to run the government."

Frank Walton, an alumnus of the Governor's cabinet, told friends: "The Reagan people are always a day late and a dollar short. Deaver and Hannaford are running everything. But no one seems to be the boss. I don't believe this body without a head can win."

Reagan's over-reliance upon his handlers led him into one major mistake that caused him to lose precious momentum at the very outset of his drive for the White House. Before a Chicago audience in September, 1975, he delivered a speech written for him by Jeffrey Bell, a zealous young conservative, calling for a massive transfer of federal programs to the states, along with the "resources" to finance them. Reagan estimated that this might reduce spending by as much as $90 billion a year, balance the budget, begin paying off the national debt, and cut the personal income-tax burden of every American by an average of 23 percent.

Stuart Spencer, the mastermind of Reagan's first campaign for the governorship, but now the chief political strategist for President Ford, seized upon the speech and turned it into a major issue in the New Hampshire primary in early 1976, charging that such a huge transfer would lead to much higher state taxes.

Reagan assured New Hampshire voters that he had no "devious plot to impose the sales or income tax" on them. He insisted that he proposed only "an orderly phased transfer" of some functions, not a single slash of $90 billion. Still, the President's backers kept harping on the theme in their efforts to paint Reagan as an impractical theorist and no match for Ford, with his long experience in government. They also raised false insinuations that his reforms would somehow imperil the Social Security system.

The President Ford Committee in Washington sent press releases to its local offices in the presidential primary states, with a space left blank for the name of the spokesman in each case. A sample release went: "Over the last 12 years, _____ said, Reagan has at various times advocated voluntary Social Security. . . ."

"Blank is a liar," Reagan angrily declared. "To strike fear in the hearts of those who depend on Social Security is the cheapest kind of demagoguery." He accused the Ford men of dishonest tactics and "dirty tricks."

But the damage was done. Ford, who had been trailing in the polls consistently before the New Hampshire primary February 24, squeaked through to victory by only 1,317 votes. He polled 54,824; Reagan, 53,507.

Hurt by his loss in New Hampshire—much more seriously than he realized at the time—Reagan found himself on the defensive in Florida, where the charges about his $90-billion transfer and Social Security changes had a devastating effect upon his support among the elderly, a powerful bloc of voters. Although his state manager, E. L. (Tommy) Thomas, blithely predicted a two-to-one victory, Reagan's lead in the polls disappeared and he was confronted with a second defeat.

At this point, leaders of conservative organizations who had been rebuffed by the Reagan strategists moved in to run their own rescue operation. They begged Reagan to drop his powder puff, put on the brass knuckles, and start attacking Ford. Morton Blackwell, one of the hardliners involved, recalls:

"After New Hampshire, where he lost an issueless campaign, I was part of the nationwide effort to make Reagan get tough. It took eight days to sell him on it. He had to be dragged, kicking and screaming, to change. It was so contrary to his 'nice guy' nature."

In the last few days before the Florida primary, when his own polls showed him about twenty points behind, Reagan tossed away his white hat and began punching Ford on defense and foreign policy. Under Ford and Kissinger, he charged, this nation had retreated, lost its military superiority over the Soviet Union, and faced grave dangers. Reagan also unveiled his dynamite charge that Kissinger's State Department was secretly plotting to "give away" the Panama Canal to the military dictator of Panama, "Fidel Castro's good friend, General Omar Torrijos," under "blackmail" threats that the Canal could be sabotaged if not transferred.

"When it comes to the Canal, we built it, we paid for it, it's ours, and we should tell Torrijos and company that we are going to keep it!" Reagan shouted, and each time he rang this alarm bell, his audience burst forth with cheers and applause.

Reagan began moving up in the polls and on election day, March 9, he lost 53 percent to 47 percent, Ford taking the lion's share of the delegates. Reagan had learned how to hit Ford on his weakest points. He repeated the attacks in Illinois, where the President, backed by the entire state Republican organization, defeated him by about three to two.

Ford's managers then began pressuring Reagan to quit. They confidently expected to crush him in the next primary, in North Carolina, and wrap up the nomination. "If we had lost North Carolina, it would have been hard to hold Ron's candidacy together," Senator Laxalt later said. "We were broke and dispirited, and people around the country were imploring him to get out. He was taking a lot of heat from those who said he was becoming a spoiler."

But Reagan's opponents, mistaking his Mr. Nice Guy image as a sign of weakness, underestimated the iron will that lurked behind his mild exterior. "The more people pushed on him," Laxalt said, "the more resentful he became." When a group of Republican governors issued a statement urging the challenger to withdraw and "work for the election of President Ford," Reagan responded with a flash of anger. "That pressure is engineered from the same place that they engineered the pressure for me not to run in the first place—the White House," he snapped. "Tell *him* to quit."

Actually, Reagan's own national strategists never expected

him to win North Carolina, where the President had a wide lead in the polls plus the strong support of Gov. James Holshouser, his Southern chairman, and the rest of the party Establishment. Sen. Jesse Helms, the only prominent state leader in Reagan's camp, mobilized a citizens' campaign for him.

The struggle over North Carolina precisely demonstrated the civil war inside the Reagan camp, the split between the elite corps in his national headquarters and the throngs of citizens in the boondocks, working for The Cause. Senator Helms and his state chairman, Tom Ellis, demanded that Reagan be allowed to appeal directly to the people through the one medium in which he excelled: television.

Helms and Ellis recalled how Reagan had launched his career with his 1964 speech on TV for Goldwater. But his media expert, Harry Treleaven, refused to place him on the screen out of fear that this might remind voters of the candidate's Hollywood career. So the televised commercials in New Hampshire and in Florida looked like newsreel films.

"I called John Sears many times and told him, 'Get that crap off TV—those terrible ads,'" Ellis recalled. "This was the year of the nonpolitician, yet the ads showed Reagan in a high school auditorium, looking just like a guy running for senior class president. All he had to do was to ride on his horse in California and talk about love and motherhood, and he would have had it locked up.

"We also begged the Reagan managers to let him attack Ford on the issues—national defense, foreign policy, Kissinger and detente—but their brain trust would look at us as if to say: 'This is a corn-fed, dumb, red-neck North Carolinian. He doesn't understand our sophisticated strategy and to hell with him.' Finally, when they realized they were getting their tail beat in Florida, as in New Hampshire, they threw in a bomb about Cuba and the Panama Canal, but it was just too damned late."

Ellis became so frustrated that he threatened to resign. "I'm through with the campaign," he told Sears at one point. "I'm not going to operate with anyone I can't trust, or who does not trust me." Sears mollified him by promising to follow his advice. Helms and Ellis then took their state campaign into their own hands.

They sent Reagan, along with Nancy and their old Hollywood friend, Jimmy Stewart, to every major city in North Carolina and to several smaller ones. Reagan flailed away at Ford on Cuba, Angola, detente, the Panama Canal, and charges that the President had misused his office by offering federal "goodies" like a Santa Claus to pick up votes.

Defying the media experts, Helms and Ellis obtained a thirty-minute speech that Reagan had videotaped in Florida and aired it on prime time on fifteen TV stations. It swung most of the undecided voters to his side and produced his first primary triumph. With 54 percent of the vote, he captured twenty-eight delegates to twenty-six for Ford.

Against the advice of those who said it was "old stuff," Reagan invested $100,000 in a nationwide TV speech. It was vintage Reagan, combining his attacks on Ford and Kissinger for weaknesses in defense and foreign policy with a call for "the restoration of American military superiority" over the Soviet Union. He ridiculed "a self-anointed elite in our nation's capital" who did not believe this nation could keep its "rendezvous with destiny."

In his spine-tingling finale, the old trouper called upon Americans to help him "make this land the shining, golden hope God intended it to be."

They responded by pouring in about $1.5 million in contributions, enough to keep Reagan's debt-burdened campaign alive through the spring primaries. His managers erred by not sending him into Wisconsin often enough; with a minimum of effort, he polled an astonishing 45 percent of the vote there, anyway, in the April 6 election. Instead, Ford walked off with the state's delegates, forty-five to nothing.

In Texas, independent conservatives, raising their own money and planning their own strategy, ran a grass roots campaign. James Lyon, a Houston banker who was Reagan's finance chairman in the state, met secretly with friends in Washington and said: "We feel that Texas is particularly important. If we're going to win, we must go outside the ranks of the regular Republican party. Only ten percent of the usual Republican vote in November will be in the primary. Activist groups—antibusing, anti-ERA, Right to Life, and Concerned Christians—will have to be brought into our camp or we'll lose."

The regular Reagan organization had kept such zealous bands of volunteers at arm's length from fear that they would run out of control. But in Texas all sorts of mavericks were welcomed into the fold; and thousands of Democrats formerly backing George Wallace switched to Reagan after the Alabama Governor lost to Jimmy Carter in the Florida and North Carolina primaries.

As a result, Reagan humiliated the President by a three-to-one margin in the "May Day Massacre" and Texas sent a 100-to-0 Reagan delegation to the Kansas City convention. The Texas momentum carried the challenger to victories in Georgia, Alabama, Indiana, and Nebraska. Ford struck back hard by collecting 65 percent of the vote in Michigan. Vice President Rockefeller released 119 technically uncommitted New York delegates to Ford so that Reagan could not take a nationwide lead in pledged convention votes.

Realizing that Ford had little chance of winning in California, his agents started a move in the legislature to change the winner-take-all rule in the primary there so that he could get at least some of the delegates. The Republican State Senate killed the scheme, and Reagan, who deeply resented Ford's maneuvers, said: "If they had succeeded in that last-minute attempt to change the California primary rules, I'll guarantee you that neither I nor anyone else could have put this party back together again."

Reagan incautiously stirred up a hornet's nest by suggesting in answer to questions before the Sacramento Press Club that the United States might join in sending peace-keeping troops to Rhodesia, the African country racked by guerrilla warfare. Ford's men leaped onto this remark as proof of their claim that the ex-Governor was another trigger-happy Goldwater. Stu Spencer rushed out new TV spots, with the President's approval, warning the California voters: "Remember: Governor Ronald Reagan couldn't start a war. President Ronald Reagan could."

Charles Black, a Reagan delegate hunter, recalls that his candidate was flying from California to Ohio for a final round of campaigning in the primary there when the Ford TV blitz began. "When the airplane taxied up at the Columbus airport," Black remembers, "I had to get on there and show Reagan this ad they were running against him. I said, 'Governor, you're not going to like this, but here's what they just put on the air in California.'"

Reagan read the line about how he, as President, "could start a war." "That damned Stu Spencer!" he exploded.

"That," said Black, "was probably the maddest I ever saw Reagan."

On June 8, Reagan achieved a decisive victory in California by a margin of 66 percent to 34 percent, and all of its 167 delegates. But, on the same day, Ford swept New Jersey's sixty-seven without a fight and all but nine from Ohio. Reagan collected 45 percent of the vote in Ohio with very little campaigning, despite the solid opposition of Gov. James Rhodes and the party Establishment. If he had filed a full slate of delegates and made more speeches in Ohio, he might have captured half of its delegates. Once again, however, his managers had misled him through another miscalculation that would prove costly at Kansas City.

Ford and Reagan flew to the Missouri state Republican convention at Springfield June 12, the President expecting an easy win with the aid of popular Gov. Christopher Bond. Too late, White House operatives found that a majority really favored Reagan, so they challenged 395 Reagan delegates. Reagan's men played rough, too. They prepared to file for a court injunction and they circulated letters denouncing this "desperate scheme to steal the convention." Some Reagan backers marched outside the hall, the Abou Ben Adhem Shrine Mosque, carrying signs that said: "THOU SHALT NOT STEAL."

They vowed that if the "steal" went through, the Reaganites would march out and reconvene in a room one floor below, dramatizing the party split in full view of the TV cameras. After all-night negotiations, the challenges were dropped. Reagan won eighteen delegates, Ford one.

In an unprecedented use of the White House for political benefits, the President summoned dozens of uncommitted delegates to have lunch, cocktails, or dinner with him at the mansion. His personal appeals amid the awesome aura of the Oval Office and the State Dining Room proved too potent for most of them to resist.

Ford courted fence-straddlers in the South and the border states by hinting that he would consider Reagan as a possible choice for the vice presidency after all, despite earlier indications that this was totally out of the question. "I exclude nobody," Ford said. "I hope that individuals, meantime, will not exclude themselves, because we want the best ticket we can get to win in November."

Harry Dent, an astute political operative in the Nixon White House, puffed the potential "Ford-Reagan ticket" among Southern delegates whom he escorted into the Oval Office for personal interviews with the President. Dent purloined the Dixie votes, one at a time, from Reagan.

By mid-July, the Ford operatives claimed they had the magic number needed to lock up the nomination: 1,130. It was all over. In desperation, John Sears told a news conference in Washington July 19 that Reagan would have 1,140 votes, counting those still undecided and others he hoped to woo away from Ford by some fiendishly clever tactics at the convention in Kansas City.

Reagan, interviewed at his Pacific Palisades home five days later, expressed deep bitterness over the tactics used by the President to take delegates away, especially the false insinuation that there could ever be that figment of the imagination, "a Ford-Reagan ticket."

Angrily, Reagan charged that Ford and his backers were telling "lies" in a nationwide effort to deceive wavering delegates into believing that they could vote for Ford and have Reagan for Vice President, too—a "dream ticket" desired by many Republicans to heal their party's growing split. Having repeatedly declared that he would never run for the vice presidency, Reagan accused his foes of a slick trick, unworthy of the White House.

"Ford," he noted sarcastically, "has been calling me unfit for the presidency and yet, in the past few days he has stated that I am qualified." Ford might as well quit trying to leave the impression that Reagan might be his running mate because "there is no circumstance under which I would." If the offer ever came, the answer would be "No."

"Let me make this plain—this is not personally directed at him," Reagan stressed. "I said 'No' in '68. There is no circumstance under which I would take that job, no matter who might offer it." Although he had told that to many undecided delegates, he had "a terrible feeling" that they thought he did not mean it.

The Democrats had nominated Jimmy Carter for the presidency at their New York City convention a few days before this interview. Reagan criticized Carter for summoning prospective running mates to his home in Georgia in "the parade to Plains . . . as if they were horses he was going to buy." He would never follow such a demeaning practice, Reagan said, if he should be the choice of the Republicans.

A month earlier, campaigning in Mississippi, some of whose thirty delegates were slipping out of his grasp, Reagan had declined to name his choice for the vice presidency because that would look like illegal "vote buying."

He would consider a vice president from the South, he said then, because that region was "vitally important to the Republican party, which for so long has been ruled by a clique of states in the Northeast." Reagan also said, "I don't believe in the old tradition of picking someone at the opposite end of the political spectrum because he can get some votes you can't get yourself."

When asked to name the men he was seriously considering as possibilities to round out his ticket, he exclaimed: "Oh, my! I don't want to do that." But he conceded that the names of John Connally, Senate Minority Leader Howard Baker, and Treasury Secretary William Simon had come up, along with some others. "I just can't discuss where I am in my ruminations at this moment," he said.

At that moment, a visitor to Pacific Palisades was waiting in another room to emerge and have lunch on the sunny patio and a long, earnest conversation with Reagan about the vice presidency. He was not a close friend; indeed, Reagan scarcely knew him. To maintain the secrecy required by Reagan's brain trust, the man had flown from Washington to Los Angeles incognito, assuming the name of his own press secretary, Troy Gustavson. "Gustavson" was really Richard Schweiker of Pennsylvania, who had the reputation of being one of the most liberal Republicans in the United States Senate.

John Sears had been dropping hints to friends about a brilliant coup which he was hatching. It was even kept a secret from Reagan himself until the last minute. Needless to add, the faithful workers for Reagan at the grass roots level were not being consulted at all. If they had been told, perhaps they might have prevented the explosion soon to ensue.

9

☆

THE
SCHWEIKER
AFFAIR

JOHN SEARS' uncanny ability to program and manipulate Ronald Reagan in the 1976 bid for the presidency became crystal clear in the Schweiker Affair. Reagan, who aspired to lead 200 million Americans, allowed himself to be led into selecting a potential running mate for the vice presidency whom he did not even know, and without consulting major figures in his own party.

In mid-July, while claiming in public that Reagan would have enough convention votes to win the presidential nomination, Sears privately admitted to a few associates that delegates were trickling away, one by one, and more would go when they realized that President Ford had an insurmountable lead. Many uncommitted delegates were nervously trying to go with the winner—as soon as they could find out who it would be.

Sears reasoned that if Reagan would suddenly announce his own choice for the vice presidency, Ford would have to do the same; and this would fracture the President's coalition by angering either the Rockefeller liberals of the East or the conservatives of the South.

Sears wanted a liberal senator from an Eastern state to balance his ticket headed by a conservative former governor from the West. He selected Sen. Richard Schweiker of Pennsylvania as if picking a name from the telephone book. He tried out the idea on two assistants, David Keene and Andy Carter, asking them, How would the conservatives working for Reagan in the South and West react when they discovered that their hero pro-

133

posed to run with "a genuine, certified Washington liberal?"

Carter thought "we'd be safe in the West and in the mountains" and Keene believed "we could hold the South" while Sears predicted his slick maneuver would bring over about thirty delegates from Pennsylvania, "collapse New Jersey, and affect New York, Delaware, and West Virginia."

Sen. Paul Laxalt, who sat next to Schweiker in the Senate and liked him, went along with the scheme. Defending it later, the Nevada senator said: "Sears and I realized that we had better do something or we would be dead in the media count ahead of Kansas City. Once the media said Ford had the magic 1,130 votes, then we'd lose the uncommitted delegates overnight. We came to the conclusion that the only 'float' was in the Northeast: Pennsylvania, New Jersey, New York. If we could keep it fluid, maybe we could put the package together.

"Reagan didn't know Schweiker at all. I told him we were seatmates, I thought he had a liberal image, primarily because of his labor voting record, but he was sound in the basic areas that counted. 'Beyond all,' I said, 'he's a very fine human being, a strong family man. If you talk with him, you'll find enough areas where you can get along.' "

Conceding that few presidential candidates would choose a running mate who was a total stranger, on the advice of a senator, Laxalt said with a touch of pride in his voice: "There are not many presidential candidates who have the relationship that Ron and I have, either. My personal assessment of Dick, he would respect."

Laxalt and Sears startled Schweiker with the offer at a secret meeting July 20 and quickly won his consent. The next day, Sears flew out to Pacific Palisades and explained the plan to Reagan. He seemed shocked. "Look, fellows," he said to Sears and Michael Deaver, according to one report, "you've got to show me more."

So they showed him the prospective partner himself to cement the strange alliance. Schweiker, upon entering Reagan's home, felt "some concern about whether or not we really could hit it off." But he found the former movie star, in shirt sleeves and slacks, "a very friendly, warm person," and even though the two men were warily sizing each other up, their six-hour parley turned into a cordial chat.

Schweiker admitted that he had voted a few years earlier for federal spending intended to solve social problems. But, by 1976, he had come to realize that the antipoverty program and others had failed, at a cost of billions. He concluded that Reagan was right: "The only way to solve the problems of the economy was to stimulate the private sector by tax incentives" and it was time to trim down the oppressive bureaucracy.

The two men also agreed upon "social" issues, both opposing gun control and federally funded abortions. They favored more defense expenditures and a firmer stand against Soviet adventurism.

Despite his initial misgivings about teaming up with a former actor, Schweiker concluded that Reagan was much more than that—a thoughtful man who had sincere concern about the country's downward drift and yearned to check it. "I found no hidden Reagan," he said. "I thought he told it like it was, right from the top." Schweiker also became convinced that Reagan could appeal to ethnic and blue-collar voters, traditionally members of the Democratic party, whom President Ford could not reach. With the Pennsylvania senator as his running mate, there was a chance of improving the Republicans' prospects in the East.

After their long conversation on the patio in Pacific Palisades, the Odd Couple moved back into the living room and Reagan concluded: "Dick and I can certainly hit it off together; we'll get along well." So their alliance was sealed. Schweiker flew back to Washington on the Red Eye Special, arriving at dawn Sunday, and the Reagan staff prepared to drop the Big Bomb the next day.

At this point, Reagan made a mistake. He did not pick up his telephone and ask any of his friends in Congress to say whether or not he should go ahead with the plan for the novel procedure of announcing a prospective running mate before the convention. The lawmakers, who certainly knew much more about Schweiker than Sears did, could have warned him that the selection of a liberal would touch off a blast of protest from the Right.

Reagan did telephone some conservative allies on Sunday night but he did not ask for their advice; he merely told them of his decision. They were flabbergasted.

"I nearly went berserk that night," Congressman Phil Crane of Illinois recalled. "I almost fell off my chair."

Sen. Jesse Helms of North Carolina remembered the precise time of his telephone call from Reagan—9:05 P.M.—"because I looked at my watch to record the time in my life when I was most shocked."

When the news flashed over the press wire tickers in the Capitol cloakrooms Monday, many members of Congress thought it must be a hoax.

"I thought somebody had perpetrated a fraud," said Tennessee Sen. Bill Brock. "I couldn't believe it."

Kentucky Congressman Gene Snyder quipped: "Reagan has just sold his last cow to buy a milking machine."

Many conservatives across the country felt baffled, bewildered, or even betrayed.

"I'm dead inside," sighed Tom Ellis of North Carolina, accusing Reagan of having figuratively "cut the heart out" of his most loyal corps of volunteers, who had helped him advance almost to the verge of the presidential nomination.

The Schweiker move provided a convenient excuse for Clarke Reed, the mercurial Mississippi Republican chairman and long-time drum-beater for Reagan, to switch under intense pressure from the President and his demon Dixie delegate hunter, Harry Dent.

Lyn Nofziger, Reagan's rumpled Sancho Panza, who had been promoting him for the White House since 1966, greeted the defections with rumbles of profane rhetoric, which he deemed suitable for traitors. "An awful lot of conservatives didn't have the balls to come out for Reagan, so they have no bitch coming over Schweiker," the paunchy ex-reporter said. "If they had helped, he would never have found it necessary to go East. You can't count on those guys. Schweiker has said he'll be bound by the Republican platform and will accept the Governor's decisions.

On major issues, Schweiker has been right—against abortion, gun control, federalized welfare."

The breakaway of some delegates in the South was supposed to be offset by dramatic gains in the East as the fruit of the bold and desperate gamble. Schweiker himself expected to cut loose a large part of his home state's 103-vote delegation and transfer it from Ford to Reagan. The senator believed that his close friend, Drew Lewis, Ford's Pennsylvania chairman, would welcome a Reagan-Schweiker ticket.

Schweiker telephoned Lewis and pleaded with him to come over and give Pennsylvania the prospect of having the second man on the Republican ticket. For four hours, the two comrades remained on the telephone line, Schweiker desperately begging Lewis to switch in the belief that twenty to thirty other members of his delegation would follow suit.

But the Pennsylvanians were under strong pressure from Senate Minority Leader Hugh Scott to stay with Ford. In the end, Lewis said "No." "I had promised the President that I would deliver ninety votes to him," he explained, and he had to keep that promise.

Without Lewis, the whole rationale of the Schweiker choice disappeared. The dramatic movement of Eastern delegates to Reagan never happened. Reagan firmed up his wavering forces on the right to block any further erosion. So many conservatives were unhappy, however, that they were tempted to seek an alternative to both Reagan and Ford in a Third Man choice. Thus began a sudden boomlet to draft New York's conservative Sen. James L. Buckley as a dark horse.

Sen. Jesse Helms said he and a few other conservative senators casually began promoting Buckley during a conversation one afternoon on the Senate floor. They were worried about polls showing that 45 percent of the Reagan backers would not vote for Ford and an equal number of Ford supporters would boycott Reagan; so the grim prospect of certain defeat led to a talk of a possible compromise nominee who might heal the party breach.

"Do you know who is the most popular political figure in

Massachusetts?" asked Sen. Clifford Hansen of Wyoming, and then supplied the answer: "Jim Buckley."

"Old Jim is a consistent, honest, pleasant, decent, responsible individual," Helms agreed, "unscarred by the Ford-Reagan fisticuffs."

The senators began promoting a draft and soon it caught fire. On August 10, Buckley came to Helms and said: "I've been getting calls from Ford people and Reagan people, asking me to run for President. I have talked it over with my wife and I have decided neither to encourage nor discourage it."

"He didn't say, 'Jesse, go out and blow the bugle,'" Helms conceded, but no stronger signal was necessary.

The North Carolina senator perceived that if Buckley worked hard among the wavering delegates at Kansas City, he could siphon off enough "soft" supporters of both Reagan and Ford to prevent anyone from winning on the first ballot. Then, delegates legally bound to Ford for the first ballot could switch to Reagan on the second and nominate him. North Carolina and Kentucky were examples of delegations almost evenly split on the first ballot but free to go all the way to Reagan after that.

After Buckley gave him the green light, Helms telephoned the news to Reagan who, according to the senator, was "puzzled and surprised" and said, "Gosh!"

Ford's men reacted with an outward show of nonchalance but a private display of panic. They feared that Buckley could draw away enough votes from both contenders to bring about a deadlock.

The Republican bosses in New York State moved quickly to puncture Buckley's little balloon. Richard Rosenbaum, the party chairman handpicked by Vice President Rockefeller, telephoned the senator to "close the door" on the presidential race at once, or he would face big trouble trying to get re-elected in November.

But Buckley, defying the warning, told Illinois Congressman Philip Crane to launch the boom. "When I reached Kansas City," Crane recalled, "I was convinced that John Sears had blown the Reagan campaign. His choice of Schweiker was a desperate move, a political disaster. I felt that Reagan would lose unless we could deadlock the convention and throw it into a second ballot. Obviously, we could not have a deadlock with only two candidates, so we brought out a third one, Buckley."

Crane resigned from the Reagan campaign and on August 14, two days before the convention's opening session, started his Draft Buckley Committee. "I lined up six Reagan delegates and six Ford delegates to go for Buckley," the congressman said. "We could have had twenty to fifty on the first roll call. That would have been enough to prevent a first ballot victory for Ford. Later, Buckley could have switched his votes to Reagan, nominated him, and thus staked out first claim on the vice presidency."

Boss Rosenbaum threatened to kill Buckley politically if he did not quit the presidential race instantly. This time the Rockefeller envoy did not merely give the senator some friendly advice, he gave direct orders: Get out of Ford's way or get out of the Senate.

Within hours after Crane had unveiled his "Draft" committee, Buckley bowed out. "There was not enough time," he said, "to mobilize potential support in an effective and resourceful way."

Rosenbaum knew the real reason. "Buckley got out just in the nick of time," said the tall, bald chairman, nicknamed "the Prussian."

Rosenbaum also refused to let Reagan speak to the New York delegation in a last-minute attempt to pry a few votes loose for himself. When the tiny band of Reaganites in the delegation shouted protests, the boss muzzled them by shouting: "This is not bean bag we're playing here in Kansas City!"

Whether he headed the ticket or not, Reagan came to Kansas City determined to have his own conservative ideas embodied in the platform. In this endeavor, he followed the advice of hardliners such as Senator Helms and Congressman Crane despite the Sears faction's efforts to go along with the President's aides in writing a moderate platform that either Ford or Reagan could run on, for the sake of party unity.

Sears ordered strict control clamped on the Reagan Irregulars, who clamored for a conflict on the issues and a dramatic battle on the convention floor. Under Helms' leadership, conservatives agreed upon twenty-two proposals for much stronger language in the platform. At a motel east of Kansas City, the North Carolina delegation's headquarters hummed with activity as a rival to the official Reagan command post in the Alameda Plaza Hotel south of the city.

Helms' forces hammered out a plank repudiating the Ford-Kissinger foreign policy of detente, arms control concessions to the Soviet Union, negotiations for transferring the Panama Canal. Their language would have been a direct slap in the faces of the President and of the Secretary of State. Reagan's aides—Ed Meese, Martin Anderson, and Pete Hannaford—had a late-night meeting with the Helms men in an effort to tone down the "Morality in Foreign Policy" plank.

The compromise version amounted to a tap on the wrist for Ford and for Kissinger. It criticized detente, the Helsinki Pact, and one-way concessions on arms cutbacks. It also praised Aleksandr Solzhenitsyn, a reminder that Ford had refused to receive the famed Russian emigré-author at the White House for fear of angering Moscow.

On domestic issues, the amended platform conformed more closely to Reagan's own speeches. It opposed "federalizing welfare and the guaranteed annual income." It pleased the foes of abortion by saying "The Republican party . . . supports the efforts of those who seek enactment of a constitutional amendment to restore the right to life of unborn children."

Although his own brain trust had originally gone along with the weaker platform drafted by the White House, Reagan would proudly say later: "The rank and file wrote that platform in a grass roots revolution against the document handed down by the party hierarchy."

As Tom Ellis, the North Carolina guerrilla fighter, said: "The platform had been written by President Ford's people and considered by the Reagan staff and they expected the delegates to put the rubber stamp on it. Instead, bless Pete, these good conservatives, who had backed Governor Reagan, fought for a Republican platform that we could stand on."

But Sears ignored Ellis and the other Reagan Irregulars from the grass roots and drove ahead with his own pet scheme, Rule 16–C, which he counted on as a master stroke for victory. This rules change would have made Ford reveal his choice for the vice presidency before the balloting for President.

Sears believed that if Ford could be thus smoked out in advance and required to disclose his favorite, he would anger either the Southern conservatives, who had been wooed away by promises that Ford would choose Reagan or John Connally or some other conservative; or the Northern liberals, who had been privately assured that Ford would never, never take Connally with his Watergate Era "milk money" taint, but that the Number Two slot would go to some moderate like Bill Ruckelshaus or Elliot Richardson.

Either way Ford jumped, he was bound to lose some delegates, Sears surmised. So he played a lone hand in the Kansas City poker game, bet the family plantation on a single turn of the cards, Rule 16–C—and lost the whole pot. The new rule was rejected on August 17, the second night of the convention, by a vote of 1,180 to 1,069.

Senator Laxalt later defended the Rule 16–C maneuver. "I thought it was worth the gamble," he said. "We were short on votes. The only way we could beat the President was to force him to name his 'bride.' So it didn't work. So, what the devil? We stayed alive."

It was after midnight, following the Rule 16–C fight, when the weary delegates began debating the "Morality in Foreign Policy" provisions in the platform. Many of Ford's advisers fumed over the language, calling it a slap at the President and at Kissinger. They wanted to fight the plank on the floor—which was exactly what Senator Helms' forces were eager to see, a battle that would blow the convention wide open. However, the strategists in the "Sky Suite" high above the floor persuaded Ford to swallow the harsh words rather than risk a debate that could trigger violent emotions and even give Reagan a last, slim chance at victory.

Down on the floor, Tom Ellis had made the proper arrangements for a roll call vote on the "Morality in Foreign Policy" amendment. He had the support of eight state delegations, the number required to force a roll call, and Convention Chairman John Rhodes had been so notified. But in the early hours of Wednesday morning, the plank was rushed through by voice vote. Ellis was standing on his chair in the North Carolina delegation, shouting for a roll call. But Rhodes, the usually mild congressman from Arizona, gaveled him down.

"Railroad! Railroad!" Ellis screamed. "You have broken the rules!"

Senator Helms stalked out of the convention and growled: "It's all over unless John Sears can pull a rabbit out of a hat—and I don't see any rabbits hopping around this convention hall."

Indeed, Sears' hat was empty at breakfasttime when Reagan and his top command discussed last-ditch moves they might make to snatch the presidential nomination away from Ford. Was there still a chance that the Mississippi delegation, which had gone against the proposed Rule 16–C, could be moved back to Reagan? Most of the thirty Mississippians still liked Reagan, although they were cool to his choice of Schweiker for the ticket.

Schweiker came in and suddenly volunteered to withdraw as the vice presidential candidate. "Governor," he said, "I sense that I may be the problem for you, particularly in Mississippi. If it would help your interest—and I think it would—I'd be happy to call a press conference and walk away from this thing."

Reagan looked Schweiker straight in the eye and said: "Senator, we came to Kansas City together and we're going to leave Kansas City together."

"That's the Reagan style," said Senator Laxalt, who witnessed the incident. "I'm not sure every politician would have said that. The Governor proved to me anew his loyalty and basic integrity. It's one of the enduring things that have caused Dick to be so loyal to him since."

Knowing their cause was lost, zealous Reaganites staged a

brave show of defiance in the convention hall Wednesday night, blowing two-foot-long plastic horns in an ear-splitting filibuster that accomplished little except to delay the vote. The final count was Ford, 1,187; Reagan, 1,070; Elliot Richardson, one; and one abstention.

After midnight, the President summoned his long black limousine and rode to the Alameda Plaza Hotel, where he made the gracious gesture of calling upon his defeated rival and asking his advice about the vice presidential nominee. Reagan had long ago ruled himself out and White House aides said he sent them word that the President might as well not come down at all if he intended to make the offer. Nancy Reagan wouldn't hear of it.

In the wee small hours, delegates from several states began belatedly organizing a drive to draft Reagan for the vice presidency, anyway, by a vote on the convention floor. But the Governor nipped that in the bud.

Ford actually wanted to stick to his original idea of a Ford-Rockefeller ticket, but the furious, red-faced horn-blowing Reaganite delegates had frightened his staff into believing that they would stampede out of the hall in furious protest against such an outrage. Rocky had not added to his own prestige when he snatched a placard away from a delegate and thrust it beneath his own seat, whereupon another delegate, Douglas Bischoff of Utah, seized the Vice President's private telephone and jerked it loose. So the convivial Veep was out of the question.

Senate Minority Leader Howard Baker of Tennessee thought he had a firm promise of second place on the ticket—Rocky had even thrown a breakfast in his honor—but, after an all-night round of agonized discussions with his advisers, the President chose Sen. Robert Dole of Kansas.

Thereupon some wag in the press corps wisecracked: "The perfect Republican ticket: Dull and Dole."

Ford's acceptance speech was one of his best, but Reagan's impromptu remarks were even more eloquent. To shouts of "Viva! Olé!" from his loyal followers, the loser made a gracious plea for a united campaign.

"Reagan could get a standing ovation in a graveyard," said

California State Sen. H. L. Richardson. "Ford puts you to sleep in the third paragraph."

When the Governor bade farewell to his campaigners in an emotional scene at the Alameda Plaza, many were weeping openly. "We lost," he said, "but the cause—the cause goes on." He remembered a line from an old Scottish ballad: "I'll lay me down and bleed awhile; though I am wounded, I am not slain. I shall rise and fight again."

"It's just one more battle in a long war and it's going to go on as long as we all live," he said. "Nancy and I, we aren't going to go back and sit in a rocking chair and say, 'Well, that's all for us.'"

Although his followers wept in sorrow and frustration, their battered old hero accepted his defeat with stoic calm and a serenity that arose from his faith in his own destiny.

"If you've done your best, you've done everything you can for something you believe in, and it doesn't turn out that is the course you follow," he said, "then I believe that means the Lord has a different purpose in mind for you."

Reagan, admitting he had been "naive," had lost a lot of his innocence at Kansas City as he saw with his own eyes how politicians used their muscle to block him from taking over the Republican party, which they had controlled for so many years as their personal fiefdom. He did not know how to cope with them then, but he learned. His primary victories convinced him that he really represented the hopes and dreams and basic beliefs of a majority of Americans.

He had made a basic mistake by failing to lead those people, by delegating too much authority to his managers and allowing himself to be manipulated as the "star" of the show, not the main strategist making the major decisions. This practice of letting his aides have excessive power disturbed many of Reagan's most loyal followers. They began to wonder if he would also run the presidency the same way, if he ever achieved it.

In the immediate aftermath of Kansas City, another race for the White House seemed an impossible dream. Whether Ford or

Carter won the fall election, Reagan would be sixty-nine in 1980, and there was a clamor for "new faces" in his party. Still, the old cowhand was not quite ready to ride off into the sunset. He cherished his dream of the presidency . . . and watched . . . and waited to see what the Good Lord might have in mind for him to do next.

10

☆

THE
COMEBACK
TRAIL

IN THE AGONIZING aftermath of Kansas City, Ronald Reagan had good reason to believe that he would never seek the presidency again. He would keep on fighting for his principles, which he and his followers had hammered into the Republican platform, but at sixty-five he could see that the party would be inclined to turn to a younger leader four years in the future. He told his faithful friend Paul Laxalt that this was the end of the trail.

"After the convention, he had pretty much decided that was it," the Nevada senator said. "Everybody assumed at that point that he had run his last race and I think Ron and Nancy felt that, too."

Still bitter over Reagan's almost-successful attempt to topple him, President Ford began his fall campaign by ignoring his fallen foe. Reagan and his aides were left completely out of the early strategy sessions of the Ford camp; only a month later did the President, striving to catch up with Jimmy Carter, finally ask Reagan for help.

Out on the road again, Reagan campaigned, not so much for Ford as for the party and its platform, with its pledges of free enterprise, fiscal responsibility, firm defense and foreign policies. He found throngs of followers cheering him with as much zeal as if he had won. Once again, in an echo of the bedlam in the convention hall, he heard the faithful crying "Viva! Olé!" and tooting their ridiculous, defiant plastic horns.

At Springfield, Missouri, more than 1,000 people paid fifty

dollars a ticket to attend a dinner at which they gave him standing ovations and hundreds swarmed about him for autographs. At Indianapolis, his speech before 2,000 Republicans was interrupted fourteen times by applause. At Winston-Salem, North Carolina, the cheering and horn-blowing Republicans at a dinner honoring Reagan showed an emotional intensity sadly lacking in rallies for the victorious President Ford.

In each case, the old trouper repeated the familiar lines that bored the traveling press corps. Samples: "Status quo: That's Latin for 'the mess we're in.' The difference betwen them and us," he would say, referring to the Democrats, "is that *we* want to check government spending and *they* want to spend government checks."

Reagan viewed his barnstorming efforts as helping the Republicans to stay alive as a national party even though Ford lost the presidency to Carter, and the Democrats kept control of both houses of Congress. Carter, after frittering away his huge early lead, finally squeaked through to victory with 297 electoral votes to 241. The former Georgia Governor recaptured the onetime "Solid South" for the Democrats, carrying every Dixie state except Virginia, and that made the difference.

Reagan, citing his own popularity in the region, said in a post-election interview that he could have won the South and the election if he had been the nominee. The polls showed that "Watergate had been the Number One issue in the minds of those who voted and that would not have been possible if I was the candidate," he said in a Mississippi interview.

Bitter over his defeat, the President claimed that Reagan had caused it in part by knocking him around in the primaries and then failing to give him all-out support in the autumn campaign. Reagan retorted that because of his own efforts, his followers had stuck with the Republican ticket; they had delivered California's big bloc of electoral votes and all the rest of the West except Hawaii, so there was no basis for Ford's attempt to spread the blame.

. Noting that Ford had polled nearly 50 percent of the popular vote although registered Republicans made up only 20 percent of the electorate, Reagan said this proved that his party should reach out immediately to the many Democrats and independents who had voted for the President. Then, together, they could build the New Majority coalition, which lingered in his mind as a shimmering vision for the future.

"The party wasn't quite ready this year to rechristen itself and to offer a permanent home to conservative independents and Democrats," he said. "It did take a big first step when its rank and file hammered out a platform which recognizes that a majority of Americans, according to public opinion polls, today consider themselves conservatives."

Refusing to "rule out or rule in" another bid for the White House in 1980, Reagan said in a Buffalo, New York, interview in November: "This is the only prediction I can make with certainty: I heard, saw, and felt this struggle for Republican reformation this fall as I campaigned back and forth across the country. The message I got was that if the party didn't win this one, it should reshape itself into a clear-cut alternative to the Democrats. I intend to be in the thick of that effort."

"I have never had any great overpowering hunger for holding public office," he said at Jackson, Mississippi, in December. "My feeling about 1980 is that whoever is best able to carry on the causes that I believe in, that's the way it should be."

Without fanfare, Reagan slipped into Washington on January 15, 1977. President Ford was packing up to leave the White House five days thence, ending an eight-year era of Republican rule in the executive branch. The hotels of the capital city were filling up with convivial Democrats, joyfully anticipating the inauguration of Jimmy Carter. They believed that he would usher in a long epoch of Democratic party domination, like the twenty-year reign that Franklin D. Roosevelt had begun with his New Deal in the Depression days of 1933.

Once an ardent apostle of F.D.R., Reagan had closely studied the way his former hero had formed the coalition that had produced his unprecedented success in politics. After long research and reflection, Reagan had determined how he would assemble his own coalition to create a Conservative Age.

While hardly anyone in the media paid attention, he spoke to the Intercollegiate Studies Institute at a Mayflower Hotel banquet that January night. The conservatives, he said, were no longer a little "cult" or a minority of a minority party, but a potential majority of all Americans if they could only be pulled together into a new and lasting alliance.

"The New Republican Party I envision will not, and cannot, be limited to the country club-Big Business image that for reasons both fair and unfair it is burdened with today," he declared. "It is going to have room for the man and woman in the factories, for the farmer, for the cop on the beat, and the millions of Americans who may never have thought of joining our party before. If we are to attract more working men and women, we must welcome them, not only as rank-and-file members but as leaders and as candidates."

Republicans, he said, must speak to all the people in plain language about their most pressing problems of inflation and jobs and make an especially strong appeal to win back the black Americans who are "taken for granted by the Democrats."

"I refuse to believe," the onetime actor said, "that the Good Lord divided this world into Republicans, who defend basic values, and Democrats, who win elections. We have to find the tough, bright young men and women who are tired of the clichés and the pomposity and the mind-numbing economic idiocy of the liberals in Washington."

"Little more than a decade ago," he went on, "more than two thirds of Americans believed the federal government could solve all our problems with its multitude of bureaus, agencies, and programs without restricting our freedom or bankrupting the nation.

"We warned of things to come; of the danger inherent in unwarranted government involvement in things not in its proper province. And today more than two thirds of our citizens are telling us, and each other, that social engineering by the federal government has failed. The Great Society is great only in power, in size, and in cost. Freedom has been diminished and we stand on the brink of economic ruin."

Reagan called upon his party to say:

"We, the members of the New Republican party, believe that the preservation and enhancement of the values that strengthen and protect individual freedom, family life, communities and neighborhoods, and the liberty of our beloved nation should be at the heart of any legislative or political program presented to the American people.

"The United States must always stand for peace and liberty in the world and the rights of the individual," he said. "Given that there are other nations with potentially hostile design, we recognize that we can reach our goals only while maintaining a superior national defense, second to none.

"When we are maligned as having little thought or compassion for people, let us denounce the slander for what it is," the conservative leader said. "Concern for the people is at the very heart of conservatism. Concern for the dignity of all men; that those in need shall be helped to become independent—not lifetime recipients of a dole; concern that those who labor and produce will not be robbed of the fruit of their toil or their liberty. Concern that we shall not forfeit the dream that gave birth to this nation— the dream that we can be as a shining city upon a hill. . . . Believing in that dream, I became a Republican and because of that dream, I am a conservative."

Reagan returned to Washington on February 5, 1977, and delivered the same speech almost word for word at a national rally of conservatives. This time the media paid some attention— especially to his startling demand that the Republicans must shake off their image as the errand boys for Big Business.

The New York *Daily News* featured the story with the speaker's picture under a two-column headline, "SHUCK BIG BIZ IMAGE, REAGAN COUNSELS GOP." A few political columnists saw the White Knight of the Right striving to break free from his stereotype and reach out to a majority of the voters in one last quest for the presidency in 1980.

To his zealous acolytes in the Young Americans for Freedom, the American Conservative Union, and allied organizations, Reagan administered a stiff dose of Common Sense medicine. They must, he said, build a "new conservative majority, not based on abstract theorizing of the kind that turns off the American people. Whatever the word may have meant in the past, *today* conservatism means principles evolving from experience and a belief in change when necessary." In brief, he meant that the conservatives must no longer defend a sterile status quo but welcome change.

Reagan preached the new gospel in huddles with Republican senators behind closed doors at the Capitol. One participant said: "Half of the time was spent by the senators and Reagan dumping on Big Business for its lack of support for conservatives in the last election."

Looking to the future, Reagan unveiled his new organization, Citizens for the Republic (CFTR), billed as "a multi-candidate political action committee," the successor to the Citizens for Reagan of the '76 campaign. The ever-faithful Lyn Nofziger closed down the old group and opened the new one as its executive director, with headquarters in Santa Monica, California. John Laxalt, the Nevada senator's brother, became the CFTR's Washington representative. Clearly, the Reagan team was already aiming at 1980; and a quiet struggle for control of the Republican party began.

Bill Brock, beaten by Democrat Jim Sasser in a bid for election to a second term as U.S. senator from Tennessee, became the new Republican national chairman. He defeated Reagan's personal choice, Utah Chairman Richard Richards, in a hard-fought battle at a Republican National Committee meeting in January. Brock had a conservative voting record but was acceptable to the Ford-Rockefeller forces, who were determined to keep the chairmanship out of the hands of the Reaganites.

Brock candidly told the Republicans, "Our party is in shambles in some of our states," and the 1976 election returns showed it becoming steadily weaker at the grass roots, in state legislatures and local governments, almost everywhere except in the West. But he rejected the gloomy predictions that they were tottering toward the graveyard to join the Federalists and the Whigs. "I am bone weary of all the talk about the demise of our party," Brock said. He began rebuilding the party in every state, reaching out to the same groups of voters whom Reagan had called upon to make up the New Majority.

But the chairman and his large staff of assistants at the Republican National Committee (RNC) headquarters on Capitol Hill had no intention of constructing a vehicle to place Ronald Reagan in the White House. They persisted in viewing him as only a right-wing splinter candidate who could not win a national election. They prepared the way for the party to offer a "new face," such as George Bush or Senate Minority Leader Howard Baker, at the top of its ticket, or else renominate the ever-reliable Gerald R. Ford.

There was no large faction promoting Reagan at the RNC offices. On the contrary, Senator Laxalt charged that the whole place was "a nest of anti-Reagan people." They looked askance at the Citizens for the Republic and its million-dollar kitty of leftover 1976 campaign funds, fearing that CFTR would become a launching pad for another Reagan bid for the White House.

Reagan, in the eyes of the Republican Establishment, had one redeeming feature: He devoted his formidable speech-making and money-raising talents to Republicans and showed no interest in helping to elect any conservative Democrats as some New Right organizations did. Chairman Brock complained that the single-issue splinter groups drained money and workers away from the Republican party.

The uneasy alliance between the "conservative movement" people at the heart of Reagan's faction and the moderates running the RNC split apart in the fight over the Panama Canal treaties. Reagan continued his strong opposition to "giving away" the Canal to the "tin-horn dictator," Gen. Omar Torrijos, and his regime in Panama, while ex-President Ford, Henry Kissinger, and other Establishment figures in the Republican party helped President Carter's efforts to win Senate ratification of the treaties.

At Brock's request, Reagan allowed his signature to be used on letters from the Republican party, pleading for money to finance a nationwide grass roots fight against the treaties signed by Carter and Torrijos. Reagan's October 25, 1977, letter told the reader:

"I need your immediate help to prevent our country from making one of the most serious mistakes in its two-hundred-year history. . . . Unless you and I act now, one of the most vital shipping and defense waterways will be in the complete control of the anti-American, pro-Marxist dictator, General Torrijos. You and I just can't let that happen."

Reagan called for "millions of Americans" to send funds to help Republicans oppose the Carter treaties. In a second letter, he said "the Republican National Committee and the National Republican Congressional Committee have joined together to establish an Emergency Panama Canal Fund," to beat the treaties and to "elect more Republicans to Congress who will vote against any giveaway schemes." Reagan also mentioned plans to "place ads in national magazines and major newspapers" to alert the people to oppose the "dangerous" pacts.

Along with each letter went another one signed by Brock, specifically endorsing Reagan's plea and saying: "We must counter a well-orchestrated, powerful lobbying assault led by Mr. Carter and the liberal Democrats in Congress."

Reagan's appeals proved most successful, pulling about three quarters of a million dollars into the Republicans' treasury. Senator Laxalt then asked for $50,000 from this fund to help cover the cost of sending a "truth squad" of speakers aboard a chartered plane on a cross-country barnstorming tour to arouse public opposition to the Canal treaties.

So Reagan believed the money he raised by his letters would really be used to oppose Senate ratification. Yet, upon visiting Washington in early December, 1977, he found that his party had no plans whatever for an antitreaty campaign. On the contrary, the RNC staff was busily boosting former President Ford, who was powerfully aiding in Carter's drive for Senate approval of the pacts.

Reagan and Laxalt made a joint telephone call from the senator's office, urgently asking Brock to release the requested $50,000. Brock demurred, saying he could not give money to an "outside" group, the Committee to Save the Panama Canal, sponsoring the air caravan's tour.

"Baloney!" Reagan and Laxalt replied (or, actually, a profane variation thereof) and accused Brock of hiding behind excuses. They told him to get the RNC's approval for the fund transfer by sending mailgrams to the members, who had unanimously opposed the treaties at a recent meeting in New Orleans.

His temper rising, Reagan reminded the chairman that the Kansas City convention had also opposed surrendering the Canal to Panama. Despite his defeat by Ford, Reagan recalled, he had been trying to show his loyalty to the party by being helpful with such things as his fund-raising letters. Instead of assisting the RNC with its budget problems, he said, he could have collected the money for his own Committee for the Republic, and the RNC would not have received a dime of it.

Laxalt could hardly believe his ears when he heard his usually mild-mannered friend pouring out expletives over the telephone —words that the Nevada senator had never suspected of being in the former film star's vocabulary. "He was a pretty hot Irishman," Laxalt said later. "I've never seen him quite so excited."

With his keen sense of honor and integrity, Reagan was furious upon discovering that the party hacks were cynically using his good name to raise money under false pretenses. "My credibility is involved in this," he protested. "Letters with my name on them have gone all across the country asking for money to help fight the treaties. Now we discover that money raised by the letters will not be used for that purpose. And, worse than that, we discover that the national party has no plans to campaign against the treaties."

When he learned that another antitreaty letter was about to go out over his signature, Reagan ordered Lyn Nofziger to stop any further mailings by the Republican committees. Never again would he allow himself to be so betrayed by the RNC.

"Ford is the problem," Senator Laxalt surmised. The former President was pressuring Brock to straddle the Canal issue. On that same weekend in December, Ford met with other treaty advocates at the Washington home of Averell Harriman, the aged Gray Eminence of the liberal Democrats, plotting strategy to guide the pacts through the Senate.

Brock's close friend Howard Baker later helped Carter to achieve the necessary two-thirds majority, with a few face-saving revisions. Laxalt grimly vowed that any senator who voted for giving away the Panama Canal would never be nominated by the Republicans for the presidency.

Belatedly realizing that alienating Reagan could damage the Republicans' prospects in future elections, Brock moved to mollify him with assurances of goodwill and appreciation for all of his valuable services to the party. Reagan, ever the Good Guy in the White Hat, cooled off after his explosion of Irish temper and forgave the chairman. So peace was restored on the surface. But Ford's support of the Panama Canal transfer widened the gulf between him and Reagan. Ford confided to friends that he would do almost anything to stop Reagan from becoming the presidential nominee in 1980—even, if necessary, acceding to a Ford-for-President draft.

By the spring of 1978, Reagan had privately determined to seek the presidency again. But he kept his decision a secret for months while he waged an intense undercover drive to keep his faithful conservative friends from drifting away to younger rivals. John Connally, Senator Bob Dole of Kansas, and Congressman Philip Crane of Illinois were three of the contenders who hoped to win the nomination by presenting themselves as more vigorous versions of Reagan, the Elder Statesman. Crane claimed that he didn't expect Reagan would actually run, so it was imperative for the conservatives to have a fall-back candidate—Crane.

Reagan flew to Washington to reassure some of his influential friends that they need not look elsewhere for a candidate in the 1980 White House race. On July 26, he met in a private dining room in the Senate wing of the Capitol with the Kingston Group, the central strategic planning committee of the New Right.

Under sharp questioning, Reagan quickly found out that these people would be reluctant to support him again if he chose John Sears a second time as his campaign manager. They blamed Sears for the mistakes that cost Reagan the nomination before.

When asked, point-blank, "Will John Sears be your campaign

manager?" the candidate replied: "No, there will be a different campaign organization." He said Sears' "talents and abilities" would be used again, but in another role, not yet defined.

Reagan also smoothed the ruffled feathers of those who complained that Sears was already sounding off about a switch in Reagan's long-standing policy of defending the Republic of China on Taiwan; that Reagan would even visit the Communist rulers of Mainland China.

"John is not authorized to speak for me," Reagan said. "It is absolutely untrue that I am going to Peking. I have not altered one bit in saying this country must not abandon its friends on Taiwan or weaken our mutual defense treaty with them."

Reagan said he had learned from the mistakes of his 1976 campaign, when he had made a late start because he was honestly reluctant to run against President Ford and be branded "a spoiler." "This time, when I will be the candidate, things will be different," he promised. He would have no hesitation about attacking Jimmy Carter, whose presidency he branded "the worst disaster this country has ever known."

Because of the Democrats' deficit spending policies, he predicted, "we're in for an economic bellyache in 1980."

Reagan defended his selection of Senator Schweiker for the vice presidency but conceded that he had acted without consulting enough advisers. Next time, he said, he would confer with a wide range of party leaders before making a final decision.

Reagan assured the conservatives that he would "never compromise" on their shared principles; that he would continue to express them in his speeches, and "to hell with whether they make somebody mad or not."

One conservative complained that "we are almost shut out of the Republican National Committee staff" and asked Reagan to commit himself to "clean house" there after the election.

"You have such a commitment," Reagan replied. "The RNC is the weakest link in the whole chain. There's a New Majority out there but it is not reflected at the RNC headquarters."

During this Washington visit, Reagan also met privately with

Congressman Crane and gave him a clear signal of his own intentions to run again in 1980, saying: "On a scale of one to ten, Phil, I am at ten and a half."

But Crane, who had backed Reagan in two unsuccessful bids for the presidency, was tired of playing a supporting role and sought to be a star himself. "I paid my dues longer than a lot of these people around Reagan," Crane said later. "I helped to form a committee in Illinois for him in 1968, and in 1975 I was the second member of Congress to get behind him. I met with him as a courtesy to reassure him that I was not running against him or anybody else, I was running against the Democratic party."

On August 2, Crane announced his candidacy and became the first to enter the Republican race, in a move that threatened to split some conservatives away from Reagan.

Kevin Phillips, the columnist, hailed Crane's entry as a "very real threat" to Reagan and said some New Right activists were backing Crane because "they think a weak-willed, one-term Reagan administration would be a waste of time or worse. They see little benefit to themselves or their goals even in a Reagan presidency."

11

☆

LOCHINVAR
RETURNS

RONALD REAGAN, who sought the presidency in 1976 as the Robin Hood of the Right, leading a band of rebels in an almost-successful bid to topple the incumbent President, dressed up in a different costume as his followers launched the unofficial phase of his new campaign. This time they presented him as a moderate, genial, dynamic champion who could lead a united Republican party to victory as Dwight D. Eisenhower did in 1952.

"Not since General Eisenhower's first election has there been such a perfect 'fit' between the man and the public mood as there is today with Governor Reagan and the American people," Sen. Paul Laxalt said as he unveiled the Reagan for President Committee in Washington on March 5, 1979. He spoke to a standing room-only crowd in the Eisenhower Lounge of the Capitol Hill Club, the favorite haunt of the Republican Party Establishment.

With Laxalt were more than a dozen senators and congressmen, mostly conservatives. But, to stress his candidate's appeal to moderates, the Nevada senator released an impressive list of 365 big-name supporters, about a fourth of whom had backed former President Ford in 1976.

Among the stars in Reagan's new supporting cast for the drama of 1980 were four members of Ford's cabinet: Treasury Secretary William Simon, Agriculture Secretary Earl Butz, Interior Secretary Stanley Hathaway, and Health, Education and Welfare Secretary Caspar Weinberger.

"Our doors will be open to every American who knows the

time has come when we must again put a true giant in the White House," Laxalt said. In a jab at President Carter, he went on: "At a time of dangerous weakness and confusion in the presidency, Ronald Reagan would provide a welcome change as a 'take charge' President."

While Reagan's role as the New Eisenhower undoubtedly gave him an image that would appeal to a much broader constituency than before, it also turned off some of his old friends on the Right. Notably absent from the ceremonies in the Eisenhower Lounge were Sens. Jesse Helms of North Carolina and Strom Thurmond of South Carolina. Both said it was too early for them to take a stand. Both were being ardently courted by John B. Connally, who hoped to seize much of Reagan's base in the South in promoting his own bid for the presidential nomination.

Despite Reagan's personal assurances that John Sears would not be the boss of his new campaign, many conservatives expressed concern when the Mastermind of 1976 popped up at the top of the "management group" presented by Senator Laxalt as the team that would be in charge of everything. Sears had the title of "executive vice chairman," technically subordinate to Chairman Laxalt and equal to Michael K. Deaver, the deputy chairman for operations. Lyn Nofziger filled an unaccustomed role as fund-raiser with the title of deputy chairman for finance, while Ed Meese and Jim Lake were presented as "senior consultants," Martin Anderson as research director and Charles Black, a former aide to Senator Helms, more recently an employee of the Republican National Committee, emerged as Reagan's national political director.

Congressmen Steve Symms of Idaho and Bob Dornan of California were among the conservatives who insisted that Sears must not be allowed to seize total control of the campaign again. "Reagan has promised me that Sears will not be the manager, and we will hold him to it," Symms said. Dornan said: "Reagan has the nomination for 1980 if he keeps his health. He has the organization and he picked up a lot of I.O.U.'s from Republican candidates by campaigning for them in the fall elections."

Regardless of his title and his supposedly subordinate role,

Sears quickly began dictating the campaign strategy. He determined to have his candidate pre-empt the field as the early front-runner in hopes of discouraging his opponents from uniting behind any one man in a "stop-Reagan" drive. The moderate Republicans, despite all of the efforts to paint Reagan as a middle-of-the-roader, viewed him as a second Barry Goldwater who would lead their party to defeat as the Arizona senator did in losing to Lyndon Johnson. Nearly all of the Republican governors yearned for someone other than Reagan at the top of their ticket and a few were willing to be drafted themselves.

Govs. William Milliken of Michigan, James Thompson of Illinois, Robert Ray of Iowa, James Rhodes of Ohio, and Richard Thornburgh of Pennsylvania were among those milling about in search of an alternative nominee. Before many months went by, the Republican field became crowded with presidential contenders as Reagan, Connally, and Crane were joined by George Bush, the former ambassador and Central Intelligence Agency director; Senate Minority Leader Howard Baker of Tennessee; Sen. Bob Dole of Kansas; Congressman John Anderson of Illinois; and others.

Early in the race, Reagan's operatives resolved not to repeat the mistakes they had made in 1976 when they had written off a large part of the North as inhospitable to their conservative candidate and let Ford collect a big block of delegates that proved decisive at the Kansas City convention. Senator Schweiker agreed to become the chairman of Reagan's campaign in the Northeast, but only after extracting a solemn promise that this time there would be a strong, well-financed drive to carry that region. Schweiker foresaw that Reagan could surprise the experts by capturing at least half of the delegates from New York and Pennsylvania in 1980, although both states had been delivered to Ford through the influence of the late Vice President Nelson Rockefeller and his allies.

Roger Stone, former chairman of the Young Republican National Federation, began organizing for Reagan in the Northeast early in 1979, lining up county Republican chairmen in New York City, New Jersey, and Connecticut. Stone recruited a majority of

the Republicans in the legislature of Connecticut, the state where
George Bush, son of Connecticut's late U.S. Sen. Prescott Bush,
had grown up.

Reagan gained another influential recruit from the Republican
Establishment when Delaware's Congressman Tom Evans came
aboard as his senior policy adviser. Evans, a former national cochairman of the party, had made a seconding speech for Ford's
nomination at the Kansas City convention. Now, however, the
congressman opposed an incipient movement to draft Ford again.
Evans was impressed by Reagan's eight-year record as governor
of California and agreed with his stands in favor of a stronger
national defense, a better intelligence system, and limits on the
federal bureaucracy.

In his home state, Reagan and his associates had to fight to
save the Republicans' traditional "winner take all" rule, which
awarded all of California's 168 national convention votes to the
candidate coming in first in the presidential primary. Because of
his great popularity, Reagan expected to lead the field in the 1980
primary, just as he had defeated Ford in 1976, and take all the
delegates.

Backers of George Bush and John Connally fought to scrap
the rule and divide the delegates in direct ratio to the primary
votes of each contender. That would give the challengers at least
a share of the California bloc. The showdown came at the Republican Central Committee convention in San Diego on September 16, 1979.

Former Congressman Charles Wiggins led the attempt to
junk the "winner take all" rule. Senate Republican Leader William
Campbell denounced the move as "a direct political ploy to dilute
the strength of Ronald Reagan at the national convention."
Reagan won a decisive victory as the state committee kept the
rule by a vote of 675 to 277, or nearly three to one. "This is truly
Reagan country," Wiggins said after the vote. "Reagan chose to
make this a test of his popularity, and he's pretty popular around
here."

With the Far West as his rock-solid base of strength, and the
Deep South resisting the siren songs of Connally, Reagan concen-

trated on the Northeast where, as he told columnist John Lofton, the media still failed to tell the people the true story of his eight-year record as a compassionate, effective governor. "Every time I cross the Mississippi River and come East I find there is this picture of me as some kind of Neanderthal nut who is going to put people up against the wall," Reagan said.

"I'm trying to get people to see my record and not this false image they have. We reformed welfare. We saved billions of dollars for the taxpayer. But there are people in the East who think I threw people in the street and let them starve."

Reagan resented the reports that he was retreating from some of his hard-line stands: a superior national defense, across-the-board tax cuts, and reductions in the oppressive bureaucracy. "Every time I read those things," he said, "I get madder than hell."

As if to stress his appeal to the Northeast, the Lochinvar from the West chose New York City as the place for officially launching his presidential campaign, which actually had been going on for months. In a speech at a fund-raising dinner in Manhattan November 13 and in a taped version of the same address for a nation-wide television audience, Reagan called for this nation to rebuild its strength at home and its influence for peace abroad.

Challenging President Carter's claim that the people suffered from some sort of "malaise" of the spirit, the old evangelist said: "The crisis we face is not the result of any failure of the American spirit; it is a failure of our leaders to establish rational goals and give our people something to order their lives by.

"The confidence we have lost is confidence in our government's policies," he said. "Our unease can almost be called bewilderment at how our defense strength has deteriorated.

"The great productivity of our industry is surpassed by virtually all the major nations who compete with us for world markets. And our currency is no longer the stable measure of value it once was.

"I believe," Reagan said, "this nation hungers for a spiritual revival; hungers to once again see honor placed above political expediency; to see government once again the protector of our liberties, not the distributor of gifts and privilege. Government should uphold and not undermine those institutions which are custodians of the very values upon which civilization is founded—religion, education, and, above all, family." These were familiar themes, sure to strengthen the candidate's appeal to his New American Majority concerned about family-related issues in this campaign.

Reagan concluded with his most familiar quotation of all, as he recalled that John Winthrop told the little band of Pilgrims approaching the coast of Massachusetts in 1620, "We shall be as a city upon a hill." Then he closed with his own revised version of the lines from his old hero, Franklin D. Roosevelt: "A troubled and afflicted mankind looks to us, pleading for us to keep our rendezvous with destiny."

At a Washington press conference the next day, Reagan introduced New York Congressman Jack Kemp as his policy development chairman. This was a coup that strengthened his bid for votes in the Northeast through an alliance with a younger politician (age forty-four) who had shown how a Republican could carry a Buffalo congressional district populated by blue-collar Democrats.

Kemp, a Los Angeles native and onetime aide to Reagan in the governor's office, starred as a professional football quarterback for the San Diego Chargers and the Buffalo Bills before going to Congress, where he made a name for himself as coauthor of the Kemp-Roth tax-cut bill. He welcomed the speculation that he might become the Republicans' choice for the vice presidency to provide a youthful counterbalance to the elderly nominee from California. On the other hand, objections were raised to a ticket teaming an over-the-hill quarterback with a former motion picture star.

Some reporters raised questions about Reagan's health and vigor and about reports that he had to take frequent naps to keep going on his speaking tours. He replied that his wife tried to coax him into catnaps on the campaign plane by saying, "Close your eyes and sleep," but he was usually not sleepy. "My idea of a day off is to get up to the ranch and cut wood," he said. "I have an awful lot of wood to cut to build a fence there."

"Do you have all the vigor you need for a campaign?" someone asked. "Yes," the candidate replied. "The whole issue of my age will be resolved when people see that I can go the distance. If I were a betting man, I'd bet that I won't have to be helped off the track." (This remark could be construed as a crack at President Carter, who had collapsed while jogging a few weeks before.)

On the surface, Reagan seemed to be racing far ahead of his younger rivals on the track in the opening days of his campaign, as friendly crowds greeted him on his first swing around the country. He won a straw vote among Florida Republicans on November 17, with Connally trailing in second place despite a lavish outlay of money, and Bush was third. Behind the scenes, however, Reagan's aides were bickering with one another in a power struggle that threatened serious trouble for him in the future.

There was a basic split between the Californians, who had been promoting their former Governor's White House dreams for years, and the outside professionals, headed by John Sears, who had worked with other candidates in the past and had not staked their entire careers on Reagan. Sears' main allies were Charles Black, the national political director, and Jim Lake, the press secretary. Sears had sold the three of them to the candidate as a "package" of experts to engineer his nomination and election.

Reagan believed he had kept his promise to the conservatives that he would not make Sears his campaign manager but would use a management committee instead. Sears still tried to be the boss, however. He complained that the Californians—Ed Meese and Mike Deaver—reported directly to the former Governor, who made some major decisions about hiring people and spending money without consulting Sears.

Black, backing Sears, charged that "we had a horribly poor return" on direct mail solicitations, of about fifty cents received for every dollar spent, when Lyn Nofziger was running that. It was an entirely new field of work for the former newspaperman, who had been handling public relations and the Committee for the Republic. He did his best, but Sears determined to get rid of him by offering to make him director of the Texas and California primary campaigns. Nofziger, who suspected that Deaver was undercutting him by backing Sears, had enough of these Borgia Palace maneuvers and in August he quit.

Deaver took over the fund-raising chores and he, too, soon found himself accused of failures. Black said: "We had a Frank Sinatra concert in Boston and two Wayne Newton concerts in Texas and the big announcement dinner in New York. Mike was in charge of all those. They appeared to the public to be great fund-raising successes but, in actual fact, we grossed about one point one million dollars at a cost of a million dollars."

Deaver believed that Sears and Black were blaming him for the financial problems as an excuse to drive him out whereas, in his own opinion, "we could never raise the kind of money Sears and Black were spending."

Reagan deplored the feuding, which intensified through the autumn, but was too kindhearted and easygoing to stop it. Finally, he called his assistants to his Pacific Palisades home on November 26, the Sunday after Thanksgiving Day, in an effort to restore some peace and harmony.

Upon arriving, Deaver found Sears, Black, and Lake already there and lined up in a solid phalanx against him. Sears, in effect, handed the candidate an ultimatum: If he kept Deaver, he would lose Sears, Black, and Lake. Deaver, who had loyally promoted Reagan's presidential hopes through the years, withdrew rather than make his old friend face up to the decision. Reagan accepted Deaver's resignation with great regret, and Sears seized total control of the campaign.

Newsday reported that after Deaver left, Reagan turned to Sears, Black, and Lake and said: "You were not big enough to give in. Mike was the only guy big enough to walk away. You are small, petty men."

Since Pete Hannaford had earlier returned to the Deaver-

Hannaford public relations firm, Reagan had only one close associate left from his old days as governor: Ed Meese, his chief of staff. Soon Meese came under fire from Sears and Company on charges that he was not properly coordinating the policy and issues division or giving the candidate up-to-date briefings on the road.

"We didn't have position papers out, even though we had been begging for them and promising them for a long time," Black said later. "The Governor just did not have good, thorough issue briefings. He does a lot of his own reading and writing. But, when you're running for President, you don't have time to do your own research. Meese was in charge but we could not get him to move. We could not even get Meese to devote full time to the campaign. He would teach a law class and spend a lot of time in San Diego. Our attitude was that when Reagan was on the road, his chief policy adviser must be with him because all kinds of things can come up that need quick answers. Ed was on the road about half the time but not always with Reagan."

So the friction between the Sears bloc and Meese went on as Reagan prepared for his first popularity test of 1980, the Iowa caucuses. Since he had delegated so much authority to his staff, he was unprepared for the shock that would soon shake him out of his dreams of an easy victory.

12

☆

"I AM PAYING
FOR THIS
MICROPHONE!"

THE IMPERIAL PRESIDENCY phase of Ronald Reagan's 1980 campaign began in Iowa in January and ended in defeat.

His strategists misread the true situation inside the state, where the precinct caucuses would provide the first battleground for the Republican presidential nomination. They underestimated the threat posed by George Bush, although the former Central Intelligence Agency director and ambassador had been crisscrossing Iowa for months, shaking thousands of hands, energetically trying to rise from the obscurity that made his rating "just an asterisk" in the early public opinion polls, as he liked to quip. Those polls showed Reagan coasting along like an emperor far above the common herd of plebeians panting along behind him, his scores ranging in the 40 percent to 50 percent bracket while Bush at the outset rated little better than 3 percent.

Bush's surprising victories in several straw votes at fund-raising events started rumors that the onetime Texas congressman was recruiting a cadre of volunteers while the overconfident Reaganites were slow in organizing their own people at the grass roots.

But John Sears and his political director, Charles Black, refused to become alarmed. They noted that only 20,000 out of almost half a million registered Republicans in Iowa had turned out for the caucuses in the 1976 Ford-Reagan battle and the total this time should roughly double because of the larger field of contestants and the greater coverage assured by the national media since Jimmy Carter had used the Iowa caucuses as a launching pad four years before to blast out of nowhere into the national spotlight.

Considering this "a traditional caucus situation," Black calculated that his agents must simply locate 25,000 Reagan voters in Iowa and deliver them to the caucuses and that would lock it up. So the Reagan men brought their candidate into the state for only a few brief visits, like a monarch occasionally looking in to see if his faithful subjects were happy and content. In all, Reagan spent only forty-one hours in Iowa whereas Bush devoted thirty-one days to his exhausting campaign there.

With serene self-confidence, Sears believed that Reagan was virtually assured of the nomination if he followed a low-profile script that would keep him out of press conferences and debates where he might make some mistake that would cost him votes.

Following Sears' directives, Reagan did not deign to appear in a Des Moines debate with all the other Republican contenders, his excuse being that such discussions were divisive. But his managers, with far less lofty motives, were really afraid that Reagan, nearing his sixty-ninth birthday, would look old in contrast to his younger competitors, especially the tanned and handsome Phil Crane, the ruggedly virile John Connally, the slim jogger Bush, and the winsome, boyish Howard Baker. Sears, who underestimated Reagan's quick wit, also feared that his candidate might make some hard-line statement that would mar the moderate image that the master strategist was so carefully cultivating for him to make him acceptable to the party Establishment.

Black later summed up the reasoning behind the decision to keep Reagan out of the Iowa debate:

"You'd have had Reagan, with forty percent in the polls, sitting up there with John Anderson and Phil Crane and Bob Dole, who had less than one percent, let alone John Connally, who had the capacity to unload on you at any one time. The guy next to you can really blow you away and you have to wait three minutes apiece for seven more people to talk before you can get back at him." The truth was that Sears and Black feared Reagan's foes might "blow him away."

With imperial hauteur, Sears explained Reagan's above-the-masses attitude by saying: "It wouldn't do any good to have him going to coffees and shaking hands like the others. People will get the idea he's an ordinary man, like the rest of us."

After the debate, in which all his rivals made a big issue of his absence, Reagan took a nose dive in a Des Moines newspaper poll, dropping from 50 percent to 26 percent. Too late, his managers realized that the Iowa contest, which they had mistakenly viewed as only a series of caucuses involving small groups of Republican professionals, had been transformed into a mini-primary involving ordinary voters by the thousands.

Bush made the most of the change, mailing his brochures to every Republican household in the state. "We didn't do that, because we didn't think ninety percent of these people were even prospects to come to the caucuses," Black later explained. "We didn't do any TV advertising. Reagan did a live half-hour broadcast on the Saturday night before the caucuses but that was to fire up our precinct workers rather than to attract general voters."

It was too late now to repair the damage caused by the impression that Emperor Reagan was taking the good folks in Iowa for granted. On the night of January 21, Sears, Black, and their colleagues assembled at their Des Moines headquarters and watched the returns come in. At first, Reagan seemed to be exceeding the quotas set for him, but then he began losing. Black added some of the figures and found to his dismay that the turnout was not a mere 40,000 voters, as he had expected, but more than 112,000. Bush came in first by two percentage points.

Bush's surprising victory propelled him into the front-runner's status, made him an instant hero in the national media, and threatened Reagan with disaster. Tom Pettit proclaimed on the NBC–TV network the morning after: "Ronald Reagan is dead."

Lyn Nofziger, secretly rejoicing that his old enemies on the Reagan staff had flopped by pursuing a "Rose Garden strategy" as if their candidate were already President, wisecracked from the sidelines: "They were taking Reagan into Iowa to be crowned. They forgot that to have a Rose Garden strategy, you've got to have a Rose Garden." Reagan, who had gone to the movies in

California on the night of the Iowa caucuses, looked on television like a man who had been knocked down by a car but was too stunned to realize how badly he had been hurt.

From all over the country, his loyal followers began telephoning him with angry protests against the imperial strategy that had led to his defeat. Some called upon him to fire John Sears. But Reagan, having approved his managers' decisions in advance, accepted his own share of the blame for the mistake. Sen. Paul Laxalt, who never believed Sears had the executive ability to run a successful campaign, seized this opportunity to work for a shake-up in the staff. Sears explained that Reagan had to think in "national" terms about contests in thirty-five states and could not spare the time for only one. The Nevada senator retorted that if Reagan lost the next round in the New Hampshire primary, he need not worry about campaigning in all those other states; he would be finished.

Most of the three dozen House members supporting Reagan's bid for the presidency had a brutally frank, private gripe session with Black in a Capitol hideaway office January 24. They said Reagan must give up any notion that Iowa marked only a minor setback; they called it a danger sign of a fatal flaw in the strategy of treating Reagan as the inevitable nominee who did not have to campaign as vigorously as his lesser rivals.

"We don't have a monarchy in this country," said the congressmen's leader, Tom Evans of Delaware. "The Governor must no longer be wrapped in cellophane. He must go out among the people, let them see him and touch him and ask questions about his views. He is our greatest resource and we must have him take off the wraps."

The congressmen stressed that Sears should stop making statements and let the people see Reagan instead of keeping him locked in a closet. Their message to Sears, through Black, was: "Maintain a much lower profile. Keep your head down, or it may be cut off."

Black recalled: "The biggest criticism John got in that meeting was that he was too visible. The congressmen said: 'Dammit, instead of seeing Reagan on the tube campaigning in Iowa for the past month, all we've seen is Sears there explaining why Reagan was *not* campaigning.' The gist of the members' comments was: 'For God's sake, get out there and have Reagan work harder and put Sears in the background.'"

"We concluded," Evans said, "that if Reagan lost the New Hampshire and South Carolina primaries, back to back, he would be out—even if he later won in Florida."

In response to his repeated requests for a face-to-face meeting with his elusive candidate to express the House members' grave concerns, Evans had an hour-long talk with Reagan during a flight between Newark, New Jersey, and Greenville, South Carolina, January 28. "Governor Reagan," the congressman said, "I want you to know that after the loss in Iowa, we are even more fervently in support of you. But we feel strongly that you should alter the direction of your campaign. Frankly, all of us are supporting *you* as our nominee for President and we are *not* supporting John Sears. We've been hearing a great deal from John Sears on television and elsewhere, but we want to hear from you."

Reagan did not resent the criticism. He agreed with it. So did his wife, who listened to the conversation on the plane. "You're absolutely right," Nancy Reagan told Evans. "Get John Sears off television; put Ron on. Go out with the people."

"Yes, let's do it," Reagan agreed. "Let's go out with the people."

So he did. He told his staff, "Now we've got darned near everything riding on New Hampshire and we've got to go at it. I'm ready; that's what I want to do."

Reagan doubled his schedule of speeches in New Hampshire. He barnstormed all over the state for nearly three weeks, visiting many little towns by bus, while Nancy Reagan and various other surrogates sought to reach every possible group of voters. Instead of coming in by the side door of an auditorium, rattling off his old familiar speech, and dashing out the same door, Reagan would mingle with the people. Nancy would field questions—often hostile ones—from high school students, without losing her poise.

At Memorial High School in Manchester, one boy asked: "If

Reagan becomes President, what is he going to do about the oil companies and rising prices?"

"First of all, he believes that government should get out of the way—" Mrs. Reagan began.

"No, they shouldn't," the youth cut her off. "My brother runs a gas station. Since the first of February, gas has gone up sixteen cents!"

Nancy stood her ground. "We have a lot of oil in Alaska and Mexico and various states, but the government won't let us get it out," she said.

Asked what her husband would do to stop inflation, she answered: "He would stop printing all that printing press money. He would propose an across-the-board tax cut for everybody, immediately." Federal curbs on campaign expenditures, she said, were "crazy."

Nancy strongly defended her "Ronnie" in his opposition to the Equal Rights Amendment when she was challenged by an irate woman teacher. Mrs. Reagan advocated guaranteeing women's rights by state law rather than the constitutional amendment. "Ronnie did it by statute in California," she said. The teacher was not persuaded. "I've heard some words," she said in a parting thrust, "but I need some action."

Nancy also said: "Abortion is taking human life. I can't understand women who say they should have control over their own body; they forget that within the mother's body there is another human being, a person with a soul."

The Right to Life organizations were delighted to find Nancy working with them against abortion. She also attended a conference of the "Moral Majority," another of the many conservative groups clamoring to be heard by the Reagan entourage, but left out in the cold before the post-Iowa change in strategy.

Gerald Carmen, the former New Hampshire Republican state chairman, who had retired from his business to run the Reagan campaign in the Northeast, built a network of volunteers, including the single-issue groups, and directed it from a crowded office in downtown Manchester, where organized chaos reigned supreme. The Bush workers also had a smooth machine directed by former Gov. Hugh Gregg, who had run Reagan's 1976 campaign in the state. They also had an army of volunteers promoting the slogan, "Go with the Front-runner."

In early February, Bush was running far out in front with his "Big Mo," the momentum from his Iowa triumph apparently propelling him toward another victory, which could even knock Reagan out of the race. Reagan was trailing by at least ten points in his own staff's polling estimates and worrying about a dangerous financial crunch. William J. Casey, a former Securities and Exchange Commission chairman and a member of Reagan's national advisory committee, reviewed the campaign records in California and brought back the grim news that Reagan's men had spent $12 million. If they kept on pouring out money at that rate, they would reach the federal limit of $16.9 million by April.

John Sears was trying to bring Casey in as an issues expert to replace Ed Meese. But Reagan had another idea: Casey, a distinguished New York lawyer, might take over the direction of the whole campaign.

Reagan had an acrimonious meeting with Sears at the Sheraton Rolling Green Inn in Andover, Massachusetts, Friday night, February 15. Sears, with Charles Black and Jim Lake backing him, complained to Reagan that Meese was not adequately briefing the candidate on issues. As Black recalled it, "we said, 'Either Ed has got to do this job or somebody else does, but for Christ's sake, let's do something about it.'"

According to Black, Sears had overheard Meese telling another staff member a few days before, "You just low-key it and mind your manners for a couple of weeks because it will be all right. These guys are all leaving." Sears, Black, and Lake assumed that they were the "guys" whom Meese intended to move out. This is Black's account of the stormy session in Andover, which ran four hours, from 10:00 P.M. to 2:00 A.M.:

Reagan hotly denied that Meese had ever mentioned any scheme for removing his three arch critics from the team. "That's not true, that's not true," Reagan said. "There is no plot to get rid of you guys. Ed is loyal and is doing the best he can for me. By God, if you guys are out to get Ed, I'm not going to stand for that!"

Sears, with his typically cool hauteur, replied: "Governor, if you're asking me to work with Ed on the same basis that we have been, without the job getting done, I can't do that."

By another account, Reagan roared: "You did in Mike Deaver but, by God, you're not going to get Ed Meese!"

Reagan became so violently angry that at one point Lake feared he might even strike Sears.

At the height of the dispute, Nancy Reagan intervened as a peacemaker, saying: "We're not going to settle this. Why don't we agree we're going to talk about this the day after New Hampshire?" There was a general agreement, then, to have a moratorium until after the primary February 26.

Sears, Black, and Lake still believed that Meese would try to protect his own place at Reagan's right hand by getting rid of them. Rather than be fired, they thought of quitting. But they dropped the idea because, Black said, "I think Reagan would have lost New Hampshire if we'd done that."

Still trailing Bush, Reagan began closing the gap with a capable performance in a Manchester debate involving the entire cast of Republican contenders, and he agreed to a one-on-one contest with Bush at Nashua on Saturday night, February 23, sponsored by the local newspaper, the *Telegraph*. The Federal Election Commission ruled it would be an illegal corporate political gift if the paper paid for the debate. So Gerald Carmen proposed that Reagan and Bush divide the bill. Bush refused to chip in, and Carmen quickly sent the Nashua *Telegraph* a check to cover the whole cost, $3,500; then arranged to invite all the other candidates to take part, too.

John Anderson, Howard Baker, Bob Dole, and Phil Crane all showed up (John Connally was campaigning in South Carolina) and joined Reagan in a classroom at the Nashua High School. A crowd of about 2,000 gathered in the gymnasium across the hall, eagerly awaiting a free-for-all that would later become famous as

"The Saturday Night Massacre." Bush occupied another classroom with his national campaign director, James Baker; press
secretary, Pete Teeley; and New Hampshire chairman, Hugh
Gregg. Meanwhile, Reagan aides and lawyers were demanding
that *Telegraph* editor Jon Breen change the ground rules and allow all candidates to participate.

But Breen and Gregg refused. "The format has been set,
everyone has agreed to it," Breen said, "and, dammit, we're not
going to change it at the last minute."

Lake and Black checked with Bush's aides and brought back
the word that he refused to meet with the other candidates. This
caused them to seethe with indignation and wounded egos. Jim
Baker said Bush wouldn't go to Reagan's classroom because the
count would be five to one against him.

Sen. Gordon Humphrey then went as an emissary on the
theory that Bush would at least speak to the Republican senator
from New Hampshire. The two men met outside the door leading
into the gymnasium, where the crowd was becoming noisy and
excited as the debate was already half an hour late.

"George, let's talk this over," Senator Humphrey said.

"I don't need a lecture from you on party unity," Bush
snapped. "There's nothing to say."

Then Bush strode into the gym, up to the stage and seated
himself in one of the two chairs reserved for the candidates.
Reagan soon marched onto the stage with the four other contenders, his mouth set in a thin, straight line that showed he was
trying hard to restrain his hot Irish temper.

While Reagan took the other chair at the front of the platform, Anderson, Baker, Dole, and Crane lined up like four
wooden Indians at the back, while the audience shouted, "Get
them chairs, get them chairs!" Bush sat in stony silence with his
back to the four, refusing to greet them or to shake their hands.
It was an incredible scene: two United States senators and two
congressmen, all serious aspirants for the presidency, treated as
interlopers in a New Hampshire high school gym, and required
to keep silent.

Reagan asked for a few minutes to explain the situation. He thought editor Breen, the moderator, had agreed. But when the former Governor of California began speaking, Breen shouted: "Will the sound man please turn Mr. Reagan's mike off?"

The crowd gasped in disbelief—then rebuked Breen's rude and arrogant act with a loud chorus: "BOO! BOO! BOO! BOO!"

Red-faced with fury, Reagan seized his microphone and proclaimed :"I am paying for this microphone, Mr. Green!"

As the old lion from Hollywood roared, the audience roared back with cheers, yells, and applause. Although he had the editor's name wrong, Reagan was precisely right in his response, in one of the most dramatic moments of live theater to mark this or any other campaign.

He emerged as a dynamic, commanding figure, fighting for his rivals' right to free speech against the arrogance of a petty tyrant who was trying to silence them. Some associates said they had never before seen him so furious with righteous indignation.

With his microphone intact, Reagan explained how he had "volunteered to pick up the tab" for the debate and thus became "the sponsor of this program" and invited all the other candidates. "These gentlemen came out with me so that you would know that we are all together," he said, "and willing to debate."

"Then why can't they debate?" someone shouted.

Bush said the Nashua *Telegraph* had made the rules and as a guest of the paper he would obey them.

Dole tried to put in a few words, but Breen cut him off. Then Anderson, Baker, Dole, and Crane walked out. They were embarrassed, humiliated, and hurt—and they would not forget.

Going past Bush, Dole muttered, "George, there'll be another day."

Back in their classroom, the four exiles assailed Bush and Breen as "dictators." "Is this America?" Dole shouted. "I've never been treated like this in my life! We don't want a king; we want a President."

"We were just dirt as far as Bush was concerned," the Kansas senator complained. "Of course, he's rich and went to the right schools . . ."

Bush may be the front-runner, as proclaimed by the media

after Iowa, Senator Baker said, but after this performance, he may lose his "crown."

"I agree with Howard," Dole said. "Bush wins in Iowa, the press nominates him, he thinks it's over."

When asked if the four would support Bush if he should be the nominee, Anderson replied that the question was "academic" —Bush would not win.

Leaving the gymnasium after the debate, Reagan's supporters were ecstatic over his performance and his line that would echo through the campaign: "I paid for this microphone, Mr. Green!" California Congressman Bob Dornan, a former TV commentator, exulted: "If we could just make Ron mad a few more times, we could put him in the White House!"

Bush compounded his mistake by flying home to Texas to rest while Reagan remained in New Hampshire through election day, campaigning for the last available vote. So the voters saw not only the old actor's great performance with the Nashua microphone every time they turned on their TV sets; they also saw Reagan in an overcoat, asking for votes, and Bush back home in Houston, jogging.

On Tuesday, Reagan rode on his campaign bus to greet voters at three polling places, accompanied by his aides, Black and Lake. In the early afternoon, the bus arrived at the Holiday Inn in Manchester, the headquarters for the night. Before entering the motel, Reagan said to Lake, "Jim, can I see you and Charlie and John, say, around two thirty?" Lake said, "Sure."

Sears, who was lunching with a reporter, joined his two comrades at the candidate's suite, where they found him waiting with Nancy Reagan and Bill Casey. As Black recalls the scene, Reagan began by saying, "Well, you guys know we have this problem, and it has to be resolved, and you won't like it, but I'm going to resolve it."

He handed Sears a press release that stated Casey had been named executive vice chairman. That had been Sears' official title. Sears thus learned that he had "resigned."

"I'm not surprised," Sears said and gave the press release to Lake, who handed it to Black.

Black was afraid the release would say that Sears was out but his two associates were not, because the Californians in the Reagan camp had said "it is just John who is the problem" and only he would have to go.

Black put the press release face down on the coffee table without looking at it and said: "Governor, before I read it, I'd just like you to know that I resign."

Then he picked up the paper and found out that his demonstration of loyalty to Sears had been unnecessary: "The release said right there that I had resigned."

Lake let Reagan know that the three dismissed officials blamed their troubles on their conflict with Meese, and that Casey could expect the same. Casey requested some records in Black's files and the political director replied that, of course, he would supply them.

After a few moments of strained conversation, the trio left with polite promises of friendship but private vows to protect their own reputations.

Richard Wirthlin's polls had shown Reagan overcoming Bush's lead but the final results of the primary were a stunning surprise: Reagan swept the entire field, polling a clear majority of the votes, or 50 percent plus. Bush came in a poor second with only 22 percent; Baker, third with 13 percent; Anderson, fourth with 10 percent. Connally and Crane had a pitiful two percent apiece while Dole had less than 1 percent and quickly dropped out of the race.

Reagan carried Manchester, the state's largest city and industrial center, by an incredible margin of eight to one, as the blue-collar voters responded to his appeals on the social issues and his proposal for income tax cuts. He owed much to the powerful support of the Manchester *Union Leader* and its publisher, William Loeb, who issued a daily blast against Bush. Reagan had tried his new strategy of reaching out to zealous volunteers and under the leadership of Gerald Carmen it had succeeded beyond anyone's dreams. Carmen, the chief architect of the victory, said: "I think George Bush is mortally wounded and not just in New

Hampshire. We always knew if we could puncture his balloon, there would be nothing there."

"This is the first and it sure is the best," Reagan proclaimed as he and Nancy, smiling triumphantly, thanked a crowd of well-wishers who jammed a Holiday Inn ballroom late on election night. "I don't know about the hierarchy or the upper regions, I only know about the people. Now, tomorrow, Nancy and I are flying over to Vermont, and we won't need a plane."

13

☆

THE
"DRAFT FORD" MANEUVER

By DISMISSING JOHN SEARS, Ronald Reagan emerged at last as a strong man in firm command of his own presidential campaign. The veteran Hollywood trouper resolved, thenceforth, to run the show his way by mingling directly with the voters in the style that brought about his stunning victory in the New Hampshire primary.

For too long, Sears had been allowed to cultivate his media image as the Mastermind, the puppeteer who pulled the strings and manipulated his marionette. Mingling with political writers in convivial luncheons and late-night poker games, the strategist had hinted that he would really be the power behind the throne in a Reagan administration.

The prospect of the White House being run by this cold, calculating Svengali, who had learned his political tricks from Richard Nixon, was enough to drive many prospective supporters away. Conservatives were dismayed because Sears rebuffed their offers of help and kept trying to remodel Reagan into a moderate. Grass roots volunteers voiced anger and frustration over inadequate help from the national campaign headquarters.

By firing Sears even before the polls closed in New Hampshire, Reagan showed that he had become the master in his own house. A week later, he scored well in two other New England primaries, squeezing in first in Vermont and a close third in Massachusetts. Bush barely won in Massachusetts and Anderson was runner-up. Reagan carried the blue-collar wards in Boston, where most voters shared his adamant opposition to abortion on demand. The Right to Life volunteers, who deserved much of the credit for his respectable showing in a liberal state, welcomed the change in his campaign tactics. New lines of communication opened between the conservative candidate and his foot soldiers out in the field.

Reagan and his aides sent urgent messages to conservatives across the country that they would be welcomed into the active ranks again, and the man with the most additional power in his shaken-up high command would be his chairman, Paul Laxalt.

The Nevada senator's warnings in the past had gone unheeded as the Reaganites poured out millions of dollars with a lavish hand. Coming in as Sears' replacement, William Casey took over a controller's tough task of slashing the budget, shrinking the payroll, and enabling Reagan to survive the long series of remaining primaries without running out of money.

Bush regained some of his momentum by coming in first in Massachusetts, his native state. Before his fall in New Hampshire, he had dreamed of sweeping the New England primaries, carrying those in Florida and Illinois, and locking up the nomination by April or early May. Now Anderson, the white-haired formerly conservative congressman from Illinois, suddenly became the new Guru of the Eastern liberals and the bright new star on television. Disheartened by his also-ran showings, Senator Baker pulled out of the race.

The stage was now set for Republican regulars to bring forth their favorite potential candidate: Gerald Ford.

The former President, playing golf at his sunny Rancho Mirage home in California, far away from the snowy, frigid East, nevertheless was keeping in close touch with his cronies who proposed to offer him as the one man who could bring about party unity and ultimate victory in November.

For months, Ford had been indulging occasionally in the fantasy of a triumphant return to the White House. It was only natural for him to cherish the daydream in which his party, deadlocked over several rivals for the prize at the Detroit convention in July, would turn once more to Good Old Jerry.

Although he enjoyed a millionaire's easy life with golf in California and skiing at his chalet in Colorado, Ford was not totally content with his leisure. He yearned for vindication. It was hard to forget that he had lost the White House by a margin of only 297 electoral votes to 241. On paper, at least, he could regain it by carrying the states he had won before and picking up any combination of twenty-nine more electoral votes from states he had narrowly lost—for instance, Ohio with twenty-five plus Mississippi with seven.

Ford also indicated frequently to friends that he was determined to keep Reagan from being the Republicans' nominee. His announced reason was that Reagan was too conservative to beat President Carter. But there was a deeper motive: He still cherished a bitter belief that Reagan, by bloodying him in the primaries and not campaigning hard enough for him in the fall, had caused his defeat.

So the ex-President ached to regain the White House and to get even with Reagan by blocking him out of it. But Ford refused to pay the high price required. He shrank from engaging in the primaries, where he would have to slug it out with several rivals and with no assurance that he would not again be humiliated by Reagan in such major states as Texas and California.

Ford's best chance lay in staying above the battle, encouraging a large number of contenders to take part, in the hope that they could produce the deadlock that could lead to a call from the party for him to be its nominee. But Reagan's New Hampshire comeback, Baker's pullout, and the weakness of Connally, Dole, and Crane made it clear that only Bush and Anderson were left to stop the front-runner.

So anti-Reagan Republicans from all parts of the country called upon Ford to leap into the race, even at this late date. Michigan's Gov. William Milliken telephoned Rancho Mirage and offered to round up support from various other governors in the Eastern and Midwestern industrial states who were afraid that Reagan would be a loser at the head of their party ticket.

Ford coyly responded by saying in a newspaper interview that he would run if his party would push him into it. "If there was an honest to goodness, bona fide urging by a broad-based group in my party, I would respond," he said. While not "scheming or conniving" for the nomination, he made it clear that he was eager to head off Reagan. "Every place I go, there is the growing, growing sentiment that Governor Reagan cannot win the election," he said. "I hear more and more often that we don't want, can't afford, to have a replay of 1964."

Reagan tartly retorted that Ford should "pack his long johns and come out here on the campaign trail with us."

"If he wants the nomination, he's going to have to compete like everyone else—and it's tough out there," Bush said. Connally ridiculed the Ford Draft idea as "sheer fantasy."

Robert Barrett, Ford's chief of staff, began cranking up the mechanism of a Draft Ford Committee. John O. Marsh, a former Ford White House aide and Democratic congressman from Virginia, now a Washington lawyer, flew out to Rancho Mirage and took part in the planning sessions. On March 6, the committee came out into the open. It was headed by Thomas Reed, a one-time Secretary of the Air Force, now a real estate promoter in California and Northern Virginia. Among the big-name Republicans on the list were Harvey Firestone, Ford's next-door neighbor, and Max Fisher, a Detroit millionaire.

John Sears, still sore after being booted out by Reagan, flew to Rancho Mirage on March 7, an unhappy jockey looking for a new mount to ride in the presidential sweepstakes. He had an amicable private chat with Ford about a new alliance and the prospects of a late-starting challenge to stop Reagan.

Sears, the eager convert, laid out the statistics of the primaries that the former President would have to win to avoid being beaten by the California challenger he had narrowly defeated in 1976. "The odds are very tough," Ford concluded, "but it's possible, with the right campaign, to get the nomination even with a late entry. At this stage, the mathematics are somewhat difficult, but it is a volatile political year."

Sears advised Ford to make his decision quickly, before the filing deadlines for the primaries in several major states. "I think Mr. Ford could be nominated if he decided to run," his new friend said.

Henry Kissinger also flew out to Rancho Mirage and called for the ex-President to run again. The former Secretary of State was entranced by the vision of a Restoration in which he would restore a stable foreign policy in the wake of Carter's many mistakes. The Soviet invasion of Afghanistan, the threat to Persian Gulf oil, the long captivity of the American hostages in Iran, were all grist for Kissinger's mill. Now the SALT II treaty with Moscow, based on the SALT I pact, which was among Kissinger's proudest achievements, was stalled in a hostile Senate with no prospect of being ratified.

The pressures on Ford increased after Reagan swept the South Carolina primary March 8, wrecking the hopes of John Connally, who came in second, and further damaging the image of Bush, a weak third. To the surprise of even his own managers, Reagan won a clear majority, 54 percent, while Connally, who had been predicting a victory for himself, polled only 30 percent and Bush, a mere 15 percent. Connally, who had pinned his hopes on a South Carolina triumph to begin chipping away at Reagan's base in the South, was so crushed that he withdrew from the race.

The silver-haired Texan, once the heavy favorite of his many friends in the executive suites of Big Business, had poured $10 million into his drive for the White House, yet he had only one delegate to show for all his efforts. In throwing in the towel, Connally conceded that Reagan was "still the champ."

On March 11, Reagan won three more primaries, in Florida, Georgia, and Alabama, leaving Bush further behind and Anderson looking even weaker. In Florida, where he had lost to Ford four years before, the former California Governor racked up 57 percent of the vote to 30 percent for Bush and only 9 percent for Anderson. Clearly, Reagan could count on overwhelming support all across the South, as well as the West, so it seemed clear that, barring some stumble or upset, he would be hard to stop.

Bracing himself for a last-minute challenge by Ford, Reagan said: "He's dabbled both feet in the water up to his knees. Yes, I think it's going to happen."

The former President sounded like a man eager to plunge into the race when he spent three days in Washington in mid-March. He received a standing ovation at a party fund-raising dinner in response to his bristling speech on the theme of "Carter must go." The ovation for the tanned and vigorous speaker was so great that it worried Reagan backers in the crowd. California's peppery Sen. S. I. Hayakawa said: "This dinner has turned into a Ford pep rally."

Huddling privately with friends, Ford closely studied the statistics that indicated he might win the nomination by carrying several big states that had late primaries. Thomas Reed, the Draft Ford Committee leader, said Ford must sweep the "Big Eight": New York, New Jersey, Pennsylvania, Illinois, Ohio, Michigan, Texas, and California.

He could not personally win Illinois, of course, because it was too late to enter its March 18 primary. But his advisers hoped that Anderson, who was leading in the polls there, would give Reagan a sharp setback in the year's first primary battle in a large Midwestern industrial state.

Reed even made the astonishing claim that Ford could take away the big bloc of 168 California delegates that Reagan's forces had presumably locked up by enforcing the old winner-take-all rule there. Although Ford, when he was President, had lost the state by two to one to its former Governor in 1976, Reed insisted that the Squire of Rancho Mirage could win it this time, saying: "Having been national committeeman in California and run some elections there, and having looked at enough data in California, I would have no hesitancy in taking responsibility for a campaign for Ford head-to-head against Reagan."

Congressman Bob Wilson of California was so impressed that he declared: "Ford is running, and it looks good." Wilson called for a "hurry-up" effort to file a slate of delegates in the California primary before the March 21 deadline.

Ford hoped that many Republican congressmen, who had been his friends since his days as their minority leader, would swiftly rally around the call to draft him. Several did, but others hung back because they were pledged to various active contenders already in the race and thus could not honorably switch.

Reagan men in the House fought back by arguing that it was too late to stop their candidate now. Bob Walker of Pennsylvania said Reagan would get many more delegates in the Keystone State, as well as in New York and in New Jersey, than in 1976 when most of them were delivered to Ford by Nelson Rockefeller. The whole political picture in the East has changed, Walker said. "Rocky is dead."

Tom Evans of Delaware warned Ford's pollster, Bob Teeter, that the latest polling figures proved Reagan would surely be the winner, no matter how much money and effort might be expended for Ford. Evans called Guy Vander Jagt, a Michigan congressman and longtime associate of Ford's, and told him: "Guy, I can show you figures that Reagan is going to be the nominee. So why put the former President into the primaries? It could only be divisive; it would be terrible." Shortly thereafter, Vander Jagt appeared on television and said Ford should stay out.

Bob Bauman, a Maryland congressman, warned that a Ford candidacy "would split the party worse than in 1964 and leave a lot of blood on the floor." Other members said Ford would be viewed as a "spoiler" who entered the race only to stop Reagan. So, instead of creating harmony, he would cause discord. Instead of unifying his party, he would divide it. Furthermore, he would have to win every major primary and that was quite unlikely. He would simply suffer an embarrassing rebuff.

The "draft Ford" movement gained so much momentum that it worried the Reagan forces greatly. Congressman Evans telephoned Nancy Reagan, who was campaigning with her husband in Florida, and said: "Don't worry, Nancy, about this, because the polling we've done informally shows a majority of the House members believe Governor Reagan will be our nominee and Ford entering the race would be counterproductive."

"Ford was like an old racehorse; he wanted to run again," the Delaware congressman said. "I really think he had made a decision to run, contingent upon strong support in Congress, but he didn't get it." The final crusher to his hopes came when most of the Republican governors hung back from making a clarion call for him to rush to his party's rescue. So, on March 15, after returning to Rancho Mirage, the former President met with his advisers and faced the cold, hard truth: His dream of being summoned back through an "honest to goodness, bona fide" draft had become a mirage.

It was an emotional scene. One participant said Ford burst into tears as he made the decision which he called "the toughest" one in his lifetime. "I have reached a final and certain decision," he announced. "Betty agreed with it. . . . America needs a new President. I have determined that I can best help that cause by not being a candidate for President, which might further divide my party.

"I am not a candidate. I will not become a candidate. I will support the nominee of my party with all the energy I have. America is in deep, deep trouble and needs the help of all of us."

Although the challenge by Ford thus faded away, Reagan faced a potentially serious setback in Illinois, where Anderson hung on to a lead in the polls and picked up the editorial endorsement of both the Chicago *Tribune* and the *Sun-Times*. The maverick congressman had considerable support in his home district, the Rockford area, and appealed to independents and Democrats to cross over and vote for him.

Phil Crane, the rival Illinois congressman in the presidential race, realized that his own hopes were trickling down the drain. So he resolved to help Reagan chop down Anderson, in a joint debate, on the issue of loyalty to the Republican party. Crane had obtained a copy of a fund-raising letter that had been sent out over Anderson's signature to aid in the re-election of several senators, all liberal Democrats who were targeted for defeat by the Right to Life forces for advocating abortion.

Among the senators to benefit from the Anderson letter were George McGovern of South Dakota, John Culver of Iowa, Birch Bayh of Indiana, and Frank Church of Idaho—all anathema to regular Republicans.

Crane told Reagan, who had never heard of the letter before: "I'm going after John on this. You can take the high road and play the role of statesman tonight." Reagan smiled and followed the scenario. He twitted Anderson for having said he'd rather have Teddy Kennedy as President than Reagan. With mock incredulity, Reagan asked: "You really would find Teddy Kennedy preferable to me?" The audience roared with laughter.

Crane delivered the rabbit punch by flashing the letter that showed Anderson was helping to raise money for liberal Democrats in the Senate, at the same time seeking votes from Republicans in Illinois. "You should have seen his face!" the mischievous Crane exulted later. "It caught him off guard. It showed that John was making a rifle-shot appeal to McGovern Democrats. That was when John Anderson crossed the Rubicon and read himself out of the Republican party.

"Oh, I enjoyed that night," Crane said. "It was almost worth twenty months of campaigning. I kind of did myself in, but I wasn't going anywhere by that time, anyway. I had made up my mind that after Illinois I'd throw in the sponge and back Reagan."

After the debate, Anderson began slipping. On March 18, Reagan won the primary in Illinois, his native state, with 48 percent of the total vote, Anderson coming in second with 37 percent and Bush, a poor third with only 11 percent, Crane trailing far in the rear with 2 percent. Thousands of Democrats and independents crossed over into the Republican primary. Most of them supported Anderson but Reagan also obtained a share of them, chiefly through his appeals to blue-collar workers and the "pro-life" forces.

Thanks to the fine organization assembled by his state campaign manager, Don Totten, Reagan scored a solid triumph and punctured the old charge that he was too weak to carry a large Northern state. "It's a great boost," he said, "to move into the industrial Midwest and take a state like Illinois."

Anderson vowed to fight on and "to peel Ronald Reagan's fingers away from that nomination, one by one."

Throughout the following week, Bush campaigned furiously in Connecticut on the theme, "Welcome home, George," reminding the voters that he had grown up in Fairfield County as the son of Sen. Prescott Bush and was graduated from Yale University before moving to Texas to strike it rich in the oil business.

His frenzied electioneering paid off. Bush staged a comeback by coming in first in Connecticut on March 25 with 39 percent of the vote, Reagan finishing second with 34 percent and Anderson, third with 22 percent. But, on the same day, Reagan locked up the lion's share of the delegates in New York, where he had been almost frozen out by the party machine in 1976. New York liked to go with the winner, and as incredible as the prospect had seemed to its liberal Republican leadership only a few weeks before, this time the sure-money bets had to be placed on the conservative former actor from Hollywood.

,Anderson hoped the liberals would respond to his calls for austerity and sacrifice and a fifty-cents-per-gallon increase in the gasoline tax. But the April 1 primary in Wisconsin gave Reagan still another Midwest victory with 40 percent of the total vote, Bush coming in second with 31 percent and Anderson, third with 28 percent. Anderson's poor showing killed his hopes for the Republican nomination. Soon, with his 0–7 record in the primaries, he dropped out of the Republican race and started running as an independent. In that role, he would turn out to be—quite unintentionally—a very helpful friend of Ronald Reagan's.

14

☆

FRANKLIN DELANO REAGAN

As HE MARCHED through the spring primaries on his way to the Republican nomination, Ronald Reagan sought to broaden his party's base by appealing directly to blue-collar workers, despite their union leaders' efforts to keep them locked inside the Democratic fold.

Reagan accused President Carter of deliberately squeezing the nation into a recession and throwing 2 million people out of work through high interest rates imposed, along with tight credit restrictions, in a panicky attempt to check the inflationary spiral, which was soaring toward the 20 percent mark. In a typical display of his New Populism at Philadelphia April 16, Reagan assailed the President's "new" economic policy as only the latest in a series of bewildering zigzags and blamed him for a sharp drop in car sales with resulting layoffs in American automobile factories.

Carter's anti-inflation plan is "deceitful" and destructive, the challenger charged at a rowdy, raucous Republican dinner. "He says he's going to balance the budget yet—by increasing the take from our pockets, in taxes, of almost a hundred billion dollars in the coming year." (Cheers and whistles.)

"The way to fight inflation is to whittle down the size of the federal government, remove the layers of fat, and then cut the income taxes across the board for everybody in this country!" (Cheers, whistles, and applause.)

"It is time to energize the economy by lifting the burden of taxation from the backs of the working and middle class!" (Wild whoops and applause.)

Calling for "the moral and military rearmament of the United States for the difficult, dangerous days ahead," Reagan declared: "If anyone talks of a strong defense, they say we are trying to promote a war. That is a libel and a lie!"

Reagan's strategy of seeking votes in the Northeast, where he had been woefully weak four years before, began paying dividends when he collected most of the delegates from New York, now freed from the grip of the old Rockefeller machine. Then New Jersey's party leaders assured him of at least sixty of their sixty-six convention votes in the June 3 primary and Reagan responded: "I want the party to quit writing off the Northeast and I intend to bring the Northeast home to the Republican party."

Harking back to his days as an ardent Franklin D. Roosevelt Democrat, Reagan remembered that F.D.R. had beaten President Herbert Hoover in 1932 by blaming him for the "Hoover Depression." The Republicans went into decline and almost into oblivion, as a whole generation of voters associated the word "Republican" with unemployment and Big Business, a party insensitive to the needs of the common people. Reagan set out in 1980 to achieve a "1932" in reverse.

This time, Carter appeared as the incompetent President unable to cope with a depression while millions of Americans were out of work. Senator Edward M. Kennedy, in his unsuccessful bid to take the Democratic nomination away from the President, also attacked him that way. Carroll O'Connor, television's Archie Bunker, appeared in pro-Kennedy TV commercials branding Carter as "the new Herbert Hoover."

Reagan courted the real voters of the Archie Bunker School by appealing to them as a fellow advocate of the social values they held most dear: the church, the home, the family, and the flag—and rock-solid opposition to abortion on demand.

In a pitch for the pro-life voters, he said in Philadelphia: "The American people today—and it crosses party lines—are ready to shelter and protect the least protected among us, and I believe that specifically includes the unborn."

The fight over the inflation issue brought about an ironic reversal of roles. Carter, the Democrat, imposed the tight money policies advocated for so many years by the Old Guard Republicans; while Reagan, the onetime New Deal Democrat, soon to become the Republicans' nominee, advocated the novel ideas of the Kemp-Roth Bill, calling for a 30 percent reduction in income taxes over a three-year period.

Reagan, in his enthusiasm for new ideas, embraced Prof. Arthur Laffer's theory of the "Laffer Curve," in the belief that lower tax rates would stimulate the economy to produce more wealth and more revenues. Congressman Jack Kemp liked to say that the bill, which the young New Yorker cosponsored with Delaware Sen. William Roth, would produce a "bigger pie" for everyone to share.

More conservative economists who had influenced the Nixon and Ford administrations—notably Dr. Arthur Burns, Alan Greenspan, and former Treasury Secretaries George Shultz and William Simon—tried to pull Reagan away from the individual tax cuts, which they considered radical and inflationary, and steer him toward tax credits and faster write-offs on the "supply side" for modernizing industry.

The behind-the-curtain scuffling among his advisers gave rise to a spate of newspaper articles about "a battle for Reagan's mind." They left the impression that the candidate, having no Washington experience, was being pulled back and forth by the self-styled experts who knew their way around the labyrinthine corridors of power in the capital. He tried to minimize the conflict by saying it showed he did not have a closed mind, as some critics had charged, but he welcomed advice from a broad range of economists ranging all the way from Arthur Laffer to Milton Friedman.

Kemp provided a revealing account of Reagan's conversion to the Kemp-Roth philosophy in an interview tracing their association back to the days when Kemp had worked for Governor Reagan in California during off-season vacations away from professional football. The quarterback and the former film star found they had another bond besides their love of sports: "We were both expressing ideas," Kemp said, "about the American dream. We believe that everyone should not be leveled with everyone else by regulation and a tax code that redistributes income; that the real hope of America is in upward mobility, a sense of boundless opportunities, rewards, and incentives for those who are productive, who work and save."

Elected to Congress after his retirement from the Buffalo Bills, Kemp introduced a bill to create more jobs in the private sector, and Reagan endorsed it. Then, in 1978, came the Kemp-Roth measure. "Reagan supported that because he realized that progressivity in the tax code is a tax on individual effort," the congressman said. When most Republicans in Congress sponsored the bill and gave up their age-old adherence to the orthodox economics of austerity and tight money, this marked a dramatic change in their party. "It was a change for all of us," Kemp commented. "I don't like orthodoxy anywhere; it smacks of being in concrete. Reagan doesn't like it, either.

"If you ask him about that old orthodox Herbert Hoover idea that the answer to inflation is a good, old-fashioned wringing out of the economy—you know, with a little unemployment and a recession—Reagan would say to that, 'No, that's the Old Economics. I believe in the New Economics.'

"He recognizes that all of us are looking at the economic problems of the world in a different way from the 1960's. Then, we did not have inflation and high unemployment at the same time. Today we have both, something the Keynesians and the liberals told us we couldn't have.

"Reagan is the only national leader who understands that the dilemma must be cured, not just with monetary reform, but also with tax and regulatory reform. So he has a strategy for full employment without inflation, which really is unorthodox."

Kemp hotly denied the charge that Reagan was an "intellectual lightweight" who simply parroted speeches written for him by smarter men and ran into trouble when he wandered away and made ad lib. remarks not in the script. "It's outrageous," the congressman said. "Anybody—friend or critic—who knows him well enough to have talked with him or debated with him knows that Reagan is a very thoughtful, decent, honest man who likes ideas. He likes to debate ideas. He has strong ideals and a philosophical rudder that is pretty firmly directed, but he is pragmatic enough to accept new ideas."

One day in August, 1979, Congressman and Mrs. Kemp met Ronald and Nancy Reagan for lunch at a restaurant in the Wilshire Boulevard office building that is the nerve center of the Reagan-Deaver-Hannaford enterprises in Los Angeles. Reagan asked Kemp to become involved in his coming campaign for the presidency.

"My wife got a little bit embarrassed because I was asking questions about monetary, regulatory, fiscal, tax, and foreign policies, and she thought I was a little bit presumptuous in talking about those things," Kemp recalled. "But I like Reagan as a man and I wanted to know about his campaign plans. He's such an optimist, a positivist, an activist.

"We agreed that the main danger to America on the energy issue was that we were diminishing the production of new supplies. He began rattling off statistics about areas where vast hydrocarbon deposits could be the resource base for a renaissance in energy rather than a Malthusian era of limits, in which we've got to ride bikes to work, give up washers and dryers, and look upon the future of America as a pessimistic 'small is beautiful' type of thing. I was getting ready to write my book about the American renaissance. So, when John Sears came to me and said, 'We'd like to offer you a fairly high level position,' I accepted."

For three days in January, 1980, Reagan met with his chief campaign aides and advisers at a Los Angeles airport motel for all-day brainstorming sessions about major issues that would come up in the campaign. They devoted one day to foreign policy, with Richard Allen as the leading figure, and two days to economics.

The motel scene resembled a classroom, with a blackboard, and the discussions covered a wide range of conflicting ideas. Kemp was impressed by Reagan's ability to take an idea, translate it from academic double-talk, and apply it in terms of people.

"That is what gives him a special feel for politics, because people relate to that," Kemp said. "He talks about family, jobs, the neighborhood, the community, individual lives, hopes, and potential growth."

Reagan was not a student learning at the feet of the professors but a dominant figure in the brainstorming session, Kemp said. "This is Reagan's basic philosophy: We need liberalized depreciation rates for business, yes, and incentives for saving, but we also must reduce the steep nature of the graduated income tax because it is smothering incentives for people to produce.

"Reagan's plan is to expand the pie, rather than dividing up a shrinking pie. Most Republicans have thought that only machinery and plants and equipment produce, but Reagan's concept is that *people* produce. Republicans used to say, 'What's good for business is good for America, it will trickle down to everybody.' Reagan is saying, 'What's good for *people* will be good for labor and business, black people and white people, blue-collar and white-collar workers. We should aim our policies at the objective of helping people."

Kemp conceded that for years the Republicans had carried around the bad image of a party of privilege favoring Big Business, the "fat cats," and Wall Street. But, he said, "Reagan is different. His strength comes from the blue-collar worker, the small shopkeeper, those men and women who really want to aspire to more. He once said his two favorite Presidents in the twentieth century were Calvin Coolidge and John F. Kennedy. Why? Because, under both Coolidge and Kennedy, there were rising incomes, general prosperity, lower tax rates, and very little inflation. I thought it was significant that he did not name Eisenhower or Franklin D. Roosevelt.

"Reagan is like Roosevelt, the activist who restored hope after Hoover's failure to overcome the Depression. But Reagan's activism is in the private sector, rather than in spending public funds as F.D.R. did."

Just as Roosevelt brought about a political revolution when he formed his New Deal coalition that began the Democrats' long era of power, Kemp saw Reagan doing the same with his coalition combining the Republican base with independents and blue-collar Democrats. "I'm less interested in the Republican party than in the 'Renaissance of the American Dream," the congressman said. "I don't think we can get from here to there without a revolution in the Republican party."

The awesome prospect of such a revolution alarmed the regular Republicans, who hoped to regain control of the executive branch, not for the purpose of trying out any radical economic schemes but to restore good, sound government along traditional lines with themselves in charge. They sought to take over Reagan, modify his militant views in favor of individual income-tax cuts and other populist notions, and persuade him to select a moderate for Vice President.

These politicians were haunted by memories of Barry Goldwater's defeat in 1964 when the Arizona senator ran a strictly conservative campaign. The liberals of his party mutinied, some helping Lyndon Johnson to keep the presidency and others sulking in their tents, doing nothing. Reagan received many warnings that the same fate would befall him unless he chose a running mate who could mollify the unhappy moderates in the suburbs. If he did not give them the second half of the ticket, they had another option: They could vote for the independent contender, John Anderson.

The beau ideal of the moderate Republicans was George Bush, who had never lost his Connecticut accent or his Ivy League "preppy" look even after becoming a Texas oil millionaire and a Houston congressman. The dogged jogger kept hanging on in the primaries, despite all the odds against him. He defeated Reagan in Pennsylvania, gave him a scare in Texas, and clobbered him in Michigan. Unfortunately for Bush, while these achievements enhanced his image as a tireless campaigner who could pull in votes in big states crucial to victory in November, they came too late to stop Reagan from wrapping up the presidential prize.

On Memorial Day, Bush figuratively placed flowers on the grave of his presidential campaign when he officially withdrew at a gloomy Houston press conference. He had fought on in the hope of carrying his battle through the June 3 primaries in Ohio, New Jersey, and California and pulling an upset somewhere. But he was running out of money and Reagan had a lock on the nomination, anyway. Still, the gaunt, long-distance runner could lay claim to second place on the ticket as a well-deserved reward for stamina and grit.

Also acceptable to the old "Rockefeller wing," which demanded a loud voice in the Republican inner circle although no longer strong enough to dominate the party, was Howard Baker. The Tennessee senator, who had hoped to emerge as the Number One alternative to Reagan, showed surprising weaknesses in the early primaries before bowing out.

Realizing that the Democrats would surely assail Reagan as totally lacking experience in national affairs, in dealing with Congress, and especially in foreign policy, his managers agreed that he should choose a running mate with a track record in all those fields, a veteran such as Baker or Bush.

But the New Right activists mounted a furious attack on Baker, calling him totally unacceptable, and not only because he had helped Carter to win Senate approval of the Panama Canal treaties. Baker also had sinned by repeatedly voting in favor of federal funds for abortions. So the Right to Life organizations launched a campaign to block him, using the code letters "A.B.B." for "Anybody But Baker."

"Nobody was naive enough to think that antiabortionists could dictate the VP choice," the Ad Hoc Committee in Defense of Life, Inc., said in a newsletter. "But they sure could expect to *blackball* somebody, and Howard Baker's voting record on abortion was enough to accomplish this."

The Conservative Digest magazine, published by the New Right fund-raising king, Richard Viguerie, lampooned Baker with a cover cartoon showing him wearing a dunce cap. On the pages inside were columns of quotations from various critics, denouncing the senator. *Human Events*, the old-line conservative weekly newspaper, catalogued a long list of Baker's errors. Shaken by the

ferocity of his enemies' attacks, Baker virtually ruled himself out
of the race, saying he did not expect to be chosen.

Soon the A.B.B. drive of the "pro-life" groups was expanded
to make Bush a target, too. Although he opposed federal funding
of abortions, he would not back a constitutional amendment barring them outright. So he was placed on the blacklist. The Chi-
cago-based "Friends for Life" picked up a tip from associates of
Bush's brother's, a St. Louis banker, that Bush would be Reagan's
final choice.

Then the evangelical Christians, an increasingly powerful new
political force favorable to Reagan, entered the controversy over
his running mate. They especially disliked Baker and Bush.
Among their favorites were Sen. Jesse Helms and Congressman
Phil Crane, who had no chance at all; also acceptable were Sen.
Paul Laxalt, Sen. Richard Lugar of Indiana, Congressman Jack
Kemp, Congressman Guy Vander Jagt of Michigan, and former
Treasury Secretary William Simon.

Jimmy Carter's heavy emphasis on his status as a "born again"
Christian was a major factor in his 1976 victory, when he carried
ten Southern states that had given their electoral votes to President Nixon four years before. But many Bible Belt voters became
disillusioned with Brother Jimmy as he cultivated the liberal
wing of the Democratic party. They charged that he did nothing
to curb abortions; that his Internal Revenue Service tried to take
away the tax-exempt status of their church schools; and he
worked with his henchmen in Congress to kill a bill restoring
voluntary prayer in the schools. Several prominent Christian
clergymen, after cross-examining Reagan on these and other issues close to their hearts, concluded that he was "right" on all
of them.

Reagan won the enthusiastic support of the Reverend Jerry
Falwell, whose televised *Old Time Gospel Hour* reaches 18 million viewers each week. A dynamic, hard-driving promoter, Falwell started his own independent Baptist church in an abandoned
soft drink factory in Lynchburg, Virginia, in 1956 and built it
into a congregation of 17,000. Then he founded Liberty Baptist

College and, through TV and direct-mail fund-raising, created
an evangelical empire.

In 1979, Falwell formed an alliance with some New Right
strategists who earlier appeared in this narrative as the prime
movers of the abortive effort to draft Reagan as the presidential
candidate of an independent ticket for the 1976 election, only
to see him turn them down flat. Chief members of this brain
trust were Paul Weyrich, director of the Committee for the Survival of a Free Congress, and Howard Phillips, head of the
Conservative Caucus.

Weyrich, an Eastern Rite Catholic, and Phillips, who is Jewish, convinced Falwell that the elections of the 1980's could be
won by candidates who advocated the "moral" side of burning
issues affecting the family—by opposing abortion, pornography,
drugs, gay rights, and government interference with parents'
rights to educate their children.

At Weyrich's suggestion, Falwell set up a political group
called Moral Majority. Named as its director was the Reverend
Robert Billings, a former college president and unsuccessful Republican congressional candidate in Indiana. Another strong ally
was Ed McAteer, a crack salesman for the Colgate-Palmolive
Company, whose travels had made him acquainted with hundreds of ministers, a ready-made network that could be tapped
for political purposes. McAteer took charge of the nonpartisan
Religious Roundtable, including most of the preachers who starred
in TV shows plus leaders of the New Right.

With McAteer as their shepherd, a flock of Christian preachers met secretly with Republican National Chairman Bill Brock
at his Capitol Hill office May 20. Brock had invited them to
lunch to enlist their help in registering several million new
voters, nearly all of whom would be expected to turn thumbs
down on the backsliding Baptist, Jimmy Carter.

The clergymen—who included the Reverend Adrian Rogers
of Memphis, former president of the Southern Baptist Convention; Dr. Tim LaHaye of Californians for Biblical Morality; Jerry
Falwell; and James Robison, a fiery evangelist from Fort Worth,
Texas—declared that their people would vote on "principle";

they would not become a branch of any party but would back candidates who met their own rigid tests on the moral issues.

Brig. Gen. Albion W. Knight, who is also an Episcopal cleric, shocked Brock by saying there was not a dime's worth of difference between the Republicans and the Democrats on foreign policy, for both had advocated the SALT I treaty with the Soviet Union for arms control. The retired Army officer assailed Henry Kissinger's pursuit of detente with Moscow.

His face flaming red with anger, Brock fired back: "I can't believe you're saying this!"

Brock said President Ford had requested billions of dollars more for defense than the Democratic Congress would give him; that Carter had cut billions from the last Ford budget for the military, besides killing the B–1 bomber.

After this storm had calmed down, the question of the Republican vice presidential nominee arose.

"We've got to have the right man for Vice President," evangelist Robison declared, and he meant "far right." He sang the praises of Helms and Crane but evoked no favorable response from Brock. The party chairman had served alongside Baker as a senator from Tennessee and was a personal friend of Bush and of the outside possibility, ex-President Ford.

The evangelical ministers all turned thumbs down on Baker and Bush. But McAteer came away with a definite impression that Reagan would heed the regular Republicans' demand for someone of their type. "I have a queasy feeling," the former soap salesman said, "that Reagan is going to choose a moderate."

Bryce Harlow, a speech writer and trusted counselor for Presidents Eisenhower, Nixon, and Ford, promoted the idea of drafting Ford. He sent a letter to Rancho Mirage, urging the distinguished golfer there to make the great sacrifice of returning to the vice presidency. "I know this is asking a lot, but Ford has said he would do anything to save the nation from four more disastrous years of Jimmy Carter in the White House," said Harlow, a Washington lobbyist for the Procter and Gamble company. "If the Republicans lose this election, this country could be in for a long stretch of one-party rule by the Democrats."

On June 5, Reagan made a pilgrimage to Rancho Mirage, like a good Moslem going to Mecca, to bow low before Ford and beg for his aid. The ex-President played the role of cordial host; Reagan, of respectful guest. Ford laid heavy stress on his warnings that the nominee must select a moderate for the vice presidency; otherwise, many Republicans would defect to John Anderson. Reagan offered second place on his ticket to the former Chief Executive, asking him to accept as one more service to his party and to his country. Ford refused. But he insisted upon having considerable influence in the nominee's ultimate decision. Reagan, eager to have Ford's help in the campaign, quickly agreed.

Soon thereafter, Reagan faced a storm inside the Republican party as the high command of his campaign organization moved to oust Chairman Brock. Senator Laxalt led the effort, insisting that the prospective presidential nominee must immediately take control of the entire Republican National Committee headquarters by installing his own loyal people there to assure a unified, harmonious fall campaign.

"It's my conviction that you should have your own people there," the Nevada senator insisted. "It's a matter of political necessity."

While Brock had stayed neutral during the long series of primary battles, other high-echelon officials in the RNC building had not. Laxalt charged that the whole place was packed full of people who were hostile to Reagan, and it was high time to clear them out.

Laxalt also had distrusted Brock ever since their late 1977 spat over the money that Reagan had raised by signing an RNC direct-mail letter to fight the Panama Canal treaties. Brock's refusal to release a dime of the money for Laxalt's "truth squad" to fly around the country in opposition to the pacts did not endear him to either Laxalt or Reagan.

When the Reagan men began their maneuvers to dump Brock, he moved to protect his job by flying to California and persuading Reagan and campaign manager William Casey to let him stay. Brock said he had a promise that he could remain in office through the November election. But Laxalt insisted there was a "misunderstanding," that the chairman would stay only through the Detroit convention in July.

Laxalt persuaded all the high-level officials on the Reagan staff to go along with a scenario that called for Brock to step down and be succeeded by Drew Lewis, Reagan's Pennsylvania chairman. They proposed to sweeten the pill by making Brock the "chief surrogate speaker" in the fall campaign.

Brock refused. He and his friends then mounted a furious counteroffensive to save him. Several governors and senators, the Senate and House leaders of the party, and such conservatives as Sen. Orrin Hatch of Utah and Congressman Jack Kemp warned that dumping Brock would split the party and damage its prospects for victory.

At the same time, the Reagan managers were also trying to sign up Brock's closest friend and former assistant, Bill Timmons, a Washington lobbyist, to become their national political director. Timmons, who had acquired enormous influence and expertise as chief of congressional liaison in the Nixon White House, could hardly be expected to board the Reagan campaign ship while its crew was throwing Brock overboard.

In typical fashion, Reagan was cruising serenely along, up in the captain's cabin, only remotely aware of the scuffling and knife-throwing among his crew members belowdecks. He was simply following the practice that had been traditional during his years as governor, to let his aides wrestle with the problems and leave the final decision to him.

Laxalt and his allies thought they had almost won their battle against Brock when they persuaded Chief of Staff Ed Meese and Nancy Reagan to go along. But Brock then fired his heaviest artillery: Ford sent word that he would view the dismissal of Brock as not only divisive and harmful but also as "a personal affront."

The big blast from Ford achieved the desired effect. Brock and Reagan met in Los Angeles June 13 and effected a compromise to save everyone's face. Brock remained as chairman. Drew Lewis became deputy chairman and liaison man, to bring a little harmony between the Republican National Committee head-quarters and the Reagan staff. Brock's deputy, Ben Cotten, a prime target of the attempted purge, was transferred to a lesser role. Brock went along with a decision to get rid of Cochairman Mary Crisp, who had constantly criticized Reagan while championing abortion and the Equal Rights Amendment.

Crisp had made a fatal mistake by telling an interviewer that she admired John Anderson. She denied that her remarks were an endorsement of the independent candidate, but Brock opposed her re-election. She left in tears with a parting blast at her foes in Detroit, denouncing the Republicans for no longer supporting ratification of ERA in their platform. Soon thereafter, Crisp turned up, to no one's surprise, in a high place in the Anderson campaign.

15

☆

DETROIT
MELODRAMA

HOLLYWOOD NEVER FILMED a melodrama more exciting than the political cliff-hanger that Ronald Reagan produced in four unbelievable days and nights in Detroit in July, 1980.

In his eagerness to try out new ideas, the veteran motion picture star played around with startling schemes for restructuring the office of the presidency even before he had won it. He considered giving some of its powers away to the Vice President if he must pay that price to get Gerald Ford as his running mate on a "dream ticket" heralded as likely to place Reagan in the White House.

The behind-the-scenes negotiations between the Reagan forces and the Ford forces began quietly in hushed, luxurious hotel suites, but later the drama burst forth on the television networks and caused wild scenes of commotion among the delegates to the Republican National Convention.

This was the sequence of events that made political history in Detroit, based upon the recollections of the principal players in the show.

Monday, July 14

Cheering crowds and a band blaring "California, Here I Come" greeted Ronald and Nancy Reagan when they flew triumphantly into town from Los Angeles and arrived at the Renaissance Cen-

ter, overlooking the Detroit River and Canada on the distant
shore. The four gleaming steel-and-glass towers with the Detroit
Plaza Hotel in their midst symbolized the city's determination
to rise above the urban decay that had marred the once-prosper-
ous heart of the American automobile industry, now suffering
heavy unemployment in a near-depression.

Detroit had long been a stronghold of the Democrats and
their powerful ally, the United Automobile Workers union. But
the Republicans staged their convention for the first time in this
troubled city of slums and strife to show their new concern for
the blue-collar workers. They viewed the Renaissance Center
with its fantastic towers as a symbol of a Republican Renaissance
that would drive Jimmy Carter out of the White House.

Despite the primary triumphs that assured his nomination by
the convention on Wednesday night, Reagan still felt unsure of
his ability to win the November election without the solid support of a unified party. He was obliged to court the favor of the
Old Guard leaders, who looked down on him as a professional
after-dinner speaker with no experience in Washington, a super-
salesman but not a statesman. In particular, he must have the
enthusiastic backing of Gerald Ford.

Although the former President in their parley at Rancho
Mirage had firmly refused to run for the vice presidency, Reagan
was determined to make one more try for his consent, since
Richard Wirthlin's recent polls showed that Ford would add
more strength to the ticket than would any other possible choice
for second place. Reagan also harbored a few doubts about
George Bush, the favorite of his campaign staff.

Soon after they moved into their sixty-ninth–floor suite in the
Detroit Plaza, the Reagans went one flight upstairs and paid a
visit to Jerry and Betty Ford and joined in celebrating the ex-
President's sixty-seventh birthday. As a symbolic gift that was
most appropriate, Reagan handed Ford an old pipe and a tobacco
bag from a Crow Indian tribe in Montana.

This was the inscription on the peace pipe:
"These little traveling smoke kits are rare today, although

much revered in pre-reservation days. They allowed two warriors passing on the trail to stop and enjoy a smoke in peace and wish each other good fortune on the dangerous trails that lie ahead."

Ford appreciated the friendly overture from his onetime rival and consented to appear before the convention Thursday night for a display of unity with Reagan and the nominee for Vice President. Tactfully, Reagan did not make a direct bid for the former President to accept but deferred the discussion to a longer private parley on Tuesday afternoon.

Ford made a fighting speech in Joe Louis Arena on the opening night of the convention, a blistering attack upon the failures of his successor. Jimmy Carter had assailed him in 1976 with the "misery index," the total of the unemployment and the inflation rates, then 12 percent. "Just two months ago, it was twenty-four percent—twice as high," Ford said. "That's twice as many reasons that Jimmy Carter has got to go."

Then, with withering sarcasm, Ford declared: "You've all heard Carter's alibis: 'Inflation cannot be controlled. The world has changed. We can no longer protect our diplomats in foreign capitals, nor our workingmen on Detroit's assembly lines. We must lower our expectations. We must be realistic. We must prudently retreat.' Baloney!"

The delegates loved every word of it. They cheered their old friend Jerry, they gave him a delegate's gold badge, they sang "Happy Birthday" while he and Betty embraced on the podium and waved to them. They made him feel that he was not an elder statesman out of the past but a virile leader who still had a powerful appeal to millions of Americans. So the idea of making one more bid for an influential place in the government, even if it meant playing second fiddle to Ronald Reagan, no longer seemed like an impossible dream. Neither Reagan, at sixty-nine, nor Ford, at sixty-seven, needed to ride off quietly into the sunset. Perhaps they could gallop into Washington together, chase Jimmy Carter out of the White House, and run a new Republican administration.

Tuesday, July 15

Republican leaders came in a steady procession to Reagan's hotel suite to advise him about the decision he soon must make to complete the party ticket. Senators, governors, congressmen, and party officials took turns sitting in the deep red chairs in his living room, grouped about a low, round table that bore a bowl of flowers and a silver dish of the candidate's favorite jelly beans.

Reagan, relaxing on a red-and-blue checkered sofa, listened closely to his guests' appraisals of the strengths and weaknesses of various prospects on his vice presidential list.

Several of his own aides were spreading the word that Bush had the inside track and they sought to overcome objections by the conservatives. Six Republican state chairmen from the South had endorsed Bush on a cue from the Reagan GHQ. "It wasn't something we stimulated or sought or encouraged anyone to take the initiative in," the former ambassador protested. But he was glad they did it.

A boomlet was under way at the Joe Louis Arena for Congressman Jack Kemp of New York, and another for Sen. Jesse Helms, the North Carolinian who masterminded the most controversial features of the platform—the refusal to back the Equal Rights Amendment and the endorsement of the antiabortion amendment. Helms, who carried an iron hand in a velvet glove, drawled: "I got ninety-nine percent of what I wanted in the platform." It sailed through to easy passage despite indignant protests by pro-ERA and militant feminist forces.

Helms' admirers threatened to nominate him from the floor as a protest candidate if Reagan chose either Bush or Howard Baker. Victor Fediay, a close adviser to Helms, charged that at the Reagan-Ford summit conference in Rancho Mirage, "a deal was made and Bush will be the vice presidential nominee unless someone persuades Reagan that he doesn't need Ford to win the election." Fediay said Ford intended to have a controlling voice in choosing the vice presidential nominee and forcing his former

Secretary of State, Henry Kissinger, into a powerful place in a future Reagan administration.

Although he did not know of Reagan's secret intention to try once more to draft Ford himself, Helms' astute counselor hit the bull's-eye by charging that the ex-President sought to put Kissinger back in charge of the nation's foreign policy. Kissinger's own role in negotiating a Reagan-Ford alliance would soon come to light in Detroit.

In one of his Tuesday conferences, Reagan solicited advice from Sen. Strom Thurmond of South Carolina, Sen. John Tower of Texas, Gov. Pierre du Pont IV of Delaware, Gov. Charles Thone of Nebraska, Congressman Robert Michel of Illinois, and Congressman Robert Bauman of Maryland.

Reagan spoke favorably of Bush but mentioned objections raised against him: his attacks on Reagan's tax cut proposals as "voodoo economics"; his uneven performance in the debates; and the evangelical preachers' loud opposition to Bush over his refusal to endorse the constitutional amendment barring abortions.

Senator Thurmond, intimately familiar with the intense beliefs of the voters in the Bible Belt, shared their dislike of Bush on those points but liked his advocacy of a stronger national defense and his record as CIA director. Senator Tower would also accept his fellow Texan, Bush. Everyone present had believed that Ford would never run, but when Reagan asked, "What about Ford?" the response was completely positive. Senator Thurmond said it would do no harm to make the offer to the former President as a courteous gesture, at least; it would be a "dream ticket."

Tuesday Afternoon

At 3:45 P.M., Ford came down from his seventieth-floor penthouse to Reagan's suite one floor below. They met for about an hour. Once again, Reagan began courting his former adversary by saying that Ford was the one man who could add the most strength to the Republicans' ticket so that they could achieve the main goal they could certainly agree on: defeating Jimmy Carter.

"I would like you to serve on the ticket with me," Reagan said. "I know it's a difficult decision for you. It will involve some sacrifices." But, he added, Ford could perform a great service for the future of the country.

Ford replied that he had no desire to be Vice President again. Some people might say that he was too proud to step down to a secondary role but that was incorrect. He would consider it but only if absolutely sure that he could perform an active role in running the country.

Reagan offered to make him Secretary of Defense, as well as Vice President. But Ford quickly rejected that idea. He knew from experience that such a dual role would not work.

Ford wanted much more authority than he would have as the head of a single department, even such a huge one as Defense. He sought assurances that he would actually take part in major decisions affecting national policy, not be relegated to the menial tasks of making speeches and attending funerals. In his many years in Washington, he had seen more than one President promising to give the Vice President a "meaningful" role, but the promises had seldom been kept. Ford could look back upon some bitter days he had spent in the Watergate era, defending Richard Nixon.

As Chief Executive himself, Ford sought to make his own vice presidential appointee, Nelson Rockefeller, a partner. They had a harmonious personal relationship but could not prevent hostility between their rival staffs. Members of the White House Palace Guard considered the President supremely important and the Vice President as only one more assistant in the Old Executive Office Building, available to do odd jobs and run errands for their boss. Having been both President and Vice President, Ford was not burning with ambition to be either one again.

Ford again mentioned the Twelfth Amendment, which provides that if the candidates for President and for Vice President are residents of the same state, the electors of that state cannot vote for both. That indicated that the electors of California could not legally cast their ballots for Reagan and Ford, so the Republicans would risk losing forty-five precious electoral votes.

Reagan had come prepared with a memorandum drafted by his legal advisers to show how they could skirt the constitutional problem. Ford could move his voting residence back to Michigan or to Vail, Colorado, where he owned a condominium at a ski resort, but he feared the press would scorn that as a "gimmick."

Ford accepted the memo and promised to think about it, but he said: "Ron, I have to tell you I don't think it will work."

"Well, just take the memo and think it over," his persistent suitor said, "and don't answer right now."

The two veteran political warriors parted as much better friends than they had been before. Like a couple of soldiers recalling their combat experiences, they developed new respect for each other, if not affection. Ford was impressed by Reagan's sincerity but still held back from saying "Yes."

Late Tuesday afternoon, Ford conferred with John Marsh and Robert Barrett, two close associates from his White House days who were delighted with the idea of bringing about a restoration of the Old Regime, even if Reagan had to be the figurehead in the Oval Office while their boss really ran the place. Ford designated Marsh and Barrett, along with Henry Kissinger and Alan Greenspan, former chairman of his Council of Economic Advisers, to meet with three agents of Reagan's—William Casey, Edwin Meese, and Richard Wirthlin—to work out the details of a possible Reagan-Ford alliance with greatly expanded powers for the Vice President. The negotiators had their first session around a conference table in the Reagan staff's suite at the Detroit Plaza.

On Tuesday night, Jerry and Betty Ford and a few close friends dined on the yacht *Global Star*, owned by Michigan newspaper tycoon John McGoff and anchored on the Detroit River waterfront. The ex-President emphatically reiterated that he did not desire to be the vice presidential nominee.

Then, back in his hotel suite, Ford relaxed before his television set and watched Henry Kissinger addressing the convention. A few irresponsible troublemakers had threatened to boo the former Secretary of State, but Reagan's agents on the floor of the Joe Louis Arena passed the orders to the delegates: Don't boo. They didn't. Kissinger drew polite applause when he excoriated Jimmy Carter's failures in foreign policy and praised Reagan as the nation's only hope.

"The Carter administration," he said, "has managed the extraordinary feat of having, at one and the same time, the worst relations with our allies, the worst relations with our adversaries, and the most serious upheavals in the developing world since the end of the Second World War."

These multiplying crises, he charged, are the natural result of Carter's "naive philosophy which since 1977 has recoiled from power and fled from our responsibilities . . . a philosophy of abdication allied to a diplomacy of incoherence."

A new administration, Kissinger said, must carry out four urgent tasks: "To rebuild our defenses, to end Soviet expansionism, to mend our alliances, to work with men and women of goodwill in all continents to fulfill mankind's positive aspirations."

About midnight, Kissinger arrived at Ford's hotel suite where Barrett, Marsh, and Greenspan were already conferring with the former President about the offer from Reagan. Kissinger came as a spokesman for Casey and Meese, who had asked that he try to induce Ford to say "Yes."

Having successfully run his shuttle diplomacy between Israel and Egypt, arranged detente with the Soviet Union, and opened a new relationship between the United States and the People's Republic of China, the former Secretary of State was well suited for the new diplomatic task. Ford brought up the subject and they talked about it alone for nearly an hour.

Realizing that Ford had to be motivated "to give up a hell of a lot," Kissinger told him: "The country needs you." He spoke in passionate tones about the emergency facing the nation because of Carter's weak and wavering performance, which had permitted the Soviet Union to expand its power. Kissinger warned that it would be difficult to survive another four years of Carter's bungling. The Republicans must win. Reagan was not strong enough to win on his own or to govern well without wise counselors; he must have help from the former President, Kissinger maintained.

Kissinger had no assurance of returning to his former eminence as Secretary of State, although he had discussed foreign policy with Reagan the day before. "I made it clear before the appointment that I did not think this was an appropriate time for a discussion of a position," he told the press. "I am not here as a job-seeker. I will support Governor Reagan because I believe it is in the national interest to have a change of administrations; because I think the drift in our foreign policy is extremely dangerous and will produce ever accelerating crises."

His long, sometimes emotional, talk with Ford was "a very moving experience," Kissinger said. "He knew there was a national emergency and he had to decide if he wanted to go through this very uncertain process."

After two o'clock Wednesday morning, the marathon session ended without a clear change in Ford's resistance. For the first time, however, his associates thought he was saying to them, "No—but."

The subtle change in Ford's position delighted Bill Brock, who had been trying to serve as the "matchmaker" between Reagan and Ford. The national chairman and several other Republican leaders joined Reagan in his hotel suite Tuesday night to watch the convention on television and talk politics.

If the ex-President would come back and run for the vice presidency, he would make history and "the drama would be absolutely spectacular," Brock exclaimed. He was surprised to find that Reagan shared his eagerness over "the Ford option" and considered it "an intriguing idea." After midnight, Brock made a series of telephone calls, summoning party henchmen to breakfast for a discussion of ways to make Ford accept.

Wednesday Morning, July 16

In the early morning, the skies above Detroit suddenly became as black as night. Lightning flashed across the darkened clouds, heavy rains poured down, and terrific winds with the speed of a tornado shook the Renaissance Center towers. Some startled guests near the top of the Detroit Plaza hotel thought the winds sounded like a jet plane blasting by.

Amid the thunderstorm, Bill Brock presided over breakfast in his seventieth-floor suite, welcoming Gov. James Thompson of Illinois, Gov. William Clements of Texas, Senators Baker and Dole, Alan Greenspan, Congressman Michel, and two pollsters, Robert Teeter and Tully Plesser.

Ford had appeared on the NBC–TV *Today* show and, when asked if second place on the Reagan ticket would injure his pride, had replied: "Honestly, if I thought the situation would work, if all the other questions could be resolved, the problem of pride would not bother me in any way."

To Brock and his guests, this remark meant that their old pal Jerry had left a crack in the door. Teeter presented recent polling figures that showed Ford far ahead of anyone else in the strength he could bring to a Reagan ticket. Everyone except Rhodes favored a drive to bring Ford around, but the Arizona congressman refused to believe the deal would work.

Baker and Rhodes, the minority leaders of the Senate and the House respectively, were sent to Reagan and found him eager to offer inducements that would persuade the former President to accept: an office in the White House, a policy-making post as chairman of the National Security Council, perhaps a voice in the selection of the cabinet.

Brock and a few others from his Breakfast Band made a sales pitch to Ford, Governor Thompson insisting that the best way to achieve the all-important goal—defeating Jimmy Carter—was to have Reagan and Ford as a team.

Reluctantly, Ford promised to consider any detailed propositions that would come out of the parleys soon to begin between his agents and Reagan's, specifying the extra powers he would have in the vice presidency, not merely in vague general terms.

As the morning thunderstorm subsided, Reagan met in his hotel conference room with a band of New Right representatives and endured an hour-long gale of protests against the selection of Ford, Bush, or Baker.

Howard Phillips, the dark, bearlike national director of the Conservative Caucus, led off by warning that if Reagan allowed "media and other liberal power brokers" to influence his choice of a running mate, he risked losing his opportunity of taking 118 Southern electoral votes away from Jimmy Carter. The religious conservatives' enthusiasm for Reagan, he said, "would be chilled if he chose a running mate like Bush, Baker, or Ford, who favored ERA and drafting women"; that New York's forty-one votes could also be regained if John Anderson drained votes from Carter and Reagan had the support of the "pro-life" voters.

Sen. Gordon Humphrey of New Hampshire recalled that he had helped to deliver his state in Reagan's first primary victory; and the nominee must not disappoint thousands of volunteers by allowing "the Ford-Bush Republican hierarchy" to dictate the second half of his ticket.

Phyllis Schlafly, the Dragon Lady of the anti-ERA forces, cautioned Reagan to avoid disillusioning the "pro-family" voters who flocked to him out of their devotion to deeply held moral convictions against ERA, abortions, and the drafting of women.

Nellie Gray, leader of the annual March for Life in Washington, said the antiabortion movement was a powerful, growing political force that must not be ignored. Reagan, well aware of its help to him in the primaries, replied emphatically: "I know that!"

The Reverend Jerry Falwell, the evangelist with a television audience of millions, warned that the 72,000 pastors in his Moral Majority movement would lose some of their enthusiasm for Reagan if disappointed in his choice for the vice presidency.

After listening patiently to his friends' complaints, Reagan responded by saying that Senators Baker and Laxalt had been dropped off his list of potential running mates. Noting that Bush was acceptable to such conservatives as Senators Thurmond, Tower, and James McClure of Idaho, the nominee could not understand why the New Right people could not go along with him, too.

Reagan did not mention his negotiations with Ford, which were then still confidential. His guests went away downhearted, convinced that their last-minute plea had failed. "I left with a dread feeling that our appeal had fallen on deaf ears, that a 'Northeastern liberal' campaign strategy had been long decided upon and that assuming that Ford would not agree to be Governor Reagan's ticket mate, it was ninety-five percent certain that Governor Reagan would turn to George Bush as his choice," Phillips said.

Negotiations for the Treaty of Detroit began on Wednesday morning in the Reagan staff suite. Ford's men—Kissinger, Greenspan, Barrett, and Marsh—had an advantage in experience. They were all case-hardened veterans who had served in the White House and knew their way through the mazes of Washington bureaucracy. The three agents for Reagan—Casey, Meese, and Wirthlin—lacked intimate knowledge of the Executive Offices; only Casey had headed a federal agency, the Securities and Exchange Commission, besides his service as Undersecretary of State.

After a general discussion of the White House staff and its functions and the way they might be channeled through the Vice President as a sort of Deputy President, the Reagan agents concluded that they should sum up their ideas on paper. Casey said to Ford's men: "We've got to get something together to show you guys."

Reagan gave the first public hint of his intentions when he attended a luncheon at the Polish-American Century Club in Hamtramck, taking along three possible vice presidential candidates: Bush, Simon, and Kemp. When reporters asked if the rumors were correct, that he wanted Ford, he replied: "Oh, sure.

That would be the best." But he recalled that in their parley at Rancho Mirage, Ford had said no.

At 2:30 P.M. the negotiators reconvened in the Reagan staff suite. The Reagan agents brought forth a memorandum entitled, "Draft Talking Points." It was a two-page, typewritten paper produced by Meese, drawing on suggestions by Casey and other advisers including Bill Timmons, Reagan's convention manager who had been Richard Nixon's chief lobbyist with Congress.

One idea called for the Vice President to be given great power as the boss of the Executive Office of the President, supervising the Office of Management and Budget, the National Security Council, and the Council of Economic Advisers. Ford, as Vice President, would thus control the paper flow to the Oval Office and he would actually become a Deputy President, drawing upon his experience in national security issues, appropriations, and dealings with Congress.

By laying their cards face up on the table in this high-stakes poker game for executive power, Reagan's men showed their eager desire to win Ford for their ticket at almost any price. Ford's agents seized upon the opportunity to raise the ante and drive the best possible bargain. The "Draft Talking Points," they said, were all right in general terms but not specific enough. They sought to pin down in clear language the Vice President's authority in the selection of cabinet officers, and they wanted to make sure that several of Ford's closest advisers would accompany him back to the White House.

One critic of Ford's "Gang of Four" voiced suspicions that like the Bourbon exiles in France after the overthrow of Napoleon, the courtiers of the Ford White House leaped at the chance of restoring the Old Regime, regaining their own offices, secretaries, and chauffeured cars. Certainly, the former President would like to bring Jack Marsh and Bob Barrett back with him, while Alan Greenspan, his former chief economic adviser, might become Secretary of the Treasury and Henry Kissinger certainly had not closed the door against a triumphant return as Secretary of State.

One of Reagan's foreign policy advisers likened Kissinger to Talleyrand, the crafty, cynical, brilliant old courtier who had kept his head on his shoulders through the French Revolution and the turbulent years thereafter by assiduously cultivating every ruler who came to power. He swore allegiance to each in turn and leaped nimbly to kiss the hand of each successor.

Thus, Kissinger first emerged in the game of Republican power politics as the gifted Harvard University professor who became a highly paid adviser to Nelson Rockefeller, then masterminded foreign policy for Presidents Nixon and Ford amid international acclaim; and now, in the latest spin of the wheel, aspired to restore himself to that role with a new President, Reagan.

William Safire said in one of his columns that Kissinger was the only Secretary of State who ever had two Presidents serving under him. In the opinion of some detractors, the Detroit Scenario would let Kissinger once again direct foreign policy as he did when Jerry Ford sat on his knee. The difference would be that "Talleyrand" would have had a puppet on each knee—Ronnie and Jerry—while the sage ventriloquist mouthed their speeches in his delightfully droll Teutonic accent.

About 3:00 P.M., Ford's negotiators brought him the "Draft Talking Points." He read the paper carefully and commented that it seemed to sum up the assurances Reagan had given him in their discussion the previous day. Ford assumed that he would be given more authority than any previous Vice President in history, and he liked that. Apparently, he would be like the principal operating officer in a corporation while Reagan would be the head of state.

But it was still not clear that Reagan would be merely a figurehead like the British Queen while Ford would be the Prime Minister with actual power. Reagan could not possibly have consented to give away his constitutional authority in such a manner, and there is no evidence that he even considered doing so. Ford doubted that Reagan's agents really meant to go that far, either, despite their pathetic eagerness to create the "dream ticket" to win the election. From his own sad experience, Ford knew that every Vice President must play second fiddle; and he had no intention of being Throttlebottom to Reagan's Wintergreen.

Ford reiterated his doubts when a delegation of Republican

leaders came to his suite and begged him to say "Yes." Among them were Senators Baker and Dole, National Chairman Brock, Governor Thompson of Illinois, former Sen. Robert Griffin of Michigan, and the House minority whip, Robert Michel of Illinois.

"We frankly considered the difficulties of trying to restructure the presidency by using the Vice President in a more supportive role," Brock said later. "The excitement I felt was that because of Ford's background and experience, we could make the presidency into a more workable office. We could lighten the President's burden of minutiae and day-to-day routine to give him more time to think and *be* the President. Governor Reagan showed what a large person he is by even discussing the subject, while Ford indicated a rather remarkable demeanor, too, in being willing to consider something for the benefit of his country that clearly was not in his personal interest or his range of desire."

Ford emphasized that he was quite happy with his life as a former President, free from the burdens and aggravations of high office, with ample income and time to enjoy a leisurely succession of days on the golf links or the ski slope, and opportunities to speak out on national issues when he pleased.

So he had few incentives to go back into harness. The Reagan people needed him; he did not need them. So he directed his negotiators to "go back and get more"—meaning more concessions and outright pledges to guarantee that as Vice President he would have a strong voice in deciding the future administration's policies.

About 3:30 P.M., the Republican leaders departed and conferred with some of Reagan's strategists, who brought them up to date on the new round of negotiations going on in Bill Casey's suite. Drafting the detailed terms proved as complex and difficult as writing the communique after a strategic arms limitations conference between the nuclear superpowers. Reagan's spokesmen were willing to grant almost anything to reach their sole objective: a victorious Reagan-Ford slate. Others in the Reagan camp, however, resisted the escalating demands for unprecedented powers for the Vice President. These men voiced suspicions about the ambitions of Greenspan and Kissinger.

Caspar Weinberger, a Reagan delegate from California and veteran of the Nixon cabinet, said the parleys were like the "negotiation of a foreign treaty," for sharing presidential authority.

About 5:00 P.M., Ford made a telephone call to Reagan, who told him to come downstairs immediately for a parley that might clarify the precise powers to be granted to the Vice President under their deal. Ford named Kissinger and Greenspan as two men he wanted in the cabinet. Some sources say the former President asked for assurances that Kissinger would become Secretary of State and Greenspan, Secretary of the Treasury; others deny there was a clear demand that Reagan pay this exact price as a quid pro quo. Reagan, as governor of California, had discussed major appointments with his lieutenant governor but had not given him any veto power over them; he made no commitments now. After about twenty minutes, Ford left.

For the first time, Reagan began to suspect that his offer to enhance the Vice President's powers, generally, was being transformed into a scheme for restoring the presidency of Gerald Ford in fact, if not in name. Reagan's innocent negotiators were being outfoxed and outtraded by the city slickers from Washington, D.C., who were using Old Jerry as a pawn in their great game to regain power.

At 7:00 P.M., Ford appeared on the nation's television screens in an interview with Walter Cronkite in the CBS "Sky Box" high above the convention floor. At the outset, the former President seemed to be turning down the offer of second place on the ticket. But as he discussed it further, he showed signs of excitement and renewed ambition.

"I would not go to Washington and be a figurehead Vice President," he said. "If I go to Washington, and I'm not saying that I am accepting, I have to go there with the belief that I will play a meaningful role across the board in the basic and the crucial and the important decisions that have to be made in a four-year period.

"It wouldn't be fair," he went on, to be only a Vice President dealing with the "ceremonial aspects" of the job. "I have to have responsible assurances."

When Cronkite suggested "something like a co-presidency," Ford did not contradict him. "That's something that Governor Reagan really ought to consider," he said. "The point you raised is a very legitimate one."

Reagan, watching the interview on the television set in his hotel suite, frowned and tightened his lips into a thin, straight line that showed his shock and anger. He was amazed that Ford would reveal their secret negotiations to an audience of millions, and apparently endorse the idea of a "co-presidency" as the basis of the deal.

"Can you believe it?" he asked his assistants. "Did you hear that?"

At the Pontchartrain Hotel near the Joe Louis Arena, George Bush also watched Ford on the screen and said glumly to his wife: "He's going to take it."

Ford's comments to Cronkite, and later to Barbara Walters on ABC, touched off a storm of rumors that swept through the convention and were multiplied by the television networks, as politicians claiming to be close advisers to Reagan confidently declared that the great "dream ticket" was all set. Although the negotiations were still going on at the Detroit Plaza, TV reporters in the excitement of pursuing the Big Story said Reagan and Ford had reached an agreement and would soon drive to the convention together to announce it.

"It was a firestorm literally feeding on its winds," Lyn Nofziger commented. "And the press, especially television, became its own victim."

Delegates went wild with jubilant cries of "It's Ford! It's Ford!" As TV seemed to give the report an air of absolute authenticity, the Reagan men back at the Detroit Plaza began to feel high-pressured by the self-fulfilling prophecy on the screen. They resisted the escalating demands from Ford's agents. They resented Kissinger's increasingly open role in the shuttle diplomacy designed in part to assure that he could again direct the nation's foreign policy.

Heeding the pleas by Kissinger, Greenspan, and his former White House aides, Ford went along with their proposals that would have given him much of his old power as Chief Executive, although these ideas were not clearly constitutional. Ford, who had had only a few hours' sleep during this feverish Convention Week, wanted a little more time to lock up the guarantees of his future authority. His agents proposed that the convention adjourn overnight so that they could finish drafting the final Treaty of Detroit.

But Reagan's men feared that such a delay would cause the convention to demand a Reagan-Ford ticket, already pronounced a certainty by the omniscient seers of the TV networks.

So, to nip that idea in the bud, Reagan telephoned Ford about 9:00 P.M. and told him the decision must be made "to-night." The ex-President, who was eating dinner in his suite and watching the increasingly wild convention on TV, gave a non-committal answer. His instincts were against saying "Yes" but he could not bring himself to say "No," either. He was holding out hope of obtaining the ironclad assurances he wanted so that he could share in the basic, crucial decisions of the Reagan White House.

As the minutes ticked by, Reagan became nervous. This was one of the greatest nights of his life, the night when the Republican convention at last would give him the presidential prize he had been seeking for twelve years. Nothing must spoil the perfection of the glorious show.

With Nancy, sons Michael and Ron, and daughters Maureen and Patti, Reagan watched the drama on the TV screen. His faithful friend, Senator Laxalt, placed his name in nomination, there were several seconding speeches, and then the roll call of the states. Montana, with its twenty votes, put him over the top with the required 998. The crowd roared; the orchestra struck up Sousa marches; and 12,000 red, white, and blue balloons fell from the ceiling.

As in the old Reagan movies, virtue had triumphed at last. The hero of this drama gave Nancy a victory kiss.

Shortly after 10:00 P.M., while TV commentators were chattering about reports that the motorcade was already forming at the Detroit Plaza to bring Reagan and Ford together to the Joe

Louis Arena, the two teams of negotiators had one more session. Casey and Meese brought Reagan the word about the final terms proposed by Ford.

About 11:00 P.M., the ex-President came down one flight to Reagan's suite and said in effect, "No, thanks." Ford instinctively felt this was not the right thing to do. After a few minutes of conversation, he left.

Reagan told an assistant: "Call George Bush."

Bush, convinced that he was out and Ford was in, had left the convention hall and retired downhearted to his Pontchartrain Hotel suite, where he eased his pain somewhat with popcorn and beer.

At 11:37 P.M. his telephone rang and he heard Reagan say: "I plan to go over to the convention and tell them you are my first choice for the nomination."

Bush's face lit up with joy, and he flashed a thumbs-up sign to his family and staff. "I must confess I'm surprised, but at the same time I'm pleased," he told Reagan. "I can campaign enthusiastically for your election and the platform. Thank you, sir!"

Then Reagan's motorcade roared from the Detroit Plaza Hotel to the Joe Louis Arena in a "midnight ride" that brought the candidate into a convention hall filled with deliriously shouting delegates eager to hear him announce his final choice. When the applause died away, he explained why he had broken precedent and come, "at this late hour," to clear up the "rumors and gossip" that the ticket would have former President Ford in "second place":

"It is true that we have gone over this, and over this, and over this, and he and I have come to the conclusion, and he believes deeply that he can be of more value as the former President campaigning his heart out, as he has pledged to do, and not as a member of the ticket.

"I respect him very much for the decision . . ."

Then, with a smile, Reagan revealed that he had chosen "a man who has great experience in government, and a man who told me that he can enthusiastically support the platform across the board . . . George Bush."

Amid a new burst of cheers, Reagan quickly concluded: "It's past the witching hour. It's late. God bless you. Good night. And we'll see you tomorrow night."

Thursday Night, July 17

In a carnival atmosphere of fun and harmony, the Republicans formally named Bush as their vice presidential candidate, giving him 1,832 votes to fifty-four for Jesse Helms, forty-two for Jack Kemp, and twenty-three for Phil Crane. Earlier, Helms had abandoned his threatened floor fight, since Bush promised to support the entire platform largely drafted by the North Carolina senator.

In a brief acceptance speech, Bush stressed his vow to endorse the platform "enthusiastically" and devote his "total energies" to Reagan's election. Then the band blared "California, Here I Come," and here came Reagan with his family. The convention rocked with a tremendous demonstration—cheers, applause, horn-blowing, and shouts of "Viva! Olé!" the battle cry of his defiant legions when he lost to Ford at Kansas City four years before. Tonight, they were victory cries, and Reagan quipped, "You're singing my song."

In a reference to a flattering film biography of him that had been shown beforehand, the veteran actor said, "My first thrill tonight was to find myself in a movie on prime time. This is the second big thrill."

Indeed, the scene was an actor's dream come true: a convention hall jammed with delegates eager to cheer his every word; and a television audience of millions, one of the largest ever to watch a presidential nominee's acceptance speech.

Pete Hannaford had carefully crafted the script, but the candidate himself made it sing, turning words into music as only a professional can. He began by stressing his favorite theme—that the Republicans, reaching out to all the people, at last were ready "to build a new consensus with all those across the land who share a community of values embodied in these words: family, work, neighborhood, peace, and freedom."

To soothe the injured feelings caused by the anti-ERA plank in the platform, Reagan promised to eliminate all discrimination against women through state and federal laws. Then he moved to a direct attack upon the Democrats and President Carter, blaming them for "three grave threats to our existence: a disintegrating economy, a weakened defense, and an energy policy based on the sharing of scarcity."

He promised to reduce the "overweight" federal bureaucracy by an immediate freeze on federal hiring; to protect Social Security; to begin a steady reduction in the heavy tax burden, starting with a 10 percent down payment in 1981; and he called for "a crusade to make America great again."

In mocking tones, Reagan declared that Carter's "amateurish and confused" administration had let America's defenses decline to the lowest ebb in a generation and yet wanted the people to vote for "four more years of weakness, indecision, mediocrity, and incompetence."

"Can anyone look at the record of this administration and say, 'Well done'?" he asked.

"No!" shouted the delegates jamming the arena.

"Can anyone compare the state of our economy when the Carter administration took office with where we are today and say, 'Keep up the good work'?"

"No!" cried the crowd.

"Can anyone look at our reduced standing in the world today and say, 'Let's have four more years of this'?"

"NO!"

As President, Reagan pledged, his Number One priority would be to work for peace. He would build up the defense forces without a draft and would "insure that the safety of our people cannot successfully be threatened by a hostile foreign power."

Then came some vintage Reagan oratory with sure appeal to the hearts of his audience:

"This evening marks the last step, save one, of a campaign that has taken Nancy and me from one end of this great land to the other. . . . It is impossible to capture in words the splendor of this vast continent which God has granted as our portion of His creation. There are no words to express the extraordinary strength and character of this breed of people we call Americans.

"Everywhere we have met thousands of Democrats, independents, and Republicans from all economic conditions and walks of life bound together in that community of shared values of family, work, neighborhood, peace, and freedom. They are concerned, yes, but they are not frightened. They are disturbed, but not dismayed. They are the kind of men and women Tom Paine had in mind when he wrote—during the darkest days of the American Revolution—'We have it in our power to begin the world over again.' "

Reagan, the former Democrat, had the audacity to quote his idol, Franklin D. Roosevelt, twice in this speech before a Republican convention, recalling F.D.R.'s 1932 pledge to reduce the federal government and his later declaration that Americans had "a rendezvous with destiny."

"Tonight," the nominee said, "let us dedicate ourselves to renewing the American compact. I ask you not simply to 'Trust me,' but to trust your values—our values—and hold me responsible for living up to them. I ask you to trust that American spirit which knows no ethnic, religious, social, political, regional, or economic boundaries; the spirit that burned with zeal in the hearts of millions of immigrants from every corner of the earth who came here in search of freedom.

"Some say that spirit no longer exists. But I have seen it. I have felt it all across the land: in the big cities, the small towns, and in rural America. The American spirit is still there, ready to blaze into life if you and I are willing to do what has to be done: the practical, down-to-earth things that will stimulate our economy, increase productivity, and put America back to work."

As he concluded his prepared remarks, Reagan paused dramatically and said, as if it were an afterthought:

"I have thought of something that is not a part of my speech and I'm worried over whether I should do it.

"Can we doubt that only a Divine Providence placed this land, this island of freedom, here as a refuge for all those people in the world who yearn to breathe freely: Jews and Christians enduring persecution behind the Iron Curtain, the boat people of Southeast Asia, of Cuba, and of Haiti, the victims of drought and famine in Africa, the freedom fighters of Afghanistan, and our own countrymen held in savage captivity?"

His voice cracked, and tears welled in his eyes as he concluded: "I'll confess that I've been a little afraid to suggest what I'm going to suggest—I'm more afraid not to—that we begin our crusade joined together in a moment of silent prayer." A hush fell over the noisy convention hall. Then Reagan added quietly: "God Bless America."

16

☆

BATTLING
"JINGLING JIMMY"

ON THE MORNING after his acceptance speech, Ronald Reagan huddled with his state campaign chairmen behind the closed doors of a Detroit Plaza hotel suite and gave a locker-room pep talk aimed at inspiring his followers to win the Big Game for the Old Gipper.

These were the hard-ball politicians who had carried him through the primaries to his triumph at Detroit, so he could speak frankly to them in private without the idealistic rhetoric reserved for the less sophisticated electorate. In plain language, Reagan warned that the Republicans must wage a long, hard fight against mean and ruthless opponents to take the White House away from Jimmy Carter.

"We're in for a rough time," he said, because the discredited President would make a "vicious, vindictive" effort to hold on to his power at any cost. "We can be completely honest in saying nasty things" about Carter's failures, Reagan said, "because they'll be true."

Reagan started out "running scared" because of concern that his lead in the polls in July could be wiped out after the quarreling Democrats united at their August convention in New York City, renominated the President, and used all the advantages of incumbency to keep their control of the federal government.

"Carter is not much of a President but he is a very shrewd and able campaigner and any opponent who underestimates his very real political capabilities is making a mistake," Ed Meese declared. Reagan's chief of staff explained:

"First, Carter is the incumbent. He can manipulate events by scheduling things to suit his political strategy.

"Second, he can exploit events that happen naturally.

"Third, Carter is still perceived by the American people as a decent and honest person, and while this may be eroding somewhat, it still is a formidable thing.

"Fourth, there are more Democrats than Republicans. We have to hold all our base and pick up Democrats and independents to win."

Meese's advice to Reagan was sound, for the Republicans needed to avoid the overconfidence that had caused their nominee, Thomas E. Dewey, to lose to Harry Truman in 1948, when the Democrats were split and their unpopular President had an even lower rating in the polls than Carter. My own view, based on my coverage of national politics since Truman's first day in the White House, was that Carter could not duplicate Truman's feat. The West, once a Democratic stronghold, now seemed solidly for Reagan, and he had good prospects of splitting the South. Furthermore, the Democrats were saddled with a recession, plus inflation, and high unemployment among industrial workers in the big Northern states, which they must carry to win the election.

"The beleaguered President, running ten points or more behind Reagan in most polls, is really assured of carrying fewer than a hundred electoral votes, far from the 270 needed to win," I wrote from Detroit on July 18. "His chances look good only in his home state, Georgia, a few other Southern states, plus Massachusetts, Rhode Island, Minnesota, West Virginia, and the District of Columbia." *

In his most euphoric moments, Carter could see himself duplicating President Lyndon B. Johnson's crushing victory over the prostrate form of Barry Goldwater in 1964, with the same tactics—depicting Reagan as an amiable but ignorant old triggerhappy jingo who could stumble into nuclear war. "Clearly," I wrote on June 20, "the Democrats intend to re-run their 1964

* Carter actually carried Georgia, Rhode Island, Minnesota, West Virginia, Maryland, Hawaii, and D.C.: forty-nine electoral votes.

campaign in which they re-elected Johnson by portraying Gold-water as a dangerous warmonger, unfit to be trusted with his finger on 'the nuclear button.' Reagan had better get braced for a revival of that old horror movie."

Sure enough, Carter kicked off the assault in his acceptance speech at the Democratic national convention in Madison Square Garden on August 14, after he had squelched Sen. Edward M. Kennedy and steamrollered a move for an "open" convention that might have chosen someone else, perhaps Secretary of State Edmund Muskie or Vice President Mondale.

After an opening fluff, in which he mistakenly identified a late Vice President as "Hubert Horatio Hornblower," Carter charged that Reagan was proposing a "radical and irresponsible" drive for a new nuclear arms race that "could put the whole world in peril."

"The life of every human being on earth can depend on the experience and judgment and vigilance of the person in the Oval Office," the President cried. He saw the election as "a stark choice between two futures," the Democrats offering economic security, justice, peace, "confidence, hope, and a good life"; the Republicans leading to despair, "surrender to the merchants of oil," plus "a bizarre program of massive tax cuts for the rich, service cuts for the poor, and massive inflation for everyone."

Having made good on his threat to Kennedy, to "whip his ass," the Chief Executive set forth with relish to do the same to his Republican foe. Carter viewed Reagan, whom he scarcely knew, as an incompetent amateur, unfit to grapple with the great problems of national security; John Anderson, the independent presidential candidate, also ridiculed Reagan as "the former leading player for Eighteenth Century-Fox" who would "get into the biggest arms race we've ever seen."

Although he had been facing the cameras since 1937, Reagan was surprised by the relentless glare of the national media, and the television networks in particular, as he began to compete head-to-head against the President of the United States. He could get away with offhand remarks and gaffes in a primary campaign and see only a ripple of comment in the local press.

Now, however, he found every little slip magnified a thousand-fold, trumpeted on the evening news shows of all three networks, and puffed up to show that he was damaging his image as a potential President.

The first major flap began August 16, when Reagan and George Bush appeared at a Los Angeles press conference to give the vice presidential candidate a well-publicized send-off on a trip to Japan and China. The journey was intended to show that a Reagan-Bush administration would have expertise in foreign affairs, and that it would make no major change in the steadily improving relationship with the People's Republic of China.

But Reagan, stubbornly loyal to his friends, the free Chinese, reiterated his intention to restore "official" diplomatic ties with their regime on Taiwan. This touched off a blast of protests from Peking, and the TV networks featured them as an embarrassment for the Republican ticket.

While this tempest was bubbling in a Chinese teapot, another quickly arose—over the Vietnam War.

At their Chicago convention August 18, Reagan told the Veterans of Foreign Wars that the 50,000 Americans killed in Vietnam had died in "a noble cause," defending a little nation against "a totalitarian neighbor bent on conquest."

"There is a lesson for all of us in Vietnam," he said. "Let us tell those who fought in that war that we will never again ask young men to fight and possibly die in a war our government is afraid to let them win."

This was vintage Reagan rhetoric. He had said it time and again to applauding audiences across the land.

This time, however, the TV networks were paying attention and so were the Associated Press and the United Press International wire services. They echoed the theme of the Chicago Tribune's headline: "REAGAN DEFENDS VIET WAR."

The furor over this small part of the VFW speech obscured its main theme: "PEACE: Restoring the Margin of Safety." Reagan's principal point was that as President, he would rebuild America's depleted military forces to avert a war. He repeated his pledge to negotiate with the Soviet Union for "an honest, verifiable reduction in nuclear weapons." But only the line about the "noble cause" in Vietnam came through the mass media.

Reagan learned from this unpleasant experience that he must keep his speeches on one simple, basic theme so that no smart-aleck TV commentator could pick up a minor point and blow it out of proportion. But he was not out of the woods yet on the China issue.

In Peking, Bush assured the officials, whom he had met while heading the United States Liaison Office there in 1975, that Reagan as President would not "turn the clock back" and restore official diplomatic relations with Taiwan. The Chinese gave the visitor a chilly reception and pronounced his mission a failure.

After Bush's return, he and Reagan once more faced the skeptical press corps in Los Angeles on August 25. Reagan admitted he had "misstated" his position. He clarified it by saying that he would carry out the act of Congress which set up an American Institute on Taiwan. By executive order, he would also do his utmost to upgrade the negotiations with the representatives of Taiwan.

His campaign manager, William Casey, loyally said that Reagan himself—and none of his advisers on foreign policy—had made the decision to alter his stand. Reagan, he said, "is not a damned puppet."

Vice President Mondale gleefully seized upon the China episode as proof of Reagan's "confusion" about foreign policy. With equal enthusiasm, the Washington *Post*'s Lou Cannon led off a dispatch by writing: "Ronald Reagan campaigned today in gloomy weather, which matched some of the omens for his own candidacy."

Next came Reagan's major mistake about the Ku Klux Klan. He said at Detroit on Labor Day that while he was speaking to working people there, Carter was "opening his campaign down in the city that gave birth to, and is the parent body of, the Ku Klux Klan." It was an off-the-cuff remark to a man in the crowd who was wearing a Jimmy Carter mask.

Reagan was wrong on two counts: First, he was inaccurate. The klan was born, not at Tuscumbia, Alabama, where Carter spoke, but at Pulaski, Tennessee. Second, it was a personal slam at the President, who was not wooing the klan but attacking it, just as Reagan himself had done earlier in spurning its proffered endorsement.

The blunder enabled Carter, figuratively, to don his Confederate uniform and rush to defend the sacred honor of the fair Southland against "slurs and innuendos." Seven Southern governors (all Democrats) demanded an apology for the "callous and opportunistic slap at the South."

Reagan quickly apologized to Tuscumbia and to Alabama's Gov. Forrest James and called upon Carter to disavow two associates, Andrew Young and Patricia Harris, for their "unfair attempt to associate my campaign with the Ku Klux Klan." Young, who had been removed as ambassador to the United Nations for backdoor dickerings with the Palestine Liberation Organization, was stirring up black voters against Reagan. Harris, the Secretary of Health and Human Services, had told the United Steelworkers in a Los Angeles speech that the klan had endorsed Reagan and the Republican platform.

In early September, Reagan's national campaign headquarters in an office building in Arlington, Virginia, just across the Potomac River from Washington, began to show some semblance of order emerging out of chaos. The staff, which had been run as a loose alliance in which various "barons" competed for their share of authority, was tightened up with more direct lines of command. Chief of Staff Edwin Meese, William Casey, and Richard Wirthlin, the chief pollster, were joined by William Timmons, as a political director, and Stuart Spencer, the mastermind of Reagan's first campaign for governor. Retired Rear Admiral Robert Garrick, who heads the West Coast office of Doremus and Company, an international public relations firm in New York, became director of research and policy development.

To protect the candidate against future slipups, Spencer joined the staff on the campaign plane, *Leadership 80*, where the major figures with Reagan were Michael Deaver, the tour director; Martin Anderson, domestic issues adviser; Lyn Nofziger, who had come back as press secretary; Jim Brady, an issues coordinator, formerly on John Connally's staff; and Ken Khachigian, a speech writer with experience in the Nixon White House.

When the headquarters moved East from the Los Angeles airport complex, the Reagans transferred their home base temporarily, also. They leased "Wexford," an estate near Leesburg, Virginia, from its millionaire-owner, William Clements, the governor of Texas.

Republican senators, worrying about Reagan's repeated gaffes and his downward plunge in the polls, summoned several of his strategists to a private luncheon in the Capitol and gave them a rough cross-examination. Senator Helms said Reagan must "stop shooting himself in the foot." Sen. Orrin Hatch of Utah said Reagan would soon move up in the polls by sticking to his prepared scripts and cutting out off-the-cuff remarks.

While a platoon of his aides sat in the audience and held their breath for fear of another slip of his tongue, Reagan cruised through a perfect performance before the B'nai B'rith convention at a Washington hotel September 3. Members of the Jewish service organization applauded thirty times during the strongly pro-Israel speech. Reagan charged that Carter's "zig-zags and flip-flops" in the United Nations, his sale of arms to the Arabs, and his overtures to the Palestine Liberation Organization had increased Soviet power in the Middle East, imperiled the United States and placed Israel in grave danger.

Carter, who addressed the B'nai B'rith the next day, drew far less applause as well as some heckling and booing, even though he had announced a new Middle East peace initiative. He said the stalled negotiations between Egypt and Israel over Palestinian autonomy would be resumed within a few weeks. The timing, one White House assistant said with a grin, was more than coincidence.

Newsweek magazine said: "The first week of the fall presidential campaign went to Jimmy Carter." It quoted one Carter strategist as saying that only the presence of John Anderson in the race "stood in the way of an overwhelming Carter victory." Such was the euphoria in the White House at that time.

Actually, Reagan was coming up more strongly than the White House experts realized. He had ended his time of fumbling and stumbling around and was moving back on the track, appealing to voters who had long been essential parts of the ruling Democratic coalition: Jewish leaders, who feared Carter would tilt against Israel in his obsessive quest for Arab oil; Roman Catholics, who shared Reagan's adamant stand against abortions; Polish, Lithuanian, Italian, Cuban, and other ethnic groups who liked his anti-Communism and his call for a stronger national defense.

In early September, Reagan ended a speech in Philadelphia with an emotional recitation of words written by John F. Kennedy that the late President had not lived to deliver. America, Kennedy had written, "is the watchman on the walls of world freedom," and Reagan called for an opportunity to lead the nation.

The Republican candidate even quoted Kennedy's brother Ted in mocking Carter as the President who was always "surprised" by crises at home and abroad. "He's due for one more surprise," Reagan shouted at Kokomo, Indiana, a "surprise on November 4, when we get government off our backs and turn the American people loose!"

By quoting the Kennedys, Reagan reached out to many blue-collar workers, normally Democrats, who were disillusioned by Carter's weak leadership in national security matters and his failure to curb double-digit inflation. Carter, as expected, won the endorsement of the national AFL-CIO hierarchy, the United Automobile Workers' chieftains and the top brass of the National Education Association. But Reagan appealed to rank-and-file members of these unions besides winning the official support of the Teamsters Union and the Maritime Union.

At Columbus, Ohio, he reminded the Teamsters that he had been six times president of the Screen Actors Guild and led its first strike; he was also the first union president ever to be a major party nominee for President of the United States. He promised that representatives of organized labor would have access to the

White House, and he would build "a Great Coalition made up of the producers of America."

To Reagan's claim that workers were suffering in a "new depression," Carter retorted that the economic slowdown was only a mild recession.

At Jersey City Reagan fired back that Carter had "taken refuge behind a dictionary."

"Well," he said, "if it's a definition he wants, I'll give him one: A recession is when your neighbor loses his job. A depression is when you lose yours. Recovery is when Jimmy Carter loses his."

Reagan stubbornly refused to retreat from his pledge for a 10 percent income tax cut in each of the ensuing three years, although the President branded it as wildly inflationary. "There is panic in the Carter White House at the prospect of modest tax reductions," Reagan said, "because the Ruling Party in Washington wants a larger share of the workers' income to spend as it pleases on expanding the federal bureaucracy."

Ridiculing the administration officials' claim that the Republicans could not balance the budget, provide for national security, and reduce the tax load, too, Reagan declared: "I say, 'Stand aside—because we can, and we will!'"

So Reagan persisted in his revolutionary efforts to change his adopted Republican party from its Big Business image to an agency speaking for the masses of working Americans. Despite Carter's appeals to the past glories of the Democratic party, the President showed he did not understand, or care about, the worries of average people who were finding it harder every week to make ends meet with budgets squeezed by rising prices and taxes.

"For the first time in the history of our country," Reagan said at Jacksonville, Florida, September 5, "we face three grave crises at the same time, each one of which is capable of destroying us: Our economy is deteriorating, our energy needs are not being met, and our military preparedness has been weakened to the point of immediate danger."

Then he accused the administration of deliberately leaking

data about the top-secret "Stealth" technology that supposedly could make American warplanes "invisible" to enemy radar. Defense Secretary Harold Brown said he confirmed the breakthrough because, somehow, it had already leaked. But Admiral Elmo R. Zumwalt, Jr., a Democrat and former chief of naval operations, charged that the President had arranged for the leaks by the Pentagon itself in a political move to "diffuse criticism" of Carter for having killed the B–1 bomber. The decision to disclose the secret gave the Soviet Union at least a five-year head start in devising countermeasures, the Admiral said, and thus the maneuver was "unbelievably harmful to the national security."

Reagan's strategists, who had a hand in orchestrating the brouhaha over "Stealth," rejoiced as it threw Carter on the defensive. "After the klan flap, bang! we hit with 'Stealth,'" one exulted. "When we drew the country's attention to the fraudulence of that move, we really did hit home."

In a carefully rehearsed tableau to show that Reagan, as President, would work in harmony with Congress—in marked contrast to Carter's feuds with his own Democratic chieftains there—the Republicans presented Reagan, Bush, their own members of Congress, and congressional candidates in a "unity" show on the Capitol steps September 15.

Senate Majority Leader Robert C. Byrd ridiculed the theatrical display in advance, saying: "They'll bring Reagan out all wrapped in cellophane after a good nap and take him out for another good nap. It will be G.E. Theater and selling Borax to create the image that there is a team." Byrd said the Republicans' decrepit movie actor could not carry the burdens of the presidency: "There will be no teleprompter when he meets with Brezhnev."

But the show was staged without a fluff, and the Democrats realized that they could not count on Reagan to lose by some fatal mistake. Their congressmen, battling for re-election and keeping much closer to the voters than was the White House Palace Guard, candidly said in the cloakrooms that Carter was in danger of defeat. They could see Reagan chipping away, little by little, at the voting blocs that traditionally had formed their party's victorious coalition.

One group remained totally loyal to the apostle of brotherly love in the White House—the blacks. They had given Carter about 90 percent of their votes in 1976 and they must turn out in even larger numbers this time to keep him in power.

On September 16, Brother Jimmy went home to the Ebenezer Baptist Church in Atlanta, the overwhelmingly black congregation of the Reverend Martin Luther King, Sr., and, speaking from the pulpit, he warned: "This meeting this morning could very well decide the outcome of this election and . . . the future of this country.

"My phone has been open to you," Carter said, "and you have never failed to use it. But if my opponent should be elected, you're going to have a hard time getting a telephone call answered at the White House."

Then, in an unmistakable slap at Reagan, Carter charged that "hatred" and "racism" had been injected into the campaign. He assailed his opponent's endorsement of "states' rights" in a Mississippi speech as marking "the rebirth of code words" for racism and once more dragged up the Ku Klux Klan.

This partisan attack from the sanctity of the pulpit, where Carter was photographed with his head bowed in prayer, evoked stern rebukes from both of Washington's daily newspapers. Even the *Post*, which seldom had a kind word for Reagan, chastised the President in a stinging editorial entitled "RUNNING MEAN."

His sanctimonious assault on Reagan, the *Post* said, fit precisely into Carter's "miserable record of personally savaging political opponents (Hubert Humphrey, Edward Kennedy) whenever the going got rough . . . He displays an alarming absence of magnanimity, generosity, and size, when he is campaigning."

The *Star* said "this squalid exercise in Dr. King's church" must be the President's last such indulgence in cheap epithets and innuendoes, unworthy of his high office.

Gerald Ford called upon Carter to apologize for "demeaning the presidency." "The American people are asking themselves,

'Is this the real Jimmy Carter?' " the former President said, brand-ing his successor "a man so desperate for re-election that he will make any statement—true or false—to reach that end."

Carter's fear of defeat was the real reason for his attack on Reagan in "one of the most vicious smears in modern political history," Sen. Paul Laxalt said. The Nevada Republican said on September 19 that the latest polls showed Reagan, after his early missteps, had moved ahead in most of the large states—California, Illinois, Ohio, Texas, and Florida—while New York and Pennsyl-vania were "dead even."

Three days later, several prominent black leaders met in Washington and grimly agreed that unless they could motivate more blacks to come out and vote for the President, he would lose the election. Dr. Benjamin Hooks, executive director of the Na-tional Association for the Advancement of Colored People, said: "At Saginaw and Flint, Michigan, yesterday, I found fifty per-cent of the automobile workers laid off. The question today is whether they will vote as their union leaders tell them." Because of the recession, inflation, and high unemployment among blacks, Dr. Hooks said, there was "much disillusionment, doubt, and despair because Carter has not fulfilled his promises."

"If a million blacks don't vote, Ronald Reagan is going to be the next President of the United States," columnist Carl Rowan said, complaining that Carter had "chickened out" under the Washington newspapers' fire and had admitted that Reagan was not a racist, after all.

Carter did not help his own prospects by boycotting the hour-long televised debate between Reagan and Anderson at Balti-more on the night of September 21. Both contenders blamed the absent President for uncontrolled inflation and pointedly re-marked that he should have been there to defend his administra-tion's policies.

The two debaters differed sharply on the tax-cut issue. Rea-gan stuck to his proposal for a 30 percent reduction over three years, although it was branded as "inflationary" by Anderson and "by the man who isn't here tonight." Anderson defended his un-popular proposal for an extra fifty-cents-per-gallon tax on gasoline, to be offset by lower Social Security levies Reagan rejected this as a further burden on consumers.

Anderson insisted upon a woman's "freedom of choice" to get rid of an unborn baby by abortion. Reagan retorted that an unborn child is "a human being" and acidly commented: "I've noted that everybody that is for abortion has already been born."

Carter had hoped that by staying away he could downgrade the debate to a mere sideshow between "two Republicans" and thus brush off Anderson as an insignificant also-ran. But the independent contender proved to be a serious, articulate man who could poll enough votes to throw several key states to Reagan, just as the Democrats feared.

The President, who considered Reagan an ignorant bumbler, also had hoped that the Republican candidate would make a fatal slip of the tongue. But no such error occurred. Reagan's aide, James Baker III, commented: "Our risk was that he would make a serious mistake with the President safe in the White House, but our candidate showed that he is reasonable, competent, compassionate, and has the vision to cope with the future."

So Carter stepped up his efforts to paint Reagan as a dangerous incompetent who could stumble into war. In Los Angeles on September 22, the President twice said the election would decide whether the American people would have "war or peace," clearly equating himself with "peace." Reagan denounced the attack as "beneath decency."

He had earlier forecast that the White House crowd would try to portray him as "a combination of Ebenezer Scrooge and the Mad Bomber."

White House Press Secretary Jody Powell said Carter would not apologize for raising questions about Reagan's past statements advocating the use of the armed forces in international disputes—for example, his comment in January that the United States should consider, as "one option," blockading Cuba in response to the Soviet invasion of Afghanistan. The President, denying any intention of depicting Reagan as a warmonger, said: "The record's there; to call for the use of military forces in a very dangerous situation has been a repeated habit of his as governor and as a candidate for President."

Some Carter assistants bragged that he had shown a shrewd sense of timing by zeroing in on the "Reagan's a warmonger" issue at the outbreak of the war between Iraq and Iran—their theory being that the voters would be reassured by Carter's coolness and neutrality and afraid that the old movie cowboy from California would respond to the Middle East crisis by shooting from the hip.

The trouble with the theory was that Carter did not look cool and calm but quite the opposite. George Bush, campaigning in Michigan, said the President was taking the low road of "sly innuendo" and "guerrilla" assault instead of making his charges face to face in the Baltimore debate. Sen. Mark Hatfield, a liberal Republican from Oregon, noted sharply that "it was President Carter, not Governor Reagan, who demanded a return to draft registration," so which candidate was really thinking about a war?

While touting himself as the "peace" candidate, the President also sought to keep the support of the evangelical Christians, who had helped him to carry every Southern state except Virginia in 1976. Many of these church people were disappointed in him and disillusioned by his tactics of courting liberal Democrats, promoters of ERA, supporters of abortion, homosexuals, and others whose policies the fundamentalists perceived as a threat to the traditional American family.

The Reverend Jerry Falwell, spiritual leader of the Moral Majority, predicted that 4 million newly registered Christian voters would be a decisive influence in the election. Carter and several advisers expressed grave concern about the new voters at a private White House strategy session August 5, called for the purpose of coping with the Falwell Menace.

The President listened to doleful reports from the Reverend Robert L. Maddox, who had left the pulpit of the Calhoun, Georgia, Baptist Church to become the religious liaison director in the White House. Maddox had one main mission—to win back the lost sheep who were straying away from the fold of Good Shepherd Carter. The statistics were chilling: While Carter drew

46 percent of the total Protestant vote in 1976, Reagan led in the latest polls among these voters, with 58 percent to Carter's 28 percent and 14 percent for Anderson.

Since the Democratic platform committed the party to a pro-abortion, pro-ERA stand and opposed the return of voluntary prayer in the schools, the evangelicals had a compelling motive to switch to the Republicans, with their "pro-life" and pro-defense stands. Carter was advised to appear at some evangelical event and to use more religious phrases in his speeches. Maddox was ordered to invite the editors of Christian magazines and newspapers to the White House and warn them that the conservative clerics were threatening social programs and breaking down the wall separating church and state.

Reagan wooed the fundamentalist Christians by fervently defending "traditional moral values" in a speech at the Religious Round Table's National Affairs Briefing, which drew 15,000 people to Dallas in the sizzling 105-degree heat of late August. His opponents for the presidency refused invitations to the combined revival and political rally.

"I know you can't endorse *me*," Reagan said to the faithful at the technically nonpartisan assembly, "but I can endorse *you*."

He drew a storm of applause by promising that as President, he would make sure that "the awesome power of government respects the rights of parents and the integrity of the family"; that he would "keep Big Government out of the school and the neighborhood and, above all, the home."

Reagan's men hired the Reverend Bob Billings away from the Moral Majority to become their liaison with the evangelical Christians. Billings, a former Indiana educator and unsuccessful candidate for Congress, had come to Washington two years earlier to mobilize a campaign against the Internal Revenue Service's attempt to take away the tax exemptions from private schools that did not meet arbitrary guidelines for racial quotas. Through his coalition of religious groups, Billings whipped up a flood of more than 100,000 letters of protest that swamped the IRS.

Billings, who likes to bang on a piano and sing old songs at social events, next turned his talents to registering fundamentalist voters, who literally believe every word of the Bible. One sunny September day, over coffee at a fast food restaurant next door to the Reagan-Bush offices in Northern Virginia, he calmly predicted that 4 million new voters would "go three to one for Reagan" and millions more who had supported Carter in 1976 would switch to the Republican candidate. These people, he said, would swing several states away from "Jingling Jimmy with his Chiclet smile," right there in his own backyard, the Deep South, and lock up the election for Reagan. "I tell our people," he said, "to 'vote for the Reagan of your choice.'"

Billings ridiculed the Gallup Poll, which claimed the President was ahead and most evangelical Christians would vote Democratic. Gallup was using out-of-date figures, he was wrong, Billings declared, "and we'll prove it to him on election day."

Carter struck back at the Moral Majority by unleashing Patricia Harris, the Secretary of Health and Human Services, who had already shown her skill at throwing mud balls with her attack linking Reagan with the klan. At Princeton University on September 23, she called the fundamentalists' political action "a serious threat to the American democratic process" and compared the TV preachers to Iran's fanatical dictator, Ayatollah Khomeini.

"I am beginning to fear," she said, "that we could have an Ayatollah Khomeini in this country but that he will not have a beard, he will have a television program."

Falwell came to Washington, stood before a battery of microphones outside the Carter cabinet member's office at the foot of Capitol Hill on September 29, and called her charges "nonsense" and "pure rubbish." He accused the secretary of making "vicious and unsubstantiated attacks on the literally millions of Jews, Catholics, Mormons, and Protestants, whose only crime has been to register and vote."

Four days later, Reagan brushed aside the objections of some nervous advisers and addressed the National Religious Broadcasters Association at Falwell's own Liberty Baptist College in Lynchburg, Virginia, warmly greeting the TV evangelist but politely disputing Falwell's claim that "God does not hear the prayers of unredeemed Gentiles or Jews."

"Since both the Christian and Judaic religions are based on the same God, the God of Moses," Reagan said, "I'm quite sure those prayers are heard." He also opposed a state-mandated prayer in the schoolrooms but favored restoring voluntary prayers. "I don't think we should have expelled God from the classroom," he said, and the broadcasters applauded.

Warned by his advisers that his "racist" and "warmonger" attacks upon Reagan were backfiring, Carter began toning down his rhetoric. But, like the alcoholic who takes one more drink, he slipped again while haranguing a throng of several hundred Cook County Democrats at a fund-raising cocktail party in the Palmer House at Chicago the night of October 6.

Carter denounced the Republicans' "radical" platform and nominee and warned: "You'll determine whether or not this America will be unified or, if I lose the election, whether Americans might be separated, black from white, Jew from Christian, North from South, rural from urban . . ."

"The President is reaching a point of hysteria," Reagan retorted the next day. "He has absolutely no evidence to substantiate such terrible claims." John Anderson, whose independent candidacy was stuck on a treadmill to nowhere, sarcastically observed in Boston that Carter's "outrageous" new attack was "really masking his own fear that he is now not going to win the election."

The White House staff quickly orchestrated a pressure campaign on reporters and TV commentators, demanding that they quit depicting Carter as "mean" and that they pick on Reagan again to put him on the defensive.

Carter tried to clean up his image in a televised interview with Barbara Walters by agreeing that he had made some mistakes in his invective. But he insisted that "when Mr. Reagan says I'm desperate or vindictive or hysterical, he shares part of the blame." The President, his surrogates, and his TV advertising blitz persistently linked the words "Reagan" and "war" in such a blatant way that the Republican candidate's advisers became alarmed, especially when polls showed Carter several points ahead among women voters who fervently yearned for peace.

At an October 14 press conference in Los Angeles, Reagan

said that he would use the armed forces in combat only as a "last resort"; that with a firmer foreign policy and greater military strength, the United States could stay out of war. He also bid for women's votes by promising that "one of the first Supreme Court vacancies in my administration will be filled by the most qualified woman I can find."

Reagan moved off the defensive on the "war and peace" issue by making a half-hour televised speech October 19 about his "Strategy of Peace for the 80's."

Carter is gambling that "his long litany of fear" will frighten enough voters to save him from defeat, but he will lose, Reagan predicted. "The American people know—to paraphrase Franklin Roosevelt—that the only thing the cause of peace has to fear is fear itself."

Then the Republican candidate quoted another Democrat, Sen. Ted Kennedy, as saying of Carter: "No President should be re-elected because he happened to be standing there when his foreign policy collapsed around him."

In a bold appeal for millions of rank-and-file Democrats' votes, Reagan said: "The Carter administration, dominated as it is by the McGovernite wing of the party, has broken sharply with the views and policies of Harry Truman, John Kennedy, and many contemporary Democratic leaders." All of those Democrats built strong defense forces through bipartisanship, and Reagan promised, as President, to restore that great tradition in national security and foreign policy.

Reagan accurately noted that Carter could not win approval of the SALT II treaty by a Senate controlled by his own party, because a majority knew it would not protect U.S. security interests.

"As President, I will make immediate preparations for negotiations on a SALT III treaty," Reagan said. "My goal is to begin arms *reductions*. My energies will be directed at reducing destructive nuclear weaponry in the world." To induce the Soviet Union to make such mutual cutbacks, he would first "restore the margin of safety for peace" by rebuilding the American armed forces, which Carter had seriously weakened in his haste to make good on a "reckless campaign promise to cut defense spending by billions of dollars."

"I have known four wars in my lifetime—I don't want to see a fifth," he said. "I pray that never again will we bleed a generation of young Americans into the sands of island beachheads, the mud of European battlefields, or the rice paddies or jungles of Asia. Whether we like it or not, it is our responsibility to preserve world peace because no one else can do it."

Early the next morning, before flying off on a Northern campaign swing, Carter fired a withering blast of ridicule from the South Lawn of the White House. He said Reagan "doesn't understand the serious consequences" of his proposals to throw SALT II "into the wastebasket," and launch a quest for "so-called nuclear superiority."

It was "extraordinarily naive" of Reagan to expect that the Soviet Union would meekly go along with such a plan, which "would be a devastating and perhaps fatal blow to the long-term process of nuclear arms control," the Chief Executive said.

He stepped up his fusillade in a fervent plea to a crowd jamming Concord Baptist Church in the heart of Brooklyn's Bedford-Stuyvesant section, one of the nation's largest black slums. He depicted Reagan as a critic of Medicare, urban aid, the minimum wage, unemployment compensation, and civil rights; and he predicted that after the November 4 election, Reagan would be "right back . . . in Hollywood as a movie actor."

In Louisville, Kentucky, the same day, Reagan said: "I've heard that Mr. Carter this morning assembled members of the press corps to tell them that Ronald Reagan did not understand. Well, you know, for once I agree with him. He's hit it right on the nose. I don't understand why we have had inflation at the highest peacetime rates in history. . . . I don't understand why his answer to inflation was to put two million people out of work. I don't understand why mortgage rates are at fourteen percent.

"I don't understand why our defenses have weakened, why American prestige has fallen abroad, why Afghanistan is now occupied by the Soviet Union, why there is massive instability in the Persian Gulf region.

"Lastly," Reagan said, "I don't understand why fifty-two Americans have been held hostage for almost a year now." The failure to free the captives in Iran was "a humiliation and a disgrace," he added, and Carter's weak foreign policy was to blame.

Reagan's broadside reflected the Republicans' increasing nervousness over a sudden rash of reports that Carter was secretly negotiating to bring the hostages home shortly before election day and thus miraculously squeak through to victory. Carter himself provided the tip-off to a deal by stating on October 20: "If Iran should release the hostages, then I will unfreeze the assets in the banks here and in Europe, drop the embargo against trade, and work toward resumption of normal commerce with Iran in the future. It is to our advantage to see a strong Iran, a united Iran." Edmund Muskie, the Secretary of State, also tilted toward Iran in its war against Iraq by saying: "We are opposed to the dismemberment of Iran."

"Jimmy Carter is so anxious to get elected, he might do anything," Gerald Ford said at St. Louis on October 21. But, the former President warned, an agreement involving military aid to Iran in the war "will plunge the United States into a quagmire in the Middle East that will be far worse than the war in Vietnam."

At Waco, Texas, the following day, Carter brought his campaign to a new level of elegance and refinement by wearing a pair of red, hand-tooled cowboy boots and shouting to the crowd: "I grew up on a farm, and I know you need high-top boots for things besides stomping Republicans. As you well know . . . Republicans have a habit of spreading a lot of horse manure around right before an election."

Carter made fun of Reagan's statement that he had "some ideas" about freeing the hostages but declined to reveal them. Sarcastically, the President compared this to Richard Nixon's "secret plan" for ending the Vietnam War.

Reagan had already accepted the general conditions laid down by Iran for turning the Americans loose; and his stand, intended to show bipartisan unity on the issue, evoked much behind-the-scenes controversy in his own camp. The advisers who recommended his action called it "a political master stroke" which prevented the Democrats from claiming that Reagan opposed the hostages' quick release.

For months, Reagan's supporters had been warning one another to expect Carter to use his immense power as Commander-in-Chief to bring about some foreign policy coup—an "October Surprise." They recalled how Senator Kennedy had been closing in on him in the Wisconsin primary race until, early in the morning of the April balloting, the President suddenly announced on television that great progress had been made toward freeing the hostages. This mysterious break in the long deadlock dominated the news all day. "It proved to be pure nonsense, but people believed it," Ed Meese remarked, and Carter won Wisconsin.

Richard Allen, Reagan's chief foreign policy adviser, coined the "October Surprise" phrase and kept repeating it until it caught on as a symbol of Carter's willingness to pull any trick in the book to win. Allen headed a working group on the issue, including Dr. Fred C. Iklé, former director of the Arms Control and Disarmament Agency; Dr. William R. Van Cleave, director of the Institute for International Studies, University of Southern California; Lt. Gen. Edward L. Rowny, U.S. Army, retired; Lawrence Silberman, former ambassador to Yugoslavia; Dr. John F. Lehman, Jr., and Dr. William R. Schneider.

These men, who had an intricate network of intelligence sources and a few "moles" inside the Carter government, met often and exchanged information. By mid-October, their private radars were picking up an array of signals indicating early action in Iran: Some very secret military planning was going on. Certain airplanes were being modified. The Air Force was preparing large cargo planes for the flight to Teheran. Contingency plans called for the hostages to be flown to an American hospital complex in West Germany for a few days before coming home.

Reagan's strategists, on his campaign plane and in their secret sessions in Northern Virginia, pondered all these reports amid gathering gloom. Just as he seemed to be locking up a majority of electoral votes, according to his own polls, there was a danger that his great prize might be snatched away by a slick maneuver. The Reaganites had dark visions—of Carter's flying overseas to

greet the freed Americans or welcoming them to the White House
in a star-spangled extravaganza that would dominate the nation's TV screens. "The Reagan aides," one Republican commented, "are scared to death."

By October 23, Washington was throbbing with rumors that
the deal was under way, and some of the captives would be free
within a few days. Carter publicly promised that, "if Iran should
release the hostages, then I would unfreeze their assets, which are
worth several billions of dollars." Among the assets were about
$400 million worth of arms—air-to-air missiles, air-to-ground mis-
siles, anti-tank weapons, cluster bombs, and spare parts for jet
fighters and tanks. Iran's armed forces desperately wanted the
weapons to carry on the war, and that was one major motive for
the bargain.

In a *New York Times* column, William Safire warned that the
American arms could "help stage a Persian carpet-bombing of
Baghdad" so Carter might embroil this country in a "Moslem war"
in his frantic efforts to gain a second term. Columnist Joseph Kraft,
no friend of Reagan's, said Carter's all-out drive to free the captives "bears all the marks of a mad electoral maneuver." In *The
Ruff Times*, Howard J. Ruff branded the deal "political insanity."

That was the atmosphere of suspense in which Carter and
Reagan met at Cleveland on the night of October 28 for their
televised debate, which was billed as the most important event of
the whole campaign, the turning point that could decide the presidential election.

17

☆

VICTORY
AT LAST

"CARTER GOES INTO DEBATE WITH LEAD IN NEW POLL," the Washington *Post* trumpeted in its main headline on Page One of October 28. The President's rising fortunes appeared to be shown in the accompanying Gallup Poll report, which indicated that he had gained six points and surged three points out in front, leading Reagan 45 to 42 percent.

So, it was with immense confidence, even cockiness, that the Chief Executive entered the Cleveland debate. He had won a similar battle of wits against Gerald Ford four years before and now wrapped himself in the mantle of the presidency as he came face to face, at last, with the aging former actor whom he privately denigrated.

Carter, who expected to score a knockout, sailed into the attack at the sound of the opening bell. He set out to show the huge television audience, estimated at 100 million people, that Reagan was too dangerous to be trusted with the grave decisions involving nuclear war. No fewer than seven times, Carter used the word "disturbing" about Reagan, four times branding his views as "dangerous."

Relentlessly, with his eyes flashing and his voice metallic, the Chief Executive hammered away with his charges that while he had been keeping the peace through his lonely decisions in the Oval Office, his rival "habitually advocated" sending American military forces into troubled regions. Carter depicted himself as striving to curb the spread of atomic weapons to terrorists, while

Reagan considered that none of our business. Although every President since Harry Truman had sought to control nuclear weapons, by agreements with the Soviet Union, Reagan would be dangerously different: He would throw the SALT II treaty "into the wastebasket" and launch a perilous nuclear arms race.

Thrown onto the defensive, Reagan protested that he had never been indifferent to the nonproliferation of nuclear weapons; that his own views had been badly distorted by the President, who was "like the witch doctor that gets mad when a good doctor comes along with a cure that'll work."

Carter tripped, however, when he said his daughter Amy had advised him that the nuclear arms race was the major issue. An audible snicker arose from the audience.

The President flailed away without mercy on domestic issues. He said Reagan favored "heartless" changes in the minimum wage; would repeal the windfall-profits tax and give billions of dollars to the major oil companies; and enact the "ridiculous, inflationary Reagan-Kemp-Roth" tax-cut bill.

Reagan replied with a rhetorical question: Why was it "inflationary" to let the people keep their own money but not "inflationary" for Carter to take it away in higher taxes and spend it?

On four different occasions, the President charged, his rival had advocated making Social Security a voluntary system, which would "very quickly bankrupt it." Reagan retorted: "That just isn't true." He promised to continue Social Security payments intact but without a further rise in payroll taxes, a burden on younger workers.

Then Carter went too far. He declared that Reagan "began his political career campaigning around this nation against Medicare," and now opposed national health insurance with emphasis on prevention of disease, outpatient care, and control of hospital costs.

Reagan listened to this tirade with an unbelieving shake of his head and an amused, tolerant smile and quipped, "There you go again!"

It was the ultimate put-down, administered by a genial, patient man to a foe who had struck him with one low blow too many. Although Carter had excelled in his attacks, he had made the mistake of excess. He won the debate on points, but lost it by engendering sympathy for his victim in the minds and hearts of the millions watching the verbal battle on their TV sets.

Reagan also scored decisively in his closing remarks when he told the voters: "Next Tuesday all of you will go to the polls; you'll stand there in the polling place and make a decision. I think when you make that decision, it might be well if you would ask yourself: Are you better off than you were four years ago? Is it easier for you to go and buy things in the stores than it was four years ago? Is there more or less unemployment in the country than there was four years ago? Is America as respected throughout the world as it was? Do you feel that our security is as safe, that we're as strong as we were four years ago? . . ."

He concluded by offering to lead a "crusade" to "take the government off the backs of the great people of the country and turn you loose again to do those things that I know you can do so well, because you did them and made this country great."

In the opinion of his managers, the real Reagan shone through on the TV screen—not the cold, heartless, "radical warmonger" of Carter's dark fantasies, but a warm, earnest, sincere, compassionate man as reassuring as Dwight D. Eisenhower. Millions of Americans, paying close attention to Reagan for the first time in their lives, began to understand him, and most of them liked him.

"I feel great," Reagan said after the ninety minutes of intellectual fencing on prime time. "It was wonderful finally to be able . . . to respond to some of the false accusations." He was not nervous while sharing the stage with the President, the veteran trouper said, "not at all. I've been on the same stage with John Wayne."

In the immediate afterglow of the debate, Carter thought he had mopped up the floor with his opponent and scored a clear triumph. So did most of the media pundits, who looked down upon Reagan as a lightweight. Euphoria reigned in the Democrats' camp. Campaign Chairman Robert Strauss said: "This ought to be the lift we need to put us over."

Then came the report from ABC News: Its telephone survey

indicated that participating callers chose Reagan by two to one over Carter as having gained more from the debate. True, this poll could be discounted as unscientific, and there had been much confusion in the call-ins.

But *The New York Times* said a varied group of residents in this area, who had watched the debate on TV in a midtown hotel room, decided by an "overwhelming" margin that Reagan had won.

Barnstorming across the map, speaking from early morning until late at night, the President intensified his campaign with such fervor that he showed signs of fatigue and his voice began to crack. Over and over, he tried to link the name of Reagan to such scare words as "radical," "nuclear war," and "holocaust." At Rochester, New York, he said: "I pray God . . . we must not get ourselves in a situation where the horrible power of atomic weaponry is unleashed on this world." He said Reagan believed "it's none of our business if a radical and terrorist nation like Libya has the atomic weapon." (This is the same Libya which paid Carter's brother Billy $220,000 for his presumed influence.)

To thousands of garment workers at a Manhattan street rally, Carter said the Democrats would control "the terrible weapons of nuclear annihilation" but Reagan would not, so he must be "sent back to Hollywood."

Carter's personal assaults finally provoked his long-suffering rival into a flash of his Irish temper. "Carter has lowered himself to a personal type of attack against me . . . based on falsehoods and distortions," Reagan said October 29 at Dallas. "He doesn't know me well enough to charge me with being a racist. He doesn't know me well enough to suggest that I am trigger-happy and would cause a war . . . saying if I were President I would separate Christians from Jews, blacks from whites. . . . I can hardly have a warm feeling in my heart for someone who's been attacking me on a personal basis for many months now in the campaign."

Carter intensified his rhetoric after receiving incredibly bad news that he was about to lose most of his own home base. Since he had already written off all the West, the loss of the Solid South

would mean he could not possibly be re-elected. Richard Wirthlin conceded the President only eight states and the District of
Columbia in late October. Total: 103 electoral votes. One con-
tributing factor was the endorsement of Reagan by Sen. Harry F.
Byrd, the Virginia independent and former Democrat who made
it respectable for many conservative Democrats to bolt. Byrd
called Carter's record "dismal."

On Halloween, the President made a flying tour of five Southern states, waving the hobgoblin of Reagan the Terrible and
pleading with his "friends and neighbors" not to repudiate their
own President, a son of the Georgia soil. At Columbia, South
Carolina, and Lakeland, Florida, he hinted for the first time at
his fears of defeat. At Memphis, Tennessee, he excoriated the
fundamentalist Christians who were turning many church members against him. At Jackson, Mississippi, he cried: "Let's win a
victory for the South!"

At a noisy rally in Houston, Texas, amid chants of "Four more
years," he begged blacks and Mexican Americans to remember it
was only the Democrats who had been "helping those who felt
the scourge of discrimination," not the rich Republicans and Ronald Reagan. The next day he barnstormed across Texas, then
spoke at two rallies in Milwaukee and addressed an Italian-Amer-
ican banquet in Chicago at fifteen minutes till midnight.

While the President grimly depicted the horrors of having a
"right wing Republican" in the Oval Office, Reagan and Gerald
Ford campaigned merrily together in Michigan as if they were
brothers, forgetting their bitter rivalry of the past. They charged
that Carter had inherited a prosperous, confident nation from
Ford and then proceeded to make a mess of everything. Ford, who
yearned for vindication, forecast Carter's doom, and Reagan for
the first time predicted: "We're going to win this thing."

At Battle Creek, where some pranksters chanted "Bonzo,
Bonzo, Bonzo!" the chimpanzee's onetime co-star flashed back:
"Well, they'd better watch out. Bonzo grew up to be King Kong!"

Like the quarterback of a football team striving for a spectacular play to achieve a last-minute victory, Carter figuratively
tried for a Long Bomb into the end zone. He looked to the Iranian

Parliament to act in favor of freeing the hostages in time to make him a hero. A hitch occurred when hard-liners boycotted an October 30 session in Teheran, blocking a quorum, but the debate took place anyway on the Sunday before the elections and conditions were officially set for releasing the Americans, who had been incarcerated almost exactly a year before.

Awakened at 4:00 A.M. Sunday in his Chicago hotel suite, the President dramatically flew back to Washington aboard Air Force One. By 8:00 A.M. he was meeting in the cabinet room with Vice President Mondale, Secretary of State Muskie, and other advisers, considering the response to the Iranians' terms. At 6:23 P.M. the President entered the White House press room and spoke to the people through television for four minutes. He said the Parliament's action was "significant" and that it offered a "positive basis" for finally freeing the hostages.

"I wish that I could predict when the hostages will return," he said. "I cannot." He stressed that regardless of the outcome of the election, Americans would be united in desiring their return only on a basis that preserves "national honor and . . . integrity."

Once more, the President appeared as the Experienced Leader Directing Foreign Policy in a Crisis, precisely the role that Ham Jordan, Jody Powell, and Bob Strauss had cut out for him to show the contrast between the lonely man in the Oval Office and the Hollywood actor outside. Jordan exuded confidence, claiming that Reagan had peaked in the debate and was sliding downhill. Pollster Pat Caddell said, "We are well ahead, two or three points," and the President commented, "Pat's polls have always been unbelievably accurate."

Recalling how Carter had profited politically from his previous moves on the hostage issue, some Republicans fretted that he might repeat the performance. Reagan's traveling companions on the campaign trail in Ohio were no longer bubbling with optimism. It was infinitely frustrating to think that Carter the Incompetent might save himself from defeat by staging another fake play with the aid of crazy old Ayatollah Khomeini and his gang in Iran. That was the prevailing view inside the Reagan camp Sunday night.

By noon Monday, as Reagan campaigned in Peoria, Illinois,

his senior strategists studied weekend polling results and found to their relief that the renewed negotiations with Iran were not giving the President a big burst of popularity after all. Reagan's men had been braced for the long-dreaded "October Surprise" ever since the outbreak of the Iran-Iraq war when Teheran began using the hostages as a bargaining chip to gain the frozen assets and U.S. arms. The Soviet Union also hoped that the release of the Americans would assure a second term for the weak and waxlike President.

If the deal could have been consummated a few days before the election, it would have allowed enough time for Carter to bring out the captives and even parade them into the White House in triumph. Now, however, the whole maneuver was back-firing, arousing new suspicions among the voters, who had feared that Carter was manipulating the issue for his own political benefit; and the latest up-to-date polling data flowing into the Reagan headquarters showed this trend.

Admiral Robert Garrick, the director of policy development and research, confided to a visitor on the eve of election day: "You won't believe this, but Governor Reagan has increased his lead nationwide to nine points and he's even ahead in New York!"

Flying home to California, Reagan had good reason to feel confident that after a dozen years of effort, he would finally win the presidency. He believed that a majority of the people would respond to his challenge to "make America great again."

"Would you laugh," he asked reporters, "if I told you that I think, maybe, they see themselves and that I'm one of them? I've never been able to detach myself or think that I, somehow, am apart from them."

His climactic rally at San Diego was a rowdy, raucous show that combined partisanship with patriotism. When one heckler persisted in interrupting him, the weary candidate snapped, "Aw, shut up!" His mother had admonished him never to say that, he added, but he felt entitled to do it just this once. The crowd roared—and later joined the Reagans in the grand finale, singing "God Bless America."

In a televised address at the close of his long campaign,

Reagan asked the nation's voters if they were more confident, or less, after four years of the Carter regime; "is our nation stronger and more capable of leading the world toward peace and freedom, or is it weaker?"

"I find no national malaise, I find nothing wrong with the American people," he said. "Oh, they are frustrated, even angry, at what has been done to this blessed land. But more than anything they are sturdy and robust as they have always been."

"Together, tonight," he said, "let us say what so many long to hear: that America is still united, still strong, still compassionate, still clinging fast to the dream of peace and freedom, still willing to stand by those who are persecuted or alone."

Carter flew all the way across the country to Oregon and Washington, hoping to shake those two states loose from Reagan's monolithic Western bloc by a bid to woo some liberal voters away from John Anderson; then Air Force One carried him back through a sleepless night to Plains, Georgia, and home. When he asked Jody Powell, "Where do we spend the night?" his press secretary responded, "Governor, this evening there ain't no tonight."

There was also to be "no tomorrow" for the Georgians' dreams of four more years in the White House. On the homeward flight from Seattle, Powell gave the bone-tired Commander-in-Chief the final word from Pat Caddell's polls: a disastrous decline for Carter, presaging sure defeat.

The President pinned his last fragile hopes on a big election day turnout of Democrats, heeding his fervent pleas to come home to their old party and help him "whup the Republicans." But millions, distressed by inflation and recession, alarmed by an uneasy feeling that their country was slipping in economic and military strength all around the world, blamed these ills on the Democrats—who, after all, had total control of Congress as well as the White House. There was no way the President and his party could escape their responsibility, any more than the hapless Herbert Hoover and the Republicans could evade their doom in the Great Depression year, 1932.

Now, in a spectacular reversal of 1932, the newly invigorated

Republicans, with their efficient army of grass roots volunteers mobilized by Chairman Bill Brock and Cochairman Betty Heitman, turned out the votes for their ticket in an awesome display of power.

Reagan, in slacks and a red checked sports shirt, and his wife, in a red-and-black plaid dress, cast their ballots at the polling place in a neighbor's house not far from their own home on San Onofre Drive in Pacific Palisades. With his confidantes Ed Meese and Michael Deaver, the candidate discussed transition planning over lunch. The house in the placid Los Angeles suburb, so serene in the sunshine, so remote from the clangor and conflict of urban America, did not look like the nerve center of a potential presidential administration. Indeed, it was difficult to realize that Out There, in communities across the nation, more than 80 million Americans were selecting their next President.

Reagan was in the shower when a telephone call came about 5:30 o'clock in the afternoon. The White House was on the line. Wrapping himself in a towel, the next President of the United States picked up the receiver and heard the thirty-ninth President conceding the election. Jimmy Carter was gracious in defeat. He extended his congratulations and offered complete cooperation in the transfer of power.

Despite the optimism of their campaign staff, the Reagans had been steeling themselves for a cliff-hanger, as predicted in most of the published polls, and a long night of tension and suspense. So they were stunned by the swift and overwhelming triumph, so far beyond their wildest dreams. Over and over, the President-elect murmured, "It's a great surprise, I just can't believe it."

The reality of the victory became more visible as the Reagans left their residence to drive to the Bel Air mansion of steel tycoon Earle Jorgensen for a buffet dinner with a few dozen other friends. Apparently, all the neighbors had gathered along the winding roads that led from San Onofre Drive to Sunset Boulevard, and children were waving and cheering. Turning into Sunset, the Reagans found the drivers of other cars tooting their horns in jubilation; it was almost like the horn-blowing chorus that traditionally greets a bride and groom.

Later in the evening, as the future President and First Lady held court in a suite at the Century Plaza Hotel, the returns pouring in by television showed the tremendous scope of the nationwide sweep.

State after state in the Northern industrial tier, which the pollsters had been listing as "leaning to Carter" or "too close to call," were toppling to Reagan in the tidal wave of his counter-revolution against Carter and the liberal Democrats. Reagan was wrapping up every state in the onetime Solid South except Carter's own Georgia. In the end, the onetime film star who had been dismissed by his enemies as too old and too conservative to win the presidency had captured it in a Roosevelt-style avalanche of electoral votes, 489 to 49. He carried forty-four states, leaving the Democrats only six plus the District of Columbia. Reagan had a clear majority of 51 percent of the popular vote to 41 percent for Carter, 7 percent for Anderson, and 1 percent for the assorted also-rans.

These are the official totals compiled by the Federal Election Commission:

Reagan: 43,899,248 votes.
Carter: 35,481,435.
Anderson: 5,719,437.
Ed Clark, Libertarian: 920,859.
Barry Commoner: 230,377.

Total votes cast: 86,495,678.
Voter turnout: 53.95 percent of eligibles.

Reagan even pulled the Republicans into control of the United States Senate for the first time in twenty-six years—by a margin of fifty-three to forty-seven—and they gained thirty-three House seats, sharply reducing the Democrats' margin in that chamber.

The battlefield was littered with big-name liberal Democrats who had fallen: Sens. George McGovern of South Dakota, Birch Bayh of Indiana, John Culver of Iowa, Frank Church of Idaho, Warren Magnuson of Washington, Gaylord Nelson of Wisconsin,

John Durkin of New Hampshire; the House Democratic whip, John Brademas of Indiana, and the Ways and Means Committee chairman, Al Ullman of Oregon.

Truly, Reagan had brought about a sea change of amazing proportions. It was not only a verdict of "no confidence" in the performance of the defeated President Carter; it was a stunning repudiation of the liberal Democrats' policies of deficit spending, high taxes, and Big Government, and their failure to cope with the twin terrors of inflation and recession, as well as their faltering mismanagement of foreign policy.

At 6:50 P.M., Pacific Time, Carter appeared on the television screen, consoling his downcast supporters at a Washington hotel, conceding his defeat and pledging his support to his successor. "I wanted to serve as President because I love this country and because I love the people of this nation," he said. "Finally, let me say that I am disappointed tonight, but I have not lost either love."

At last, the victorious Reagan came before thousands of jubilant merrymakers jamming the Century Plaza ballroom and said: "There has never been a more humbling moment in my life,"

He expressed his "immeasurable debt" of gratitude to his family, to his dedicated campaign workers, and to the voters who had produced his incredible triumph. He promised, "I will do my utmost to justify your faith." Reagan praised George and Barbara Bush and promised "a true partnership and a true friendship" with the Vice President-elect. "Nancy is going to have a new title in a couple of months," the President-elect said, "but it isn't really new, because she has been the First Lady in my house for a long time.

"I am not frightened by what lies ahead and I don't believe the American people are frightened," Reagan declared. "Together, we are going to do what has to be done. We're going to put America back to work again.

"When I accepted your nomination for President, I hesitatingly asked for your prayers at that moment," Reagan recalled. "I won't ask for them at this particular moment, but I will just say that I will be very happy to have them in the days ahead."

☆

SOURCES

SOURCES FOR CHAPTER 1

PAGE:

13—Reagan's comments about foreign policy and his vow against "kissing Brezhnev": Interview with Reagan.

14—Reagan jokes: Remarks at Philadelphia, April 16, 1980, and elsewhere. The *Texas Observer*, April 23, 1976.

17—Sen. Robert C. Byrd's comments on General Haig: December 6, 1980.

17—Reagan's attack on Carter's foreign policy: Speech to the Chicago Council on Foreign Relations, March 17, 1980.

18—Lt. Gen. Daniel Graham's analysis of Reagan: Interview with Graham.

20—"No dye": Interview with Nancy Reagan.

21—Reagan's emotional make-up: Interviews with Charles Black, Morton Blackwell, and Richard Schweiker.

23—Reagan and his ranch: Interview with Nancy Reynolds.

26—Reagan's religion: Interview with Rev. Adrian Rogers.

26—Reagan interview with George Otis, published by High Adventure Ministries, Van Nuys, California, 1976.

27—Reagan's comments about "God's miracles": *Sincerely, Ronald Reagan,* edited by Helene von Damm, Berkley Books edition, New York, 1980.

27—Reagan's remarks at Dallas, Texas, August 22, 1980.

27—"God intended this land to be free": Reagan speech, New York, September 30, 1980.

SOURCES FOR CHAPTER 2

PAGE:

29—President Reagan's reminiscences in an interview with the author.

30—Marriage of Reagan's parents: New York *Daily News*, July 17, 1980.

32—The President's recollections of Galesburg, Illinois, are in his autobiography, *Where's the Rest of Me?*, published by Duell, Sloan and Pearce, New York, 1965, pages 11–12.

30, 36—Tampico recollections, *ibid.*, pages 14–15.

39—Memories of his father, *ibid.*, pages 7–8.

SOURCES FOR CHAPTER 3

44—*Where's the Rest of Me?*, pages 23–40.

47—Reagan's first prize for acting: Interview with the author.

49—Reagan's early days in radio: Interview with the author.

52—Hollywood tryout: *Where's the Rest of Me?*, pages 71–74.

SOURCES FOR CHAPTER 4

This chapter is based chiefly upon the President's autobiography and upon the First Lady's memoir, *Nancy*, published by William Morrow & Co., New York, 1980.

SOURCES FOR CHAPTER 5

71—*Where's the Rest of Me?*, pages 251–290.

76—Cancellation of *General Electric Theater*: Interview with Congressman Phil Crane.

77—Reagan's speech for Barry Goldwater: *Ronald Reagan, a Political Biography*, by Lee Edwards. Revised edition. Nordland Publishing International, Inc., Houston, Texas, 1980, pages 77–80.

80—Reagan's campaign and election as governor of California: Edwards, pages 83–179. Also, *The Rise of Ronald Reagan*, by Bill Boyarsky. Random House, New York, 1968, pages 104–155, and

Page:

What Makes Reagan Run? by Joseph Lewis. McGraw-Hill, New York, 1968, pages 91–156.

SOURCES FOR CHAPTER 6

85—Governor Reagan's inauguration: Lewis, *op. cit.*, pages 159–161.

86—Prayer breakfast: "The Reagans and Their Pastor," by William Rose. *Christian Life* magazine, May, 1968.

86—State "looted and drained," Edwards, *op. cit.*, page 194.

88—No "honeymoon," Boyarsky, *op. cit.*, page 176, and Lewis, *op. cit.*, page 159.

88—"Kathy, those damn trucks!": *But What's He REALLY Like?* by Kathy Randall Davis. Pacific Coast Publishers, Menlo Park, California, 1970, page 69.

89—Death threats, Davis, *op. cit.*, page 47.

90—Von Damm, *op. cit.*, page 73.

91—Interview with Robert Carleson.

92—Interview with Nancy Reynolds.

93—Davis, *op. cit.*, page 36.

94—Reagan's remarks against Ku Klux Klan: von Damm, *op. cit.*, page 158.

95—Rioting at Santa Cruz: Davis, *op. cit.*, pages 42–43.

96—Interview with Sen. S. I. Hayakawa.

99—Reagan-Rockefeller encounter in New Orleans: *The Republican Battle Line*, June-July, 1968.

99—Reagan's letter to Ethel Kennedy: Davis, *op. cit.*, page 79.

100—Interview with F. Clifton White.

101—Reagan's welfare reform fight: Interview with Robert Carleson.

105—Sen. S. I. Hayakawa statement, September 17, 1979, endorsing Reagan for the presidency.

105—"Most soul-satisfying thing": von Damm, *op. cit.*, page 76.

SOURCES FOR CHAPTER 7

108—Senator Helms' pledge: Interview with Helms.

108—How Robert Walker recruited John Sears: Interview with Walker.

PAGE:

108—Sears' removal from Nixon White House staff: Interview with his successor, Harry Dent.

109—Gerald Ford's vow not to run in 1976: Interview with Ford.

109—Reagan's comments on Ford's switch to candidacy in 1976: Interview with Reagan.

110—Ford's two offers of cabinet posts to Reagan: Interview with Reagan.

111—Reagan's refusal to lead an independent ticket: Interview with Reagan.

112—COCA plans: Interview with Helms.

113—Reagan's secret session with advocates of a Reagan-Wallace ticket: Interviews with several participants in the meeting.

116—Senator Laxalt's recollection of 1975 strategy dinner: Interview with Laxalt. Frank Walton's report of his meeting with Reagan: Interview with Walton.

118—Reagan's prayers before deciding to challenge Ford: Interview with Reagan.

SOURCES FOR CHAPTER 8

122—Critiques of Reagan's campaign methods: Interviews with Robert Walker and with other associates.

124—Reagan's conversion to tough tactics: Interview with Morton Blackwell.

125—Pressure on Reagan to quit: Interview with Senator Laxalt.

126—North Carolinians' disputes with John Sears: Interviews with Helms and with Tom Ellis.

128—Dispute over TV spots on "war" issue: Interview with Charles Black.

130—Reagan's criticism of Ford's tactics: Interview with Reagan.

SOURCES FOR CHAPTER 9

133—David Keene's account of the Schweiker selection appeared in the November, 1976, edition of The Alternative. Senator Laxalt recalled his role in a 1980 interview.

134—Schweiker's recollections in a 1980 interview.

PAGE:

136—Protests against Schweiker: Interviews with Crane, Helms, Brock, and Ellis.

136—Interview with Lyn Nofziger.

137—The Buckley Boom: Interviews with Helms, Crane, and others.

142—Schweiker's offer to withdraw: Interviews with Schweiker and Laxalt.

SOURCES FOR CHAPTER 10

147—"He had run his last race": Interview with Laxalt.

148—"I could have won": Reagan interview, Jackson, Mississippi, *Daily News*, December 9, 1976.

149—Possible 1980 presidential bid: Buffalo, New York, *Evening News*, November 6, 1976.

150—Text of Reagan's speech to Intercollegiate Studies Institute, Washington, D.C., January 15, 1977.

151—Text of Reagan's speech to conservative conference in Washington, February 5 1977.

152—Text of Brock's speech to Republican National Committee, Washington, January 15, 1977.

154—Brock versus Reagan and Laxalt in spat over money to fight Panama Canal treaties: Interviews with all three participants, December, 1977.

156—Reagan's pledges to conservatives: Interviews with participants in July 26, 1978, meeting at the Capitol. Interview with Phil Crane.

SOURCES FOR CHAPTER 11

159—Reagan for President Committee list. Text of Laxalt's speech.

160—Interviews with Congressmen Symms and Dornan.

161—Interview with Senator Schweiker.

162—Interviews with Congressman Evans.

163—John Lofton's interview with Reagan, *The Republican Battle Line*, December, 1979.

163—Reagan's New York speech: Reagan for President Committee.

164—Transcript of press conference notes.

165—Interview with Charles Black.

SOURCES FOR CHAPTER 12

PAGE:

169—Interviews with Charles Black, Senator Laxalt.

172—Interviews with Congressman Tom Evans and other House members.

174—Interview with Nancy Reagan; tape recording of her exchanges with Manchester students and teachers.

174—Interviews with Gerald Carmen.

175—Interview with Charles Black.

176—Nashua debate: Interview with Sen. Gordon Humphrey. Tape recordings of the debate and arguments about it. Interviews with Baker, Crane, Dole, Bush, Anderson, and Congressman Bob Dornan.

179—Interview with Black.

180—Interview with Gerald Carmen.

181—Tape recording of Reagan's remarks to Manchester crowd.

SOURCES FOR CHAPTER 13

183—Opposition to John Sears: Interviews with Sen. Jesse Helms, Congressmen Bob Dornan of California, Mickey Edwards of Oklahoma, and others.

185—"Draft Ford" campaign: Don Hoenshell, in the Sacramento *Union*, February 17, 1980; Ford's interview, *The New York Times*, March 2, 1980.

186—Thomas Reed committee's announcement, March 6, 1980.

186—John Sears and Henry Kissinger visits to Ford: Sacramento *Union*, March 8, 1980.

188—Ovation for Ford at Washington dinner: Interviews with Sen. S. I. Hayakawa, Amb. Guilford Dudley, Congressman Bob Wilson of California, and other guests.

188—Claims of Ford victory in California: Interview with Thomas Reed.

189—Pro-Reagan congressmen's opposition to Ford: Interviews with Representatives Walker, Evans, Bauman, and others.

190—Letter embarrassing Anderson: Interview with Rep. Phil Crane.

SOURCES FOR CHAPTER 14

PAGE:

193—Statement issued by Reagan at Philadelphia, April 16, 1980. Transcript of his speech there that night.

195—Interview with Congressman Jack Kemp.

200—Newsletter of Ad Hoc Committee in Defense of Life, Inc.

200—*Conservative Digest* magazine, July, 1980, and August, 1980.

201—Interviews with Jerry Falwell, Paul Weyrich, Howard Phillips, Robert Billings, Adrian Rogers, Ed McAteer and Brig. Gen. Albion W. Knight.

203—Interview with Bryce Harlow.

204—Attempt to "dump" Bill Brock: Interviews with Brock, Sen. Paul Laxalt, Congressman Tom Evans, and Bill Timmons.

SOURCES FOR CHAPTER 15

210—Interview with George Bush.

210—Interviews with Victor Fediay, Sen. Strom Thurmond, and Reagan aides.

212—Confidential interviews with Reagan aides.

215—Kissinger's comments at Detroit press conference, July 15, 1980.

215—Interviews with Bill Brock, Sen. Howard Baker, and others.

217—Interviews with Howard Phillips, Sen. Gordon Humphrey, Phyllis Schlafly, Nellie Gray, Jerry Falwell, Andy Messing, and Michael Valerio.

219—Confidential interviews with Reagan advisers. Also Edwin Meese comments to press pool, July 17, 1980.

221—Interview with Brock.

222—Interviews with Caspar Weinberger, Donald Rumsfeld, and others.

223—Lyn Nofziger comment at press briefing.

225—Bush comments to press in Detroit.

226—Text of Reagan's acceptance speech from Reagan-Bush Committee.

SOURCES FOR CHAPTER 16

231—Reagan's remarks to his state chairmen: transcribed notes.

232—Interview with Edwin Meese.

PAGE:

232—Sacramento *Union,* July 19, 1980.

233—Transcript of President Carter's speech before the Democratic national convention, August 14, 1980.

234—Text of Reagan's speech to the Veterans of Foreign Wars at Chicago, August 18, 1980: Reagan-Bush Committee.

235—Interviews with William Casey and Richard Allen.

237—Interviews with Sens. Jesse Helms and Orrin Hatch.

237—Text of Reagan's speech to the B'nai B'rith convention: Reagan-Bush Committee.

238—Text of Reagan's speech to the Teamsters' Union: Reagan-Bush Committee.

239—Transcript of Reagan's Jersey City remarks: Reagan-Bush Committee.

239—Text of Reagan's Jacksonville speech: Reagan-Bush Committee.

240—Letter by Adm. Elmo R. Zumwalt, Jr. Confidential interviews with Reagan aides.

240—Sen. Robert C. Byrd press conference, September 13, 1980.

241—President Carter's appeal to blacks at Atlanta: *Weekly Compilation of Presidential Documents,* September 22, 1980. Volume 16, Number 38, pages 1750–55.

241—Washington *Post* and Washington *Star* editorials, September 18, 1980.

242—Interview with Sen. Paul Laxalt.

242—Comments by Dr. Benjamin Hooks and Carl Rowan at luncheon in Washington, September 22, 1980.

243—Carter's "war or peace" remarks: *Weekly Compilation of Presidential Documents,* September 29, 1980. Volume 16, Number 39, pages 1869 and 1884.

244—Sen. Mark Hatfield's statement, September 23, 1980.

244—*Moral Majority Report,* August 15, 1980.

245—Reagan's speech at Dallas, August 22, 1980: Reagan-Bush Committee.

245—Interview with Robert Billings.

246—Text of Secretary Patricia Harris' speech at Princeton, New Jersey: U.S. Department of Health and Human Services, September 23, 1980.

PAGE:

246—Falwell's reply: Text from Falwell, September 29, 1980.

247—Carter's Chicago remarks: *Weekly Compilation of Presidential Documents,* October 13, 1980. Volume 16, Number 41, page 2093.

247—Reagan's Los Angeles press conference transcript: Reagan-Bush Committee.

248—Reagan's October 19 "Strategy of Peace" speech: Reagan-Bush Committee.

249—Carter's reply to Reagan: *Weekly Compilation of Presidential Documents,* October 27, 1980. Volume 16, Number 43, pages 2343–44 and 2367. Reagan's remarks at Louisville: Reagan-Bush Committee.

250—Carter's remarks at Waco, Texas: *Weekly Compilation of Presidential Documents,* October 27, 1980, page 2415.

251—Republicans' fears of "October Surprise": Interviews with Edwin Meese, William Casey, Richard Allen, and other Reagan advisers.

SOURCES FOR CHAPTER 17

253—Text of Carter-Reagan debate: *Weekly Compilation of Presidential Documents,* November 3, 1980. Volume 16, Number 44, pages 2477–2503. ABC News survey, Associated Press, October 29, 1980.

256—Carter's speeches: *Weekly Compilation of Presidential Documents,* November 10, 1980. Volume 16, Number 45, pages 2509, 2524–26, 2535, 2548–9.

257—Interview with Richard Wirthlin. Also Sen. Harry F. Byrd statement, October 15, 1980.

257—*Weekly Compilation of Presidential Documents,* November 10, 1980. Pages 2565–2610.

259—Interview with Adm. Robert Garrick.

260—Text of Reagan's election eve speech: Reagan-Bush Committee.

262—Official returns of the 1980 presidential election, issued by the Federal Election Commission, December 31, 1980.

263—Carter's concession speech: *Weekly Compilation of Presidential Documents,* November 10, 1980, pages 2687–8. Reagan's remarks: Reagan-Bush Committee.

☆

INDEX